6 Practice Tests

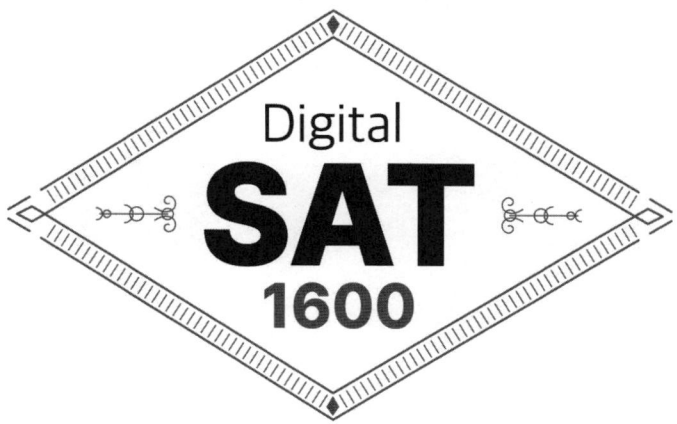

6 Practice Tests
Digital **SAT** 1600

발 행   2025년 5월 30일 초판 1쇄

저 자   Kevyn Lee
발행인   최영민
발행처   피앤피북
주 소   경기도 파주시 신촌로 16
전 화   031 − 8071 − 0088
팩 스   031 − 942 − 8688
전자우편   hermonh@naver.com
출판등록   2015년 3월 27일
등록번호   제406 − 2015 − 31호

ⓒ Kevyn Lee 2025, Printed in Korea.

ISBN   979 − 11 − 94085 − 52 − 2 (53410)

✣ 저자직강 인터넷 강의는 SAT, AP No.1 인터넷 강의 사이트인
  마스터프랩 (www.masterprep.net) 에서 보실 수 있습니다.

6 Practice Tests

Digital
SAT
1600

Reading and Writing

"Closer to the real test than Bluebook"
"Written by a Perfect Scorer on the SAT Reading
& Writing Section"

Kevyn Lee 지음

저자약력

UC Berkeley (졸) B.A. in Psychology

SAT RW 800점 만점 획득 / TOEFL 120점 만점 획득

16+ years of teaching in 대치 and 압구정

국제학교/유학생 전문 인강 1위 마스터프렙 대표강사 for SAT TOEFL and AP Psychology

(www.masterprep.net)

압구정 소재 KV EDU 개인 학원 운영

(Café.naver.com/kevynism)

SAT/TOEFL 매년 만점 배출

매년 특강 수강생 80% 이상 SAT RW 700점~800점 획득

공중파 드라마 MBC 닥터로이어 (소지섭 주연) SAT 스타강사 출현 – 국내유일 –

KV TOEFL Reading Actual Test 저자

Digital SAT 1600 시리즈 저자

A Personal Note to You, the Reader

Before you dive into the questions and drills in this book, I want to share a truth that may just change the way you prepare.

You see, there's a strange irony when it comes to the SAT. Everyone knows—whether it's basketball, painting, playing the piano, or learning to dance—that fundamentals are everything. The greatest athletes shoot thousands of free throws before game day. The best dancers rehearse their basic steps until they become second nature. Artists sketch circles and lines before they ever touch paint.

And yet, when it comes to the SAT, students rush past the fundamentals. They dive headfirst into solving problem after problem, chasing shortcuts and tricks, thinking that strategy alone will save them.

But here's the truth: *strategy is powerless without comprehension*. On the Reading & Writing section, the real test isn't how many tips you've memorized—it's how deeply you understand what you're reading. Without strong reading comprehension, even the best strategy is just guesswork.

So I urge you: don't just "do" this book. *Engage* with it. Return to the basics of language—clarity, meaning, structure, logic. Build your reading muscle with patience and purpose. Don't be afraid to slow down. Learn to read like a thinker, not a scanner. This book is your training ground, but the real work—the transformation—happens when you commit to the fundamentals.

Solve, yes. But read. Understand. Reflect. Then solve again, because in the end, mastery on the SAT, like in life, belongs to those who build on a rock, *not on sand*.

I'm rooting for you.

Kevyn Lee

독자 여러분께 드리는 글

이 책의 문제를 풀기 시작하기 전에, 한 가지 진실을 먼저 전하고 싶습니다.
이 진실은 여러분의 SAT 공부 방식 자체를 바꿔놓을지도 모릅니다.
많은 사람이 이런 말에는 쉽게 고개를 끄덕입니다.
농구든, 미술이든, 피아노든, 춤이든—*기초가 가장 중요하다*는 사실 말입니다.
위대한 농구 선수는 실전보다 연습에서 더 많은 자유투를 던지고, 최고의 무용수는 기본 스텝 하나를 수천 번 되풀이합니다.
예술가도 선과 원을 무수히 그려본 뒤에야 비로소 붓을 듭니다.
그런데 유독 SAT 앞에서는 많은 학생이 이 당연한 진리를 잊어버립니다.
문제를 많이 풀면 될 거라고, 전략만 잘 익히면 고득점이 가능하다고 믿습니다.
하지만 이건 착각입니다.

SAT Reading & Writing에서 정말 중요한 건 기술이나 전략이 아닙니다.
탄탄한 독해력, 바로 그게 가장 강력한 무기입니다.
글을 깊이 이해하지 못한 채 문제만 많이 푸는 것은, 바닥이 얕은 모래 위에 집을 짓는 것과 같습니다. 결국 무너지게 되어 있죠.
그래서 부탁드립니다. 이 책을 단순히 '풀지' 마세요. 읽으세요.
질문을 던지고, 문장의 구조를 파악하고, 논리의 흐름을 느끼며, 진짜 의미를 파고드세요.
천천히, 깊게, 제대로.
전략은 나중 일입니다. 독해력이라는 기반이 다져져야 전략도 빛을 발할 수 있습니다.
이 책은 그 기반을 단단히 다지는 훈련장이 될 것입니다.
정답에만 집착하지 마세요. 이해하고, 반성하고, 다시 풀어보세요.
결국 SAT에서도, 인생에서도, 진짜 실력은 기초 위에 지어진 사람에게 돌아갑니다.
당신을 진심으로 응원합니다.

Kevyn Lee

학부모님들께 드리는 말씀

안녕하세요.

저는 지난 16년 넘는 시간 동안 **SAT Reading & Writing** 교육에 매진해 온 선생님입니다.

이 글을 통해 SAT 교육의 현실에 대해 감히 진심을 담아 말씀드립니다.

한국의 수능과는 달리, SAT는 전적으로 비판적 사고력과 독해력을 기반으로 한 시험입니다.

그러나 한국의 SAT 교육 현실은 여전히 초창기에서 벗어나지 못한 채, 잘못된 방향으로

흘러가고 있습니다. 많은 학원과 강사들이 '전략'이라는 이름으로 문제풀이 방식만 가르치고,

학생들에게는 숙제처럼 수십, 수백 개의 문제를 던져주고, 단어 암기만을 강조합니다.

겉보기에는 열심히 공부하는 것 같지만, 실상은 학생 개개인의 근본적인 독해력과 사고력을

길러주는 교육이 아닙니다.

저는 수년간 수많은 학생을 가르치며 한 가지를 절감했습니다.

대다수 학생이 점수를 못 받는 이유는 '전략'을 몰라서가 아니라, 글을 제대로 읽고 이해하는 능력이 부족해서입니다. 그런데도 매년, 여전히 학부모님들로부터 같은 질문을 받습니다.

"문제 많이 풀고 전략만 잘 배우면 RW에서 700∼750점 이상 나올 수 있는 거죠?"

이 질문은 단순한 오해가 아니라, 이미 한국 SAT 교육산업 전체가 만들어 놓은 문화입니다.

그리고 그 문화의 가장 큰 피해자는 바로 학생들입니다.

저는 평생을 걸고 이 고정된 인식을 바꾸고 싶습니다. 그리고 그것은 단순히 한두 명의 교사나

학생의 노력만으로는 이루어질 수 없습니다. 이제는 **학부모님들의 도움이 절실히 필요합니다.**

모든 학생은 제대로 된 방식으로, 충분한 시간을 가지고, 맞춤형 독해 논리 교육을 받는다면

SAT에서 놀라운 성과를 낼 수 있습니다. 단, 지금의 학원 중심, 문제풀이 중심 시스템만으로는

절대 불가능합니다. 진정한 변화는 교육의 중심이 전략이 아닌 본질로 옮겨갈 때 시작됩니다.

그래서 저는 앞으로 학생들이 재학 중인 국제학교나 해외학교에서 SAT 독해 기반 워크숍을
직접 열고자 합니다.

**학부모님께서 다니시는 학교와 저를 연결해 주는 작은 도움이, 한국의 SAT 교육을 바꾸는
첫걸음이 될 수 있습니다.**

저는 그 변화의 시작이 되고 싶습니다. 그리고 그 변화에 함께 해주실 학부모님을 기다립니다.

감사합니다.

Kevyn Lee 드림

Table of Contents

TEST 1

TEST 2

TEST 3

Table of Contents

TEST 1

Module 1

Reading and Writing
27 Questions, 32 Minutes

DIRECTIONS

The questions in this section address a number of important reading and writing skills. Each questions includes one or more passages, which may include a table or graph. Read each passage and question carefully, and then choose the best answer to the question based on the passage(s).

All questions in this section are multiple-choice with four answer choices. Each question has a single best answer.

1

The following text is adapted from William Shakespeare's *The Tempest*.

PROSPERO: My trials have been immense, Miranda. I've faced storms and isolation on this forsaken isle, left to my own devices, with naught but my books and my thoughts. I have **endured** much suffering, but it has only strengthened my resolve.

As used in the text, what does the word "endured" most nearly mean?

A) Avoided
B) Tolerated
C) Conveyed
D) Resisted

2

Green Earth Initiative is an organization whose mission is to ensure that conservation efforts are implemented from environmentally sustainable perspectives. The organization ____ this dedication by supporting the efforts of activists like Rina Patel (Indian, environmentalist, and educator) and other prominent environmental advocates who work to preserve and protect natural habitats and resources.

Which choice completes the text with the most logical and precise word or phrase?

A) concludes
B) explains
C) precedes
D) fulfills

3

Though fewer artists display their work in the River City Art Gallery in Sacramento, California, than in the galleries of New York, Paris, or Tokyo, the River City Art Gallery has the advantage of being able to ___ emerging local artists: by connecting these artists with collectors and art critics knowledgeable about regional art trends, the River City Art Gallery can help these artists succeed.

Which choice completes the text with the most logical and precise word or phrase?

A) designate
B) nurture
C) limit
D) evaluate

4

The emphasis on accurately portraying everyday city life that is characteristic of the urban realist style can be seen in *City Streets*, painted by Daniel Reyes, which depicts street vendors selling goods along bustling sidewalks. This style can thus be seen as an effort to ___ what were viewed as the extravagances of the idealist style seen in many works by Giovanni Rossi, which instead glorified urban landscapes while ignoring any signs of poverty or decay.

Which choice completes the text with the most logical and precise word or phrase?

A) comprehend
B) promote
C) challenge
D) emphasize

5

The cheetah can run incredibly fast—up to 112 kilometers per hour (km/hr)—but it is still significantly slower than the peregrine falcon, which can dive at speeds up to 320 km/hr. The difference between these speeds is largely ___ of the fact that the adaptations that allow for flight impose fewer constraints on maximum speeds than those that are ideal for running on land.

Which choice completes the text with the most logical and precise word or phrase?

A) a result
B) a clarification
C) a rejection
D) a target

6

In what is now New Mexico, the Pueblo people maintain the Pueblo Cultural Center. Using ***ancestral wisdom to shape the presentation of exhibits, this center shares Pueblo heritage and customs with community members.*** The Navajo Nation, in Arizona, has a similar approach with its cultural center. Both centers stand in contrast to mainstream museums that aren't Indigenous-run; these museums often focus on attracting tourists and use standardized displays with minimal cultural authenticity.

Which choice best describes the function of the underlined sentence in the text as a whole?

A) It proposes enhancements to a specific tribal cultural center.
B) It invites community members to visit their cultural center.
C) It highlights how one cultural center contrasts with other cultural institutions.
D) It offers a general overview of a specific tribal cultural center.

CONTINUE

7

The National Art Gallery in Washington, D.C. has a collection of digital media that includes early computer animations from the 1980s, which visitors can view in a small theater, and interactive art installations from the 2000s, which visitors can only experience through a video recording. The gallery argues that video presentations are only for installations too complex to recreate in person, but *digital art is meant to be actively engaged with by the viewer*, an aspect that is entirely missing in a video-only format.

Which choice best describes the function of the underlined sentence in the text as a whole?

A) It highlights a characteristic of digital art that is absent in some of the pieces displayed in the gallery's exhibition.

B) It offers an assertion about digital art as a medium that both the gallery and the author agree upon.

C) It points out a misunderstanding about digital art that the author believes is apparent in the gallery's approach to exhibiting it.

D) It presents a factor that the author feels partially weakens the gallery's method of displaying digital art.

8

In the language of Xhosa, a Bantu language spoken in South Africa, *ubu* means "people," whereas *ububu* is used to refer to "a group of people." This phenomenon, in which a root element of a word is repeated, often with slight modification, within another word related to the root word, is called reduplication. In this case, the element *bu* in *ubu* gets repeated in *ububu*. There are many examples of this type of reduplication in Xhosa.

The text makes which point about the Xhosa word *ububu*?

A) It is identical in meaning to several other words in Xhosa.

B) It doesn't have a clear equivalent in English.

C) It is the only word in Xhosa that uses reduplication.

D) It contains a repetition of the element *bu* in *ubu*.

9

The Origin of Species, first published in 1859, is a groundbreaking work by Charles Darwin that explores the concept of evolution by natural selection. This book has been the subject of various interpretations. Some scientists argue that Darwin's conclusions are definitive and leave no room for doubt. Other scientists, however, suggest that the book should be viewed as a foundational text that opens up more questions than it answers, rather than as a final statement on evolution, similar to how Isaac Newton's *Principia* laid the groundwork for future scientific inquiry.

Which choice best states the main purpose of the text?

A) Many scientists consider *The Origin of Species* to be incredibly insightful, even if it leaves certain questions unanswered.

B) Scientists have differing views regarding the completeness of Darwin's theories in *The Origin of Species*.

C) The groundbreaking conclusions Darwin presents in *The Origin of Species* make it one of his most influential works.

D) Some scientists believe that *The Origin of Species* should hold the same level of importance as *Principia*, while others disagree.

10

"The Gardener's Legacy" is a 1910 story by Lucy Davis. In the story, the character of Sarah, a young girl, accidentally crushes a rosebud in her grandmother's garden while her grandmother is trimming the hedges. Davis illustrates the dedication and care with which her grandmother typically tends to her garden, writing, _____

Which quotation from "The Gardener's Legacy" most effectively illustrates the claim?

A) "[Sarah] stepped carefully onto the grass, her steps hesitant. Soon her grandmother came up with the shears, while freshly trimmed leaves fluttered to the ground."

B) "[Sarah's grandmother] was tending to the garden as delicately as if she were handling fine lace. Throughout the season, she had nurtured it in the quiet hours of early evening. Even beneath the old oak tree, the flowers were lively and full of color."

C) "[Sarah's grandmother] paused, and as the clipping ceased, one could hear the birds in the oak tree chirping in harmony."

D) "After some searching, [Sarah's grandmother] noticed the damaged flower. She turned slowly, catching sight of the girl standing a little way off, her face troubled with guilt."

TEST 01

CONTINUE

11

The following text is from Jane Austen's 1817 novel *Persuasion*. Anne Elliot, who narrates this portion of the text, reflects on her understanding of human behavior and social expectations, contrasting her insights with those of society at large.

The common person understands basic interactions and is comfortable with social rituals. The most respected socialite knows only slightly more. They might have glimpsed the intricacies of human nature, yet their understanding remains superficial. Anne, however, had observed the underlying motivations and societal pressures that shape behavior, but she was limited by convention and the narrow view of her peers. She had often felt confined by these social constraints, though she had dared to question them in private.

Which choice best describes the main idea of the text?

A) Anne became disillusioned with society when she realized that the insights of common people about behavior are often more profound than those of the elite.

B) Anne was impressed by the common person's understanding of behavior but believed her observations offered a clearer insight.

C) Anne was immediately struck by the advantages of the conventional view of observing society.

D) Anne thinks that conventional societal approaches to understanding behavior will not yield the insights she seeks.

12

The third installment in Margaret Quinn's River Valley series, A Flowing Stream, was published in 2010. The River Valley series includes five books, with a sixth planned but never completed. Like the previous books, A Flowing Stream ends abruptly, yet the next book, Rising Tides, begins precisely where A Flowing Stream ends. Thus, the abrupt ending only seems problematic if one views each book as a standalone story; the River Valley series is better understood as a single, extended narrative, similar to other continuous stories, such as John Galsworthy's The Forsyte Saga.

Which choice best states the main idea of the text?

A) Over time, the *River Valley* series has gained similar recognition among readers as works like *The Forsyte Saga* that share a similar continuous structure.

B) A certain understanding of the structure of the books in the *River Valley* series is helpful if one wants to appreciate the series as a whole.

C) Many readers consider the *River Valley* novels to be engaging despite abrupt endings within individual books.

D) *A Flowing Stream* and *Rising Tides* are two of the most intricate novels in Quinn's series due in part to their unconventional structures.

13

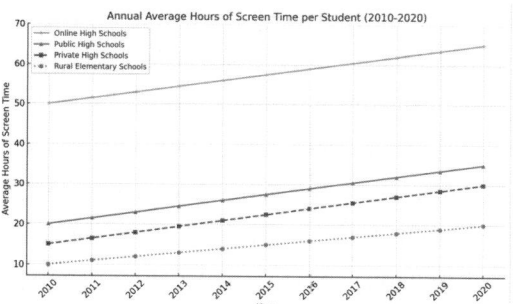

In a discussion on educational technology, a student asserts that increased screen time from 2010 to 2020 occurred not only in educational environments heavily reliant on digital resources, such as online high schools, but also in more traditional settings, such as public and private high schools and rural elementary schools, though these traditional settings experienced less dramatic increases.

Which choice best describes data from the graph that support the student's claim?

A) In at least one of the four educational settings shown, the amount of screen time was less than 20 hours per student per year at one point between 2010 and 2020.

B) Even though the amount of screen time per student per year was greater in private high schools than in online high schools throughout the period from 2010 to 2020, the amounts were nearly identical in 2016.

C) While the annual number of hours of screen time per student was always lower in rural elementary schools than in online high schools for each year between 2010 and 2020, the amount of screen time rose in both settings during this period.

D) In 2012, the amount of screen time in online high schools was less than 30 hours per student per year.

14

Table: Maximum and Minimum heights of Various Bird Species' Nests in Forests and Grasslands

species	Minimum Nest Height(meters)	Maximum Nest Height(meter)
Falco Sparnerius	3	10
Aquila chrysaetos	5	20
Cyanocitta cristata	1	15
Bubo verginianus	8	30

Some researchers suggest that with increased human activity in lowland areas (up to 12 meters above ground), certain bird species might prefer building nests in higher areas, such as forest canopies (15 to 30 meters above ground), to avoid disturbance. However, it's uncertain if all species can adapt to nesting at such heights. In 2022, Dr. Chen and her team observed bird species in both forest and grassland environments, recording their nest heights. Based on this data, the species that seems least suited for nesting in the canopy zone is:

Which choice most effectively uses data from the table to complete the statement?

A) **Cyanocitta cristata**, because its minimum nest height of 1 meter is the lowest listed.

B) **Falco sparverius**, because its maximum nest height of 10 meters is farthest from the canopy zone.

C) **Aquila chrysaetos**, because its maximum nest height of 20 meters is close to but doesn't reach the upper canopy.

D) **Bubo virginianus**, because its minimum nest height of 8 meters is within the lower area.

TEST 01

15

Psychologist Dr. Ellen Martin believes that understanding how cooperative behaviors develop in social animals could shed light on the evolution of complex societies. She and her colleagues analyzed data from various studies on how certain primates respond to different types of social interactions, including the work of Dr. Liam Rogers on gorilla bonding activities and Dr. Rachel Simmons on chimpanzee group dynamics. Martin and her colleagues concluded that both gorilla bonding activities and chimpanzee group dynamics might have contributed to the development of social behaviors in early human societies.

Which finding, if true, would most directly support Martin and her colleagues' conclusion?

A) Rogers and Simmons found that both gorillas and chimpanzees tended to display cooperative behaviors after specific social interactions.

B) Rogers found that gorillas tended to display cooperative behaviors after specific social interactions, but Simmons did not observe this in chimpanzees.

C) Simmons found that chimpanzees tended to display cooperative behaviors after specific social interactions, but Rogers did not observe this in gorillas.

D) Neither Rogers nor Simmons found that gorillas or chimpanzees tended to display cooperative behaviors after specific social interactions.

16

Like many other insect-pollinating bees on the island of Maui, the Hawaiian yellow-faced bee contributes to plant reproduction by transferring pollen from flower to flower. Ecologists have found that insect-pollinating bees help some native plants, such as the 'ilima flower, which is at risk of extinction in the wild. However, the bees tend to pollinate a larger number of flowers from invasive species, like the lantana shrub, which have larger populations and are more abundant in the wild. Therefore, it isn't surprising that _____.

Which choice most logically completes the text?

A) on Maui, native plants, such as the 'ilima flower, are already present in most of the areas where Hawaiian yellow-faced bees are likely to pollinate.

B) lantana shrubs and other invasive plants only recently began to outnumber native plants in the wild.

C) on Maui, the rate of population growth is higher for invasive plants than it is for vulnerable native plants, like the 'ilima flower.

D) the 'ilima flower and the lantana shrub are the plant species most likely to go extinct in the wild.

17

In the field of astronomy, a planet's orbital period represents the time it takes for that planet to complete one full orbit around its star. For instance, Mars has an orbital period of about 687 Earth days. James Bennett's textbook *Astronomical Stars* _____ this topic in detail.

Which choice completes the text so that it conforms to the conventions of standard English?

A) explaining
B) explains
C) to explain
D) having explained

18

A catalyst is a type of substance that ___ to increase the rate of a chemical reaction by lowering the activation energy required. In industrial applications, catalysts like platinum and palladium are often used to speed up reactions in processes like fuel production and polymerization.

Which choice completes the text so that it conforms to the conventions of standard English?

A) assisted
B) had assisted
C) assists
D) was assisting

19

Throughout history, numerous landmarks and artifacts important to American heritage—such as the Liberty Bell, Ellis Island, and the Golden Gate Bridge—have been added to a significant ___ National Register of Historic Places. New entries are selected every year by a committee that includes historian Emily Grant, archaeologist Tom Perry, and architect Sarah Lee.

Which choice completes the text so that it conforms to the conventions of standard English?

A) list: the
B) list. The
C) list; the
D) list the

20

Today, the Nobel Prize is widely regarded as the pinnacle of academic and cultural achievement, but when it was first awarded in 1901, it was a relatively modest honor. Alfred Nobel sought to promote scientific progress and humanitarian efforts by establishing an award that would recognize outstanding contributions in fields such as physics, literature, and ___ as it expanded over time, the prize came to include laureates from around the globe, including influential figures like Albert Einstein and Gabriel García Márquez.

Which choice completes the text so that it conforms to the conventions of standard English?

A) medicine
B) medicine;
C) medicine and
D) medicine,

21

In their studies, environmental ___ combine insights from biology and chemistry to understand how ecosystems function and to assess the impact of human activities on the natural world.

Which choice completes the text so that it conforms to the conventions of standard English?

A) scientists Jane Goodall and Rachel Carson

B) scientists Jane Goodall and Rachel Carson,

C) scientists Jane Goodall, and Rachel Carson

D) scientists, Jane Goodall and Rachel Carson,

22

The city of Austin, Texas, updated its water infrastructure to improve access to clean water as recently as 2021. ____ the system will likely require additional upgrades as the city's population continues to grow.

Which choice completes the text with the most logical transition?

A) Still,

B) By contrast,

C) For example,

D) Instead,

23

Tech entrepreneur Linda Chen admits that her goals were modest when she launched TechWiz, a blog covering technology trends and reviews: "I just wanted a place to share my thoughts on new gadgets." ____ her blog has grown into a valuable resource for industry insiders seeking insights on emerging technologies, software updates, and product reviews.

Which choice completes the text with the most logical transition?

A) Nevertheless,

B) Therefore,

C) Furthermore,

D) Next,

24

Dr. Emily Carter has conducted extensive research at the prestigious Climate Research Institute, one of the leading centers for environmental studies. ____ Dr. Carter focused on the impact of carbon emissions on polar ice melt, contributing critical data that enhanced our understanding of climate change dynamics.

Which choice completes the text with the most logical transition?

A) Conversely,

B) Specifically,

C) Finally,

D) Nevertheless,

25

While researching a topic, a student has taken the following notes:

- Salmon is a type of fish that contains omega-3 fatty acids, which are beneficial for heart health.
- Walnuts are a type of nut that also contains omega-3 fatty acids.
- There are 1.5 grams (g) of omega-3 per 100 grams of salmon.
- There are 0.3 g of omega-3 per 100 grams of walnuts.
- Humans cannot produce omega-3 fatty acids in their bodies, so they must get it from foods, including fish and nuts.
- Omega-3 fatty acids are associated with reduced risk of heart disease.

The student wants to make and support a claim that salmon is a better source of omega-3 than walnuts are. Which choice most effectively uses relevant information from the notes to accomplish this goal?

A) Salmon contains omega-3 fatty acids (which humans cannot produce in their bodies), and walnuts do too.

B) Walnuts contain 0.3 g of omega-3 per 100 g, but salmon is a better source of omega-3; in fact, salmon contains 1.5 g per 100 g.

C) Salmon is a better source of omega-3, which is associated with reduced risk of heart disease, than walnuts are.

D) Humans must get omega-3 from foods like salmon and walnuts because they cannot produce it in their bodies.

26

While researching a topic, a student has taken the following notes:

- Impressionist paintings often focus on capturing light and movement rather than precise details.
- Some common subjects in impressionist paintings include landscapes, urban scenes, and people.
- *Impression, Sunrise* (1872) by French artist Claude Monet is an impressionist painting that depicts a sunrise over a harbor.
- This painting emphasizes the play of light on water and the atmosphere of the scene.
- *Woman with a Parasol* (1875) is another impressionist painting by Claude Monet that portrays a woman holding a parasol in a field.
- This painting focuses on the movement of the wind and light across the landscape.

The student wants to emphasize a difference between the two paintings. Which choice most effectively uses relevant information from the notes to accomplish this goal?

A) The French artist Claude Monet created both *Impression, Sunrise* and *Woman with a Parasol* as impressionist paintings.

B) While *Impression, Sunrise* and *Woman with a Parasol* are both impressionist paintings, the former emphasizes light on water, while the latter focuses on the movement of wind across the landscape.

C) Some impressionist paintings depict outdoor scenes or natural elements, much like Claude Monet's *Impression, Sunrise*, which focuses on a harbor.

D) Claude Monet's *Impression, Sunrise* and *Woman with a Parasol* showcase the impressionist technique of capturing light and movement in scenes of nature.

27

While researching a topic, a student has taken the following notes:

- Most of the fish and coral species in the Great Barrier Reef are native.
- In a 2021 study, researchers aimed to understand the role native fish play in coral reef health.
- Researchers catalogued coral species found in proximity to native fish species.
- *Acropora millepora*, a branching coral, was one of twelve native coral species catalogued.
- *Pocillopora damicornis*, a bushy coral, was one of twenty-two non-native coral species catalogued.
- Researchers concluded that native fish significantly contribute to the maintenance of both native and non-native coral species.

The student wants to compare the number of native and non-native species catalogued. Which choice most effectively uses relevant information from the notes to accomplish this goal?

A) Coral species like *Acropora millepora* and *Pocillopora damicornis* can be found in the Great Barrier Reef, but only the former coral is native.

B) In 2021, researchers catalogued native and non-native coral species found near native fish in the Great Barrier Reef.

C) Most fish in the Great Barrier Reef are native, and researchers have concluded that they play an essential role in coral reef health.

D) When cataloguing coral species found near native fish, researchers found more non-native coral species than native species.

Module 1 answer

1

Correct Answer: B) Tolerated

 Explanation:

In the context of Prospero's speech, he reflects on suffering and solitude:

"I have endured much suffering, but it has only strengthened my resolve."

Here, *"endured"* refers to his **experience of hardship over time**, **surviving or bearing it** without giving up. This fits the meaning of **"tolerated"**—to bear something painful or unpleasant.

Why not the others?
- **A) Avoided**: If he had *avoided* suffering, he wouldn't have had to *endure* it. The entire point is that he went through it.
- **C) Conveyed**: Means *to express or communicate*. There's nothing about him *saying* or *communicating* the suffering—he *lived through* it.
- **D) Resisted**: Suggests fighting against it actively. But *endured* implies passive suffering over time—not necessarily opposition.

2

Correct Answer: D) fulfills

 Explanation:

The organization **supports activists**, meaning it *puts its mission into action* by doing concrete things. That is the very essence of the word **"fulfills"**—*to carry out or put into effect*.

Why not the others?
- **A) Concludes**: Means *ends*—doesn't fit. The sentence isn't saying the organization is ending anything.
- **B) Explains**: Doesn't capture the *action* or *commitment*. It's not just telling or clarifying.
- **C) Precedes**: Means *comes before*. There's no temporal sequence implied here.

3

Correct Answer: B) nurture

Explanation:

The gallery **helps artists grow**, especially early in their careers. It connects them to collectors and critics—this is support, development, cultivation. That's **nurture**.

Why not the others?

- **A) Designate**: Means *assign a title or role*. Not appropriate here; we're not labeling artists.
- **C) Limit**: Opposite meaning—limiting isn't helpful or supportive.
- **D) Evaluate**: Means *judge or assess*. Might be something a gallery does, but **not the central action** described in this sentence.

4

Correct Answer: C) challenge

Explanation:

Urban realism is described as contrasting with idealist style—it **shows poverty, decay, and reality**, while idealism *glorifies* and *hides flaws*. That contrast is a kind of **critique or opposition**—thus, the realist style **challenges** idealism.

Why not the others?

- **A) Comprehend**: Means to understand—not strong enough to capture opposition.
- **B) Promote**: Promote extravagances? No! Realism goes *against* that.
- **D) Emphasize**: Doesn't fit—emphasize what? If anything, it's downplaying or *refuting* the idealized view.

5

Correct Answer: A) a result

 **Explanation:**

We're comparing the cheetah and the falcon, and the difference in their speed is **caused by** how flight versus running affect physical limits. So, the difference is *a result of* that fact.

💬 **Why not the others?**

- **B) A clarification**: That would rephrase or explain—not indicate *cause*.
- **C) A rejection**: Doesn't make logical sense here.
- **D) A target**: As in a goal—not related to cause-effect.

6

Correct Answer: D) It offers a general overview of a specific tribal cultural center.

 **Explanation:**

The underlined sentence explains **what the Pueblo Cultural Center does**:

"Using ancestral wisdom to shape the presentation of exhibits, this center shares Pueblo heritage and customs⋯"

This is an **overview**—it summarizes **the center's purpose and philosophy**.

💬 **Why not the others?**

- **A) Proposes enhancements**: The sentence isn't **suggesting changes or improvements**.
- **B) Invites community members**: There's no **direct address** or call to action.
- **C) Highlights contrast**: That contrast comes **later**, in the next sentence. This one just describes the Pueblo center itself.

7

Correct Answer: D) It presents a factor that the author feels partially weakens the gallery's method of displaying digital art.

Explanation:

The sentence critiques the gallery's approach:

"Digital art is meant to be actively engaged with by the viewer...missing in a video-only format."

The gallery shows some digital art via video only—which **eliminates interactivity**, a key feature of digital art. This implies a **flaw** or **shortcoming** in the gallery's method.

Why not the others?

- **A) Highlights a characteristic···**: Yes, interactivity is highlighted, **but that's not the point of the sentence—it's a critique**, not just a description.
- **B) Offers an assertion···both agree upon**: The **gallery's position** is different—they *justify* their method.
- **C) Points out a misunderstanding···**: Doesn't fully apply. The author critiques, but doesn't claim the gallery misunderstands digital art outright.

8

Answer: D

Explanation:

The key lines:

"···ubu means 'people'···ububu is used to refer to 'a group of people.' ···this···is called reduplication. In this case, the element *bu* in *ubu* gets repeated in *ububu*."

Why not the others?

- **A) Identical in meaning···**: No. *Ububu* is related, but has a **different**, more plural meaning.
- **B) Doesn't have a clear equivalent**: The passage never claims that—it's explaining the **structure**, not the **translatability**.
- **C) Only word···that uses reduplication**: Incorrect—"there are many examples of this type" shows it's **not unique**.

9

Answer: B

Explanation:

The passage presents a **debate**:

• Some scientists see Darwin's work as **complete and conclusive**,

• Others see it as **foundational but incomplete**, akin to Newton's *Principia*.

This clearly conveys **different interpretations of the book's completeness**.

Why not the others?

• **A) Many scientists consider it insightful···:** Too narrow—misses the key **contrast**.

• **C) The groundbreaking conclusions···:** That's **background info**, not the **main point**.

• **D) Some scientists believe it should match Principia···:** Misrepresents the analogy—the **comparison to Principia** is made **to illustrate the idea of foundational work**, not a status debate.

10

Answer: B

Explanation:

This option describes **her methodical, devoted care**:

• She's gentle ("like fine lace")

• She nurtures it over time ("throughout the season")

• Even the most shaded parts thrive ("flowers were lively···")

Why not the others?

• **A)** Sets the scene and actions, but focuses more on **Sarah** and physical movements—not **devotion**.

• **C)** Highlights atmosphere (birds chirping), not **gardening habits**.

• **D)** Focuses on the **moment of conflict** (the crushed rose), not **the grandmother's care**.

29

11

Answer: D) Anne thinks that conventional societal approaches to understanding behavior will not yield the insights she seeks.

📝 **Explanation:**

The passage paints a clear contrast between **superficial social knowledge** (held by the common person and even by elite socialites) and **Anne's deeper, more introspective understanding** of human nature:

"Anne... had observed the underlying motivations and societal pressures..."

"...limited by convention and the narrow view of her peers."

"She had often felt confined by these social constraints···"

These lines reveal her **disillusionment with shallow social rituals** and her desire to see beyond them. She dares to **question convention**, even if only privately. This matches **D** exactly.

💬 **Why not the others?**

- **A)** Suggests Anne sees the common person's insights as **more profound** than the elite's. But the text doesn't elevate the common person—it says both are limited.
- **B)** Says Anne is **impressed** by the common person—but her tone is more critical or analytical, not admiring.
- **C)** Says she was **struck by the advantages** of the conventional view—but she feels **confined by it**, not inspired.

12

Answer: B) A certain understanding of the structure of the books in the River Valley series is helpful if one wants to appreciate the series as a whole.

📝 **Explanation:**

The passage discusses how the **abrupt endings** of books like *A Flowing Stream* can be misinterpreted **if read as standalones**. But:

"...the River Valley series is better understood as a single, extended narrative···"

Thus, the passage argues that to fully appreciate the series, readers must **grasp its narrative structure**—like that of *The Forsyte Saga*.

? **Why not the others?**

- **A)** Suggests *River Valley* has gained **similar recognition** as *The Forsyte Saga*. The comparison is about structure, **not prestige or popularity**.
- **C)** Talks about **engaging despite abrupt endings**—but the text doesn't mention reader opinions or praise, only **explains structure**.
- **D)** Claims *A Flowing Stream* and *Rising Tides* are the **most intricate**—this kind of judgment or ranking isn't in the passage.

13

Answer: C) **While the annual number of hours of screen time per student was always lower in rural elementary schools than in online high schools for each year between 2010 and 2020, the amount of screen time rose in both settings during this period.**

Why it's correct:

This choice directly supports the **student's central claim**:

- **Online High Schools** (digital-heavy): screen time **rose steadily** from ~50 to ~65 hours.
- **Rural Elementary Schools** (traditional): screen time **also rose**, from ~10 to ~20 hours.

Though rural schools always had **less** screen time, the **upward trend** is present in both settings—clearly reinforcing the point that **traditional schools also experienced growth in screen exposure**, just at a smaller scale.

? **Why the other choices don't work:**

- **A)** "In at least one of the four educational settings··· less than 20 hours..."
  - ✔ *True* (Rural Elementary Schools started at ~10 hours),
  - *But* it doesn't address the **student's claim about increases over time across settings**—this is just a point-in-time observation, not a trend.
- **B)** "Screen time was greater in private high schools than online high schools···"
  - This is **factually incorrect**. The graph shows that **online high schools always had the highest screen time**—private high schools are below public high schools, and **never surpass online high schools**.
- **D)** "In 2012, screen time in online high schools was less than 30 hours···"
  - Also **factually false**. In 2012, online high school students already averaged **over 50 hours** of screen time. This number is far above 30 in all years.

14

Answer: B

📝 **Why it's correct:**
- The **canopy zone begins at 15 meters**.
- **Falco sparverius** only nests between **3 and 10 meters**—it **never reaches** the canopy zone.
- This makes it **clearly the least suited** of all four species to adapt to nesting **above 15 meters**.

  💬 **Why the other choices are not correct:**
  - **A) Cyanocitta cristata (min = 1 m, max = 15 m)**
    → Yes, its **minimum** is low, but it **can just barely reach** the **lower bound of the canopy**.
    → So it's *not the least suited*—it *can* at least **enter the canopy zone**.
  - **C) Aquila chrysaetos (max = 20 m)**
    → It **does nest within** the canopy range (15–30 m).
    → Not ideal to say it's *unsuited*—it fits the **lower-middle canopy range** quite well.
  - **D) Bubo virginianus (range: 8–30 m)**
    → It nests **well into the canopy**, reaching the upper limit of 30 meters.
    → This species is **highly suited** for canopy nesting.

15

Answer: A) Rogers and Simmons found that both gorillas and chimpanzees tended to display cooperative behaviors after specific social interactions.

📝 **Explanation:**
Dr. Martin and her colleagues conclude:
"**Both** gorilla bonding activities and chimpanzee group dynamics **might have contributed** to the development of social behaviors in early human societies."
For this conclusion to be supported, both species must show **cooperative behaviors linked to social interaction**. That's exactly what **A** states:
- **Both species** displayed cooperative behaviors
- These behaviors followed **specific social interactions**

Why the others don't work:

- **B)** Only gorillas showed the behavior → contradicts the claim about **both** species
- **C)** Only chimpanzees showed it → again, not both
- **D)** Neither showed it → directly undermines the conclusion

16

Answer: C) on Maui, the rate of population growth is higher for invasive plants than it is for vulnerable native plants, like the 'ilima flower.

Explanation:

The passage tells us:

- Hawaiian yellow-faced bees help native plants **but** pollinate **more invasive species** (like lantana)
- Invasive species are **more abundant**
- Therefore, it's **not surprising** that...

So what would **logically follow** from bees pollinating invasive species more often?

➡ Invasive plants, being more frequently pollinated, will **reproduce faster**, and thus their **populations grow more quickly**.

That's precisely what **C** states.

 Why the others don't work:

- **A)** Describes native plant distribution, but doesn't address **growth trends**
- **B)** Talks about when invasive species became abundant—not relevant to **why it's unsurprising**
- **D)** Says both are likely to go extinct, which contradicts the idea that invasives are **thriving**

17

Correct Answer: B) explains

Why B is correct:

We need a verb that fits **standard present-tense narrative** for a textbook, which is still being read and referenced.

- **"Explains"** is **simple present**, and correct for general facts or summaries of current content.

The others:

- **A) explaining** → would require a helping verb (e.g., "is explaining")
- **C) to explain** → infinitive doesn't fit the sentence structure
- **D) having explained** → past perfect participle, not compatible here

18

Answer: C

✍ Why C is correct:

The sentence is in the **present tense** ("A catalyst **is**...") and describes a **general truth** in science.

- **"Assists"** keeps the verb in present tense and agrees with the subject ("a catalyst").

The others:

- **A) assisted, B) had assisted, D) was assisting** → All are **past tense** or **past progressive**, which clash with the present-tense framing.

19

Answer: A

✍ Why A is correct:

- A **colon** (:) is used properly here because the second part of the sentence **expands on or clarifies** the first.
- This construction suggests: "...a significant list: the National Register…"

The others:

- **B) list. The** → unnecessary sentence break
- **C) list; the** → a **semicolon** is too strong; it separates **independent clauses**, which isn't needed here
- **D) list the** → grammatically incorrect and lacks punctuation

20

Answer: B

 Why the Semicolon is Correct

A **semicolon (;)** is the knight in shining armor for this situation. It:
- Smoothly connects **two related independent clauses**
- Avoids the comma splice
- Keeps the flow of thought without a conjunction

Why the Other Choices Are Wrong
- **A) medicine** ← no punctuation → Incomplete; missing punctuation between two full clauses.
- **C) medicine and** → Illogical: you can't add "and" before a new sentence. Grammatically broken.
- **D) medicine,** → Comma splice! Two full clauses joined by only a comma = grammatical error.

21

Answer: A

 Explanation:

We're inserting a **noun phrase** that identifies who the environmental scientists are. The key is to **avoid unnecessary punctuation**.
- "Environmental scientists Jane Goodall and Rachel Carson" is a clean, grammatically correct noun phrase:
- **Title + names** = no commas needed if the names are **essential to the meaning**.

Why the others don't work:
- **B)** adds a comma at the end → not needed unless the names are **nonessential**, which they aren't here.
- **C)** adds a comma **between the two names** (before "and") → incorrect unless for stylistic reasons like Oxford comma in a list of 3+.
- **D)** places a comma after "scientists," creating a **comma splice** or incorrectly offsetting an essential noun phrase.

22

Answer: A

 Explanation:

This is a **contrast**: even though the system was updated recently, it **still** needs more work. "**Still,**" captures this contrast perfectly.

> [?] **Why the others don't work:**

- **B) By contrast,** → used when comparing **two different subjects** (e.g., Austin vs. another city), not the **same subject over time**.
- **C) For example,** → suggests illustration, but this isn't an example—it's a **development despite recent efforts**.
- **D) Instead,** → used when **substituting** one action for another; not relevant here.

23

Answer: A

Explanation:

We contrast Linda Chen's **modest beginnings** with the **unexpected success** of her blog. "**Nevertheless**" is the perfect word to show this **surprising result** despite humble intentions.

> [?] **Why the others don't work:**

- **B) Therefore,** → implies **causation**, but success wasn't directly caused by her modest goals.
- **C) Furthermore,** → adds info, but not **contrasting** info.
- **D) Next,** → is used for **chronological sequencing**, not contrast.

24

Answer: B

 Explanation:

We move from a **broad statement** ("extensive research") to a **precise example** of that work. **"Specifically"** signals this shift from general to detailed.

> **Why the others don't work:**

- **A) Conversely,** → implies **opposition or contrast**, which doesn't exist here.
- **C) Finally,** → suggests a concluding idea, but this isn't a wrap-up.
- **D) Nevertheless,** → introduces **contrast**, but here we're narrowing focus, not opposing the prior statement.

25

Answer: B

 Explanation:

- The student needs to **quantify** the omega-3 content in both foods to support their claim. The key fact is that **salmon contains significantly more omega-3** per 100 grams (1.5 g vs. 0.3 g in walnuts).
- **B** does this effectively by directly **comparing the omega-3 content** and making the claim that salmon is a **better source** based on that fact.

> **Why the others don't work:**

- **A)** While it mentions both salmon and walnuts, it doesn't **compare the actual amounts** of omega-3, which is essential for the claim.
- **C)** This choice mentions **heart disease** but **doesn't directly compare the amounts** of omega-3 in salmon and walnuts.
- **D)** While true, this statement **doesn't address the comparison** of omega-3 content, which is the core of the student's claim.

26

Answer: B

 Explanation:

- The student wants to highlight a **contrast** between the two paintings. **B** does this by **clearly differentiating the two**:

  -**Impression, Sunrise** focuses on **light on water**.

  -**Woman with a Parasol** focuses on the **movement of wind**.

  ❓ **Why the others don't work:**

  - **A)** It's a true statement but doesn't address **the difference** between the two paintings.
  - **C)** It focuses too much on **landscape themes** and doesn't emphasize the key **difference** in how light and movement are treated in each painting.
  - **D)** It mentions the impressionist technique but **doesn't highlight the specific contrast** • between the two paintings.

27

Answer: D

 Explanation:

- This answer **directly compares the number** of **native and non-native species** catalogued.
- The notes mention **12 native coral species** and **22 non-native coral species**, so **D** effectively communicates that **non-native species outnumber native species** in the data.

  ❓ **Why the others don't work:**

  - **A)** This talks about the **native status** of two specific corals but doesn't address the **comparison** of the total number of species catalogued.
  - **B)** While true, this doesn't highlight the **comparison of native vs. non-native species**.
  - **C)** This focuses on **fish** rather than the **coral species**, so it's not directly addressing the question about the number of coral species.

Module 2

Reading and Writing
27 Questions, 32 Minutes

DIRECTIONS

The questions in this section address a number of important reading and writing skills. Each questions includes one or more passages, which may include a table or graph. Read each passage and question carefully, and then choose the best answer to the question based on the passage(s).

All questions in this section are multiple-choice with four answer choices. Each question has a single best answer.

1

Whether the scientific contributions of a physicist such as Isaac Newton or Albert Einstein were groundbreaking or simply a natural progression of prior discoveries, their work was influenced by the prevailing theories of their time and therefore cannot be understood without a corollary understanding of the principles without which they would have been forced to ___ their hypotheses.

Which choice completes the text with the most logical and precise word or phrase?

A) dismiss
B) elaborate
C) preserve
D) simplify

2

With his critically acclaimed theories on black holes, quantum mechanics, and other complex phenomena in the realm of physics, renowned scientist Stephen Hawking has ___ unparalleled recognition as a visionary thinker.

Which choice completes the text with the most logical and precise word or phrase?

A) demanded
B) preserved
C) attained
D) rejected

3

Though many ___ investigations of the effects of dietary habits on heart health focus on individuals consuming high-fat diets, researchers Nina T. Robertson and Paul K. Young recently chose the novel path of studying individuals who consume predominantly plant-based diets, in regions such as the Mediterranean and Southeast Asia.

Which choice completes the text with the most logical and precise word or phrase?

A) unusual

B) limited

C) traditional

D) arbitrary

4

The following text is adapted from John Keats's 1819 poem *Ode to a Nightingale*.

Thou wast not born for death, immortal Bird!
No hungry generations tread thee down;
The voice I hear this passing night was heard
In ancient days by emperor and clown:
Perhaps the self-same song that found a **path**
Through the sad heart of Ruth, when, sick for home,
She stood in tears amid the alien corn.

As used in the text, what does the word "path" most nearly mean?

A) Routine

B) Consequence

C) Passage

D) Influence

5

The ancient texts of the Indus Valley Civilization—inscriptions found on seals and pottery dating back over 4,000 years—are thought of as early forms of writing today, but the question of whether the symbols were used as a functional script or served some other symbolic purpose is ___; we will never be able to answer it.

Which choice completes the text with the most logical and precise word or phrase?

A) unsolvable
B) contradictory
C) essential
D) inevitable

6

James Baldwin was a prominent African American writer and activist. Critics and readers have praised his work for addressing themes of race, sexuality, and identity in groundbreaking ways. But Baldwin is not the only writer to explore these topics in literature. In her 2017 novel *The Hate U Give*, Angie Thomas successfully brought issues of racial inequality and police brutality into the contemporary young adult fiction landscape.

Which choice best states the main purpose of the text?

A) To urge modern writers to avoid controversial social issues in literature
B) To discuss two writers who address themes of race and identity in their work
C) To argue that works addressing race are more impactful than other types of literature
D) To explain why one writer has been more widely recognized than the other

CONTINUE

7

Text 1

Efforts to develop automated systems for diagnosing rare diseases have not yielded reliable results, and we may be approaching the limit of what current technologies can achieve. However, it is not clear whether pursuing this goal is the best use of resources—researchers like Dr. Lin and Dr. Patel argue that focusing on improving the human-diagnostic process may provide better outcomes in patient care.

Text 2

Genetic disorders, which are often rare, share many overlapping symptoms, making them particularly challenging to diagnose. Recent research by Dr. Torres and her team demonstrated that by using AI to analyze genetic data as patterns in visual models, significant breakthroughs were made in distinguishing between similar disorders. This progress highlights the innovative potential of automated diagnostic systems.

Based on the texts, how would the author of Text 2 most likely respond to the claim in the underlined sentence of Text 1?

A) By arguing that humans often disagree when diagnosing rare diseases.

B) By suggesting that technology will remain secondary to human expertise in diagnosing rare diseases.

C) By criticizing earlier studies for underestimating the challenges of automating diagnostics.

D) By asserting that it may be possible to improve automated diagnostic systems.

8

The following text is adapted from Elizabeth Acevedo's 2018 novel *The Poet X*. Xiomara, a teenager living in Harlem, reflects on her relationship with her mother.

I sat at the kitchen table, surrounded by the smell of spices and stews. Mami would hum softly as she chopped vegetables, her voice rising and falling like a song I didn't know the words to. It reminded me of when I was younger and she used to sing lullabies in Spanish. Even though I didn't understand the words, the melody made me feel warm and safe, like a cozy blanket on a cold night. It wasn't just the song—it was her presence, constant and comforting.

Based on the text, what does the narrator mainly remember about the times when her mother sang to her?

A) That she enjoyed learning the meanings of the songs her mother sang

B) That her mother often sang while preparing food

C) That the sound of her mother's singing made her feel safe

D) That her mother only sang lullabies when it was cold

9

Table: Maximum and Minimum heights of Tree Species in Rainforests of South?

species	Minimum Height (meters)	Maximum Height (meter)	Range (meter)
Ceiba Pentandra	5	60	55
Swietenia macrophylla	10	45	35
Bertholletia excelsa	15	50	35
Ficus elastica	3	65	62

The table is from a 2021 study in which biologists analyzed the height ranges of different rainforest tree species in South America. Among the trees in the table, the species with the greatest range between minimum and maximum heights is ___.

Which choice most effectively uses data from the table to complete the statement?

A) Ceiba pentandra.

B) Swietenia macrophylla.

C) Bertholletia excelsa.

D) Ficus elastica.

10

Astronomers have observed an unexpected pattern in the orbits of a distant asteroid belt within another solar system. Using simulations of gravitational interactions with nearby planets and solar radiation, astrophysicist Dr. Lauren Gomez and her team suggest that this irregular pattern might be caused by a previously unseen dwarf planet affecting the belt's motion. The team recommends studying other asteroid belts in different solar systems to determine if similar objects are influencing their patterns.

Which choice best states the main idea of the text?

A) Gomez and her team were the first to confirm that many asteroid belts contain hidden dwarf planets.

B) Research has not yet identified clear evidence of a hidden dwarf planet in the distant asteroid belt.

C) Gomez and her team developed a new simulation to find dwarf planets without examining asteroid belt patterns.

D) Research has shown that an irregularity in the orbit of a distant asteroid belt might be explained by a hidden dwarf planet.

TEST 01

/// CONTINUE ➡

11

Marine biologist Dr. Carla Jensen is renowned for her innovative studies of coral reef ecosystems. Several of her most influential research papers focus on the diverse ways in which coral colonies recover after bleaching events. In a recent article, a marine science student suggests that Jensen's focus on coral recovery stems from her early experiences observing tide pools and marine life along the coast where she grew up.

Which quotation from a work by a marine biologist would be the most effective evidence for the student to include in support of this claim?

A) "Although coral reefs can appear damaged after bleaching events, some species of coral show remarkable resilience in their recovery."

B) "Many of Jensen's peers in marine biology have adopted her methods to study coral reef recovery and adaptation."

C) "Jensen's parents, who were avid scuba divers, frequently encouraged her to explore tide pools and observe the vibrant marine life as a child."

D) "Jensen showed an early interest in marine ecosystems: she began experimenting with water chemistry and marine biology while in high school."

12

Facillity	Location	Type	Average Annual Power Generation(MWh/yr)	Energy Source
highland	Texas	Wind	8,500	Wind
Sunfield	California	Solar	15,400	Sunlight
Blue Ridge	Colorado	Wind	9,200	Wind
Desert Solar	Arizona	Solar	22,000	Sunlight

A wind power facility, as the name suggests, relies on natural wind to generate electricity. Unlike solar power facilities that depend on sunlight, wind power facilities can operate during both the day and night, provided wind speeds are sufficient. On the other hand, solar power facilities can store energy in batteries during the day to meet demand at night. Despite differences in operational conditions, solar power facilities often produce more megawatt-hours of power per year (MWh/yr) than certain wind power facilities. For example, the _____

Which choice most effectively uses data from the table to complete the example?

A) Average power generated annually by the Blue Ridge facility is higher than that generated by the Highland facility.

B) Highland facility, which is wind-powered, has more turbines than any other facility in the table.

C) Wind facility with the highest average annual power generation in the table generates more electricity than the solar facility with the lowest annual power generation.

D) Average power generated annually by Desert Solar is higher than that generated by any of the wind facilities in the table.

13

In the Amazon rainforest, capuchin monkeys use two different types of tools to crack open nuts. One tool is advanced. The monkeys shape a stone into a sharp edge using a specific technique. The other tool is simpler. The monkeys find a naturally round stone on the ground. The shaped stone is harder to create but much more effective than the naturally round stone at cracking hard-shelled nuts. When studying capuchin monkeys, primatologist Sarah Lin observed that they store the shaped stones in hidden locations or carry them in their hands when not using them. The monkeys don't treat the naturally round stones the same way. This suggests to Lin that the _____.

Which choice most logically completes the text?

A) monkeys prefer to share their shaped stones but don't share the naturally round stones.

B) shaped stones are easier for most of the monkeys to carry than the naturally round stones.

C) shaped stones are more valuable to the monkeys than the naturally round stones.

D) monkeys realize that both kinds of stones are less effective than their teeth at cracking hard-shelled nuts.

14

To explore scientific advancements, Dr. Laura Kim and her colleagues analyzed a set of studies on renewable energy, including a 2020 paper by Singh et al., titled "Advances in Solar Panel Efficiency." Kim's team searched for the term "solar" in the Scopus and Web of Science databases and found that, while most papers focused on renewable energy, a few papers discussed unrelated topics like the behavior of solar flares on the sun. One possible explanation for this result is that it occurred because _____.

Which choice most logically completes the text?

A) a group of researchers had an extended discussion about solar flares during a conference on renewable energy.

B) most of the papers in the Scopus and Web of Science databases do not study solar panel efficiency or solar-related phenomena.

C) the word "solar" may not always refer to renewable energy but to other subjects like solar flares on the sun.

D) scientists working on renewable energy frequently publish papers about unrelated phenomena such as solar flares.

CONTINUE

15

In a 2015 study in Europe, Dr. Elena Moreno and her team found a positive correlation between the levels of nitrogen compounds and algae growth in coastal waters. Many other studies have produced similar findings, suggesting to some scientists that this correlation is common in coastal ecosystems worldwide. However, when Dr. Yuki Tanaka and her colleagues examined coastal waters in East Asia, they observed no significant relationship between nitrogen compounds and algae growth. If similar results are observed in other regions outside Europe, that could suggest that _____ .

Which choice most logically completes the text?

A) the nitrogen compound levels reported in Tanaka and colleagues' study were much lower than those reported in Moreno's study, even though algae growth levels were approximately the same.

B) Moreno's team may have unintentionally measured a different property of coastal waters than nitrogen compound levels and algae growth.

C) the relationship between nitrogen compounds and algae growth reported by Moreno reflects conditions that are specific to certain coastal ecosystems in Europe rather than universal patterns.

D) most of the studies conducted in Europe have measured nitrogen compound levels and algae growth with greater accuracy than was possible in Tanaka's study.

16

In the captivating 2018 exhibition *Transformative Textiles* at the Modern Art Museum in Los Angeles, artist Maria Gonzalez showcased tapestries that were ___ woven from recycled fabric scraps, such as old denim and curtains. By doing so, the Mexican-American artist inspired audiences to reconsider how discarded textiles could be repurposed into meaningful works of art.

Which choice completes the text so that it conforms to the conventions of Standard English?

A) dyed, stitched, and,

B) dyed, stitched, and

C) dyed, stitched; and

D) dyed stitched; and

17

In Japan, it's not uncommon for towns or villages to be known ___ a name that reflects their cultural heritage, local craftsmanship, or natural surroundings. For instance, the town of Yufuin has been referred to as "the Land of Hot Springs," a name that highlights its reputation for its relaxing onsen and scenic views of Mount Yufu.

Which choice completes the text so that it conforms to the conventions of Standard English?

A) by

B) by-

C) by,

D) by:

18

In 2019, James Carter ___ as an engineer at the Massachusetts Institute of Technology, developing renewable energy systems.

Which choice completes the text so that it conforms to the conventions of Standard English?

A) working

B) was working

C) to work

D) to have worked

19

The term "cyberspace" ___ first popularized in the 1984 novel *Neuromancer* by American-Canadian author William Gibson.

Which choice completes the text so that it conforms to the conventions of Standard English?

A) were

B) were being

C) was

D) have been

20

In the summer of 1985, it was impossible to escape the hit song "Summer Nights" by The Sunsets. As of July 20, the song had spent ten consecutive weeks on the Billboard Top 100 chart and ___ No. 1 on the list.

Which choice completes the text so that it conforms to the conventions of Standard English?

A) have been ranking

B) was ranked

C) were ranked

D) are ranking

21

In 1995, the United Nations recognized a section of the Amazon Rainforest as a World Heritage Site, ___ the area's unparalleled biodiversity and ecological importance.

Which choice completes the text so that it conforms to the conventions of Standard English?

A) they cite

B) cited

C) citing

D) has cited

CONTINUE

22

In 1965, researchers first discovered the molecule chlorophyllide, which they believed to be present only in plants—and, they hypothesized, exclusively in green vegetation. _____ scientists know that chlorophyllide can also exist in certain algae species, but this finding wasn't made until decades later.

Which choice completes the text with the most logical transition?

A) Nowadays,
B) For example,
C) In other terms,
D) Therefore,

23

According to conventional classifications, all celestial bodies in the solar system fall into one of three categories: planets, moons, or asteroids. The object Jupiter (discovered in ancient times), _____ is classified as a planet, while Europa (discovered in 1610) is classified as a moon.

Which choice completes the text with the most logical transition?

A) additionally,
B) likewise,
C) as an example,
D) on the other hand,

24

If you were to examine the architectural styles of the Eiffel Tower in France or the Burj Khalifa in the United Arab Emirates, you might notice that their towering structures and innovative designs make them iconic symbols of modern engineering. _____ architects often refer to these structures as marvels of human ingenuity.

Which choice completes the text with the most logical transition?

A) However,
B) Moreover,
C) Similarly,
D) Fittingly,

25

Although its compact size made it ideal for small apartments, the 2018 FlexiAir portable air conditioner lacked a built-in air purification system. ___, when designing the 2021 FlexiAir Pro model, engineers prioritized including a high-efficiency filter to address this limitation.

Which choice completes the text with the most logical transition?

A) Previously,
B) Specifically,
C) Likewise,
D) Thus,

26

While researching a topic, a student has taken the following notes:

- In urban areas, community gardens have been increasing in popularity.
- Sarah Kim and Anthony Lopez of GreenCity Initiatives studied whether community garden growth is influenced by city policies.
- Kim and Lopez analyzed reports from neighborhoods with and without city-supported garden programs, comparing the number of gardens established over a decade.
- Gardens were more prevalent in areas with supportive policies.
- Educational campaigns may have contributed to the success of these programs.

The student wants to emphasize the aim of the research study. Which choice most effectively uses relevant information from the notes to accomplish this goal?

A) Sarah Kim and Anthony Lopez, researchers at GreenCity Initiatives, wanted to investigate whether community garden growth is influenced by city policies.

B) Thanks to the work done by Sarah Kim and Anthony Lopez, we now know that educational campaigns may have contributed to the success of community gardens.

C) Researchers at GreenCity Initiatives have determined that gardens were more prevalent in areas with supportive city policies.

D) Sarah Kim and Anthony Lopez analyzed reports from neighborhoods with and without city-supported programs, comparing the number of gardens established over a decade.

27

While researching a topic, a student has taken the following notes:

- Pollination is the process by which plants transfer pollen to reproduce.
- This process often involves animals such as bees or bats.
- Bees typically pollinate during the daytime.
- This behavior helps flowering plants reproduce.
- Bats typically pollinate at night.
- This behavior helps plants in arid regions adapt to limited water availability.

The student wants to emphasize a difference between the pollination behavior of bees and that of bats. Which choice most effectively uses relevant information from the notes to accomplish this goal?

A) Both bees and bats are animals that assist in pollination, a process that enables plants to reproduce.

B) Bats typically pollinate at night, which helps plants in arid regions adapt to limited water availability.

C) Pollination, the transfer of pollen to enable plant reproduction, often involves animals such as bees and bats.

D) Bees typically pollinate during the day to help flowering plants reproduce, whereas bats pollinate at night to help plants in arid regions adapt.

TEST 01

Module 2 answer

1

Correct Answer: A) dismiss

📝 **Explanation:**

This sentence implies that **without the foundational principles**, the physicists' ideas wouldn't have held. They would have had to **abandon** their hypotheses because the necessary groundwork wasn't there.

- **"Dismiss"** = to reject or set aside → Fits the idea of being unable to proceed without foundational knowledge.

  💡 **The other options:**
  - **B) elaborate** → To add detail—illogical here.
  - **C) preserve** → To maintain—not relevant; the issue is not about keeping ideas.
  - **D) simplify** → Reducing complexity, which is unrelated to the **need for foundational support**.

2

Correct Answer: C) attained

📝 **Explanation:**

Hawking's groundbreaking work **earned** him recognition.
- **"Attained"** means **to achieve or gain** → perfect match.

  💡 **The other options:**
  - **A) demanded** → implies force or insistence, which doesn't reflect the tone.
  - **B) preserved** → means to keep something existing, not gain something new.
  - **D) rejected** → completely opposite of the sentence's meaning.

3 ....

Correct Answer: C) traditional

 Explanation:

The sentence sets up a **contrast**: the majority of studies focus on high-fat diets, but these researchers chose something **novel**. So, the existing studies must be **standard, established** ones.

• **"Traditional"** = conventional or commonly practiced → aligns with contrast to "novel."

💡 **The other options:**

• **A) unusual** → contradicts the intended contrast.

• **B) limited** → doesn't convey "standard" or "commonly done."

• **D) arbitrary** → suggests randomness, not relevance here.

4 ....

Correct Answer: C) Passage

📝 **Explanation:**

The poem speaks metaphorically: the bird's song **travels emotionally** through Ruth's heart. The "path" here is a **figurative route** through her sorrow.

• **"Passage"** captures that idea of a **movement or journey**, especially through something emotional or physical.

💡 **The other options:**

• **A) Routine** → implies regularity; not poetic or emotional.

• **B) Consequence** → incorrect meaning; not a result.

• **D) Influence** → too abstract; "path" here suggests a **traveling route**, not merely influence.

5

Correct Answer: A) unsolvable

Explanation:

The final clause ("we will never be able to answer it") makes the case clear: the question cannot be resolved.

- **"Unsolvable"** = impossible to answer or resolve → fits perfectly.

The other options:

- **B) contradictory** → means containing opposing ideas; doesn't fit the tone.
- **C) essential** → unrelated; this isn't about **importance**, but **possibility**.
- **D) inevitable** → implies certainty, not mystery.

6

Correct Answer: B) To discuss two writers who address themes of race and identity in their work

Explanation:

- The passage introduces **James Baldwin**, noting his powerful work on **race, sexuality, and identity**.
- Then it brings in **Angie Thomas**, who addresses **racial inequality and police brutality** in a modern YA novel.
- The tone is **informative**, not argumentative or comparative.
- Therefore, the passage's goal is to **highlight a thematic link** between **two different authors** from different eras.

Why the others don't work:

- **A)** The passage doesn't **urge** anything—there's no call to action or avoidance.
- **C)** There is no **value judgment** here; the author doesn't argue that race-related literature is *more impactful*.
- **D)** The passage doesn't discuss **relative recognition** at all—it treats both authors respectfully and doesn't compare fame.

7

Correct Answer: D) By asserting that it may be possible to improve automated diagnostic systems.

 Explanation:

- **Text 1** is skeptical of automated systems and suggests we may have reached their limits.
- **Text 2**, however, presents **recent breakthroughs** using AI to analyze genetic data visually, leading to **significant improvements** in distinguishing similar disorders.
- ➡ That directly **refutes the doubt** in Text 1 and supports the idea that automation **can improve and innovate**.

  💡 **Why the others don't work:**
  - **A)** While Text 1 hints at **human diagnostic focus**, Text 2 **doesn't critique human disagreements**.
  - **B)** Text 2 actually **supports automation**, so it wouldn't downplay it as "secondary."
  - **C)** There's no direct criticism of **earlier studies**—just progress being highlighted.

8

Correct Answer: C) That the sound of her mother's singing made her feel safe

 Explanation:

- The passage is emotionally reflective. Xiomara doesn't understand the words of her mother's Spanish lullabies, but:
  "the melody made me feel warm and safe, like a cozy blanket on a cold night... it was her presence, constant and comforting."
- ➡ Her memory is tied to **emotional security and comfort**, not language or specific events.

  💡 **Why the others don't work:**
  - **A)** She explicitly says she **didn't understand** the words—so it wasn't about learning meaning.
  - **B)** Her mother hums while cooking, yes, but the **main memory** is of her **singing lullabies**, not just background kitchen music.
  - **D)** The blanket imagery is **metaphorical**—there's no evidence her mother sang *only* when it was cold.

9

Correct Answer: D) Ficus elastica.

✒ Why it's correct:
- Ficus elastica has the **largest height range**:
- $65 \text{ (max)} - 3 \text{ (min)} = 62 \text{ meters}$
- This range is greater than any of the other trees listed.

  #### ♡ Why the others are wrong:
  - **A) Ceiba pentandra** → Range is $60 - 5 = 55$
  - **B) Swietenia macrophylla** → Range is $45 - 10 = 35$
  - **C) Bertholletia excelsa** → Range is $50 - 15 = 35$

10

Answer: D) Research has shown that an irregularity in the orbit of a distant asteroid belt might be explained by a hidden dwarf planet.

✒ Explanation:
- The passage **describes an observed irregular pattern** in an asteroid belt's orbit.
- Dr. Gomez and her team use **simulations** to propose that a **hidden dwarf planet** may be responsible.
- They then suggest expanding the study to **other solar systems** to see if similar patterns exist.
- ➡ This aligns exactly with **D**: a **possible explanation** for the irregular pattern is a **hidden dwarf planet**—the central idea.

  #### ♡ Why the others don't work:
  - **A)** "Confirmed that many asteroid belts contain hidden dwarf planets" →　Overstates the claim. No confirmation was made.
  - **B)** "No clear evidence⋯" →　Misleading. The passage **suggests** a plausible cause, not the absence of evidence.
  - **C)** "Developed a new simulation to find dwarf planets without examining patterns" →　Contradicts the passage. The team is **examining patterns in asteroid belts**.

54

11

Answer: C) "Jensen's parents, who were avid scuba divers, frequently encouraged her to explore tide pools and observe the vibrant marine life as a child."

 Explanation:

• The **student's claim** hinges on a **connection between childhood experiences** (tide pools/marine life) and her later research focus (coral recovery).

• **C** directly supports this by **linking her early exposure** to marine ecosystems with her later professional interest.

💡 **Why the others don't work:**

• **A)** Discusses coral resilience after bleaching, but nothing about her **background or early influence**.

• **B)** Talks about her **peers adopting her methods**—irrelevant to her **personal origin story**.

• **D)** Mentions early interest in marine biology, but not tied specifically to **tide pools or coastal observation**, which is central to the student's claim.

12

Answer: D) Average power generated annually by Desert Solar is higher than that generated by any of the wind facilities in the table.

 Why this is correct:

• Desert Solar (solar) → **22,000 MWh/yr**

• Highest wind output is Blue Ridge → **9,200 MWh/yr**

• **22,000 > 9,200** = clearly supports the idea that **some solar facilities produce more than wind facilities**.

➡ This option **directly supports** the claim in the passage by **giving a clear, data-based comparison**.

💡 **Why the other choices don't work:**

• **A)** *"Blue Ridge is higher than Highland"*
  - ✔ True (9,200 > 8,500),
  - But **both are wind** facilities—it doesn't compare solar to wind, so it's **irrelevant** to the point.

• **B)** *"Highland has more turbines"*
  - The table **doesn't include data** about the number of turbines—this is **unsupported**.

55

- **C)** *"Wind facility with the highest average generates more than the solar facility with the lowest"*
  - Blue Ridge (wind) = 9,200
  - Sunfield (solar) = 15,400

  False. The **lowest solar** still produces **more** than the **highest wind**, so this is **inaccurate**.

13

Answer: C) shaped stones are more valuable to the monkeys than the naturally round stones.

📝 **Explanation:**
- We are told the **shaped stone is more effective** but harder to make.
- Monkeys **store** or **carry** shaped stones, but they **don't do this** for the naturally round ones.
- This behavior implies that the **shaped stones have more perceived value**—they're worth the effort to protect and carry.

  💡 **Why the others don't work:**
  - **A)** No evidence is given about **sharing**—that's an unwarranted leap.
  - **B)** There's no mention that shaped stones are **easier to carry**—in fact, they may be **harder** to carry due to shaping.
  - **D)** The monkeys are using tools to **supplement** their abilities, not reject them in favor of teeth.

13

Answer: C) the word "solar" may not always refer to renewable energy but to other subjects like solar flares on the sun.

📝 **Explanation:**
- The passage says the team searched for "solar" and found some unrelated results, like **solar flares**.
- So, the confusion arises from the **ambiguity of the term "solar"**.
- **C** gives the most direct and logical reason: the word **has multiple meanings**, not just renewable energy.

  💡 Why the others don't work:
  - **A)** Conference discussions aren't related to **search engine/database results**.
  - **B)** Incorrect: most papers **do** focus on renewable energy—it's just that **some didn't**.
  - **D)** Implies that **renewable energy scientists write about solar flares**, which isn't supported and feels like a stretch.

15

Answer: C) the relationship between nitrogen compounds and algae growth reported by Moreno reflects conditions that are specific to certain coastal ecosystems in Europe rather than universal patterns.

Explanation:

- The key idea: Moreno's findings (positive correlation) do **not appear** in East Asia.
- If this pattern is repeated **elsewhere outside Europe**, then the relationship is likely **not universal**.
- **C** captures this possibility: the correlation may be **specific to European ecosystems**.

   Why the others don't work:
   - **A)** Brings in **numerical comparison** of nitrogen levels—but the **core issue is correlation**, not absolute levels.
   - **B)** Suggests an **error in measurement**, which isn't implied and is speculative.
   - **D)** Suggests European studies are more **accurate**, which is an unsupported and biased assumption.

16

Answer: B)

Explanation:

This is a **series of three past participles**: *dyed, stitched, and woven*.

- **B)** is correct because:
  - The list uses **parallel structure**
  - **No comma is needed after "and"** (that would be incorrect unless it were part of a stylistic Oxford comma in more complex structures—but this isn't one).

   Why the others are wrong:
   - **A)** Incorrect comma after "and"
   - **C & D)** Semicolons are only used in lists with internal commas or complex clauses—not needed here.

17

Answer: A)

📝 Explanation:

The idiomatic expression is:

"known **by** a name"

Much like: "She is known by her nickname."

💡 Why the others don't work:
- **B)** "by-" → punctuation error
- **C & D)** Inappropriate punctuation for this construction

18

Answer: B)

📝 Explanation:
- The time marker "**In 2019**" calls for a **past progressive tense** to describe an **ongoing action** at that time.
- "**Was working**" = correct tense and form.

💡 Why the others don't work:
- **A)** "working" → would need a helping verb
- **C)** "to work" → suggests intention, not past action
- **D)** "to have worked" → overly complex and incorrect tense

19

Answer: C)

📝 Explanation:
- "**The term**" is **singular**, so we need "**was**".
- Passive construction: *"was popularized"*

The other

- **A) were** = plural
- **B) were being** = incorrect tense and voice for a completed event in the past
- **D) have been** = present perfect, not appropriate here

20

Answer: B)

Explanation:
- This sentence is in **past perfect**: *"had spent..."* followed by a **simple past** to coordinate what happened **after**.
- **"Was ranked"** is the correct verb to indicate its **status during that period**.

   The others:
  - **A) have been ranking** → present perfect progressive = wrong tense
  - **C) were ranked** → plural verb with singular subject
  - **D) are ranking** → present tense = wrong

21

Answer: C) citing

Explanation:
- This is an example of a **participial phrase** providing **additional context**:
  "···recognized···, citing the area's unparalleled biodiversity···"
- "Citing" tells us **why** it was recognized.

  The others:
  - **A) they cite** = starts a new independent clause → incorrect
  - **B) cited** = needs its own subject
  - **D) has cited** = tense mismatch and wrong form

22

Answer: A)

 Explanation:

- The sentence presents a **contrast between past and present knowledge**.
- "**Nowadays**" clearly signals a **shift to present-day understanding** and is the most logical transition.

  💡 **Why not the others:**
  - **B) For example** → Used to introduce specific instances, not to contrast time periods.
  - **C) In other terms** → Paraphrasing phrase, not relevant here.
  - **D) Therefore** → Suggests logical consequence, not temporal contrast.

23

Answer: C) as an example.

 Explanation:

- The sentence gives **examples** of how celestial bodies are classified, following a general statement.
- "**As an example**" introduces Jupiter (and Europa) as illustrations of the prior claim.

  💡 **The others:**
  - **A) additionally** → Suggests adding another point, not illustrating.
  - **B) likewise** → Suggests similarity, but we're discussing **different categories**.
  - **D) on the other hand** → Indicates contrast, but this isn't a contradiction.

24

Answer: D) Fittingly.

📝 **Explanation:**

- The sentence follows **praise** for the structures.
- "**Fittingly**" expresses that it's **appropriate or natural** for architects to admire them.

The others:

- **A) However** → Would signal contradiction, but there's no shift in tone.
- **B) Moreover** → Adds info, but lacks the **tone of appropriateness**.
- **C) Similarly** → No comparison is being made.

25

Answer: D) Thus

📝 **Explanation:**

- We have a **cause-and-effect relationship**:   Problem in the 2018 model → Solution in the 2021 model
- **"Thus"** shows a logical result.

 The others:

- **A) Previously** → Doesn't imply causation
- **B) Specifically** → Adds detail, but doesn't show **result**
- **C) Likewise** → Suggests similarity, not cause and correction

26

Answer: A)

📝 **Explanation:**

- **A clearly states the research purpose**—what the researchers **wanted to find out**.
- This directly aligns with the instruction to **emphasize the aim**.

💡 **The others:**

- **B)** Shifts focus to **educational campaigns**, which were only a **possible factor**.
- **C)** States a conclusion, not the research's original **purpose**.
- **D)** Describes **methodology**, not the **goal**.

27

Answer: D)

📝 **Explanation:**

• Only **D** includes: 1. **Bees' daytime pollination**

2. **Bats' nighttime pollination**

3. **Distinct effects and environments**

→ A **clear contrast**, exactly as requested.

💡 **The others:**

• **A)** General info about pollination, no comparison.

• **B)** Only gives info about **bats**, no **contrast**.

• **C)** Defines pollination, no **difference** between species.

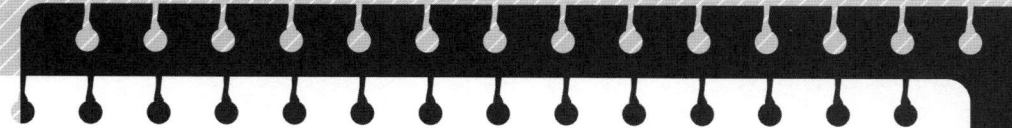

TEST 2

Module 1

Reading and Writing
27 Questions, 32 Minutes

TEST 02

DIRECTIONS

The questions in this section address a number of important reading and writing skills. Each questions includes one or more passages, which may include a table or graph. Read each passage and question carefully, and then choose the best answer to the question based on the passage(s).

All questions in this section are multiple-choice with four answer choices. Each question has a single best answer.

1

The following text is from Sarah Lee's 1947 novel Shadows in the Forest. The story takes place in a village surrounded by a dense forest.

The young hunter crouched low, adjusting his stance to stay hidden in the undergrowth, his eyes narrowing as he scanned the area with a determined gaze. In the silence, he could sense the tension in the air, the weight of the hunt pressing on his shoulders. The elder hunter watched from a distance, noting the youth's determination. He **registered** approval.

As used in the text, what does the word "registered" most nearly mean?

A) acknowledged

B) admired

C) neglected

D) expressed

2

Although fewer visitors explore the Chaco Canyon in New Mexico compared to popular sites in Yellowstone, Yosemite, or the Grand Canyon, the Chaco Canyon offers the benefit of preserving historical artifacts that represent cultural influences _____ the Southwestern United States. This dedication to specific, gradually unfolding historical narratives enriches the experience for archaeologists and history enthusiasts alike.

Which choice completes the text with the most logical and precise word or phrase?

A) unrelated to

B) prohibitive in

C) characteristic of

D) unchanging in

3

Marcus Gray, who volunteered for several environmental projects across Europe, South America, and Africa, undoubtedly contributed significantly, but to _____ a meaningful impact on a global scale, almost nothing is more influential than rallying communities to work together. For example, people will always remember that Sylvia Johnson was the first organizer to initiate a cross-border tree-planting movement across multiple nations.

Which choice completes the text with the most logical and precise word or phrase?

A) recognize

B) disregard

C) restrain

D) establish

4

In a study by Rachel N. Lee, Jason T. Davis, and their team, residents of Lyon, France, and of Naples, Italy, were surveyed about their use of public libraries in their cities. Of the 1,200 respondents from Lyon, 52.3% indicated that they frequently visit the city's libraries, while of the 850 respondents from Naples, 43.2% reported the same. *It may be tempting to assume the difference is due to varying hours of operation at these libraries;* however, given that the libraries in Naples are open more hours per week than those in Lyon, access alone can't account for the difference in library usage.

Which choice best describes the function of the underlined portion in the text as a whole?

A) It introduces a contrasting example to the situation described earlier in the text.

B) It provides background information to help clarify the extent of the researchers' study.

C) It marks a transition from discussing the researchers' findings to analyzing their approach.

D) It presents a possible reason for the team's findings that the text proceeds to challenge.

5

The following text is from Eleanor M. Price's 1912 book *Reflections on Nature.*

We are creatures of the earth, we men and women. We thrive in green spaces and peace. That is why we seek out forests and mountains, and the city feels more and more distant with each passing season. In the freshness of dawn—when nature stirs awake around us—we find comfort in the quiet lakes and high cliffs. But in the bustle of midday, when the world is full of noise, oh! the solitude vanishes, and we feel like fish out of water. Then we yearn for the rustling leaves, the whispering winds, and the soothing hum of nature's harmony.

Which choice best states the main purpose of the text?

A) To convey that the hectic pace of urban life can make people long for their childhood

B) To warn people to take time to appreciate the unique traits of urban settings

C) To explore common reasons why individuals are drawn to spend time in rural landscapes

D) To suggest that most individuals prefer cities over tranquil lakes

6

Eagles and dolphins are known to have advanced echolocation abilities, which help them navigate and detect prey in complex environments. Rabbits and turtles, however, are generally thought to lack this capability. Many scientists once believed the same about bats, but Dr. Alice Thompson and her team decided to investigate if this assumption was accurate. The team observed how bats wearing specialized sound-detecting devices responded to echoes in a simulated cave environment. Bats adjusted their flight paths based on the echoes, suggesting their echolocation is more like that of dolphins and eagles than that of rabbits or turtles.

Which choice best describes the main idea of the text?

A) Bats have more sophisticated echolocation than dolphins or eagles.

B) Thompson's team created sound-detecting devices for bats.

C) Initially, Thompson's team thought bats lacked echolocation abilities similar to dolphins, but this belief changed over time.

D) The findings of Thompson's team suggest that, like dolphins and eagles, bats may possess advanced echolocation.

TEST 02

CONTINUE

7

President Andrew Jackson is most famous for his role in the Indian Removal Act, a controversial policy that led to the forced relocation of Native American tribes, known as the Trail of Tears. Jackson's legacy is complex: he is also recognized for his efforts in reducing national debt and implementing the Spoils System, which redefined political appointments but raised questions about favoritism and corruption. Despite these achievements, his presidency is often overshadowed by the contentious policies that shaped his reputation.

Which choice best states the main idea of the text?

A) The Indian Removal Act was a significant policy during Andrew Jackson's presidency.

B) Andrew Jackson is commonly associated with a controversial policy, but this often obscures some of his other notable contributions.

C) Some of Andrew Jackson's policies influenced the governance of later administrations.

D) Andrew Jackson's legacy is primarily defined by his stance on Native American relations.

8

Echoes of the Past is a 1910 novel by Samuel Green. In one section, Green uses figurative language to connect the narrator's bustling city life in New York and the quiet countryside of the narrator's childhood, writing:

Which quotation from *Echoes of the Past* most effectively illustrates the claim?

A) "The [train] whistles cut through the city air, their sound like the shattering of cups and plates. I find them oddly soothing."

B) "And when the wind blows from the north, the scent of pine and earth drifts over the crowded avenues of [New York City] like a memory of home."

C) "I whispered a tune, with a hint of longing, a song from my youth."

D) "The old oaks had once lined the paths; [Central Park] was dotted with them."

9

Many people believe that gentle nature sounds, like the rustling of leaves or flowing water, contain auditory qualities that are universally soothing to people of all ages. In a study, Dr. Emma L. Harper and her team played both a recording of a gentle river sound and a recording of city traffic noise to a group of participants. The researchers also monitored the participants' blood pressure, as lower blood pressure is considered a measure of relaxation. They claim that the river sound did indeed help the participants feel more relaxed.

Which finding, if true, would most directly support Harper and colleagues' claim?

A) The participants' blood pressure readings were more erratic during the river sound than during the traffic noise.

B) Participants preferred the river sound over the traffic noise when asked which sound made them feel more at ease.

C) Participants' blood pressure was noticeably lower during the river sound than during the traffic noise.

D) Both the river sound and the traffic noise recordings were played at a similar volume level.

10

Contribution of Three Key Sectors to Texas Economy in 2018

Sector	Approximate contribution
Technology	$25,610,000,000
Agriculture	$12,450,000,000
Education/Health Services	$10,320,000,000

The technology industry in Texas generates a substantial amount of revenue, as do the agriculture and education/health services sectors. When the contributions of these sectors are compared, the impact of the agriculture sector on the Texas economy in 2018 _____

Which choice uses data from the table to most effectively complete the comparison?

A) surpassed the contribution made by education/health services but fell short of that made by technology.

B) exceeded the contribution made by both technology and education/health services.

C) was greater than the contribution made by technology but equal to that made by education/health services.

D) was lower than the contribution made by either education/health services or technology.

CONTINUE

11

Wind flowing around an obstacle creates eddies (patterns of swirling air) of varying size; by detecting these eddies, birds can determine the size and position of the obstacle. Research conducted by Dr. Michael Yates and Dr. Sarah Lin using models of three wing shapes—narrow, intermediate, and wide—showed that for large eddies, birds with intermediate wings would be better able than narrow-winged birds to distinguish between eddies and general turbulence in the air. A second research team has hypothesized that in foggy conditions, intermediate-winged birds will be more likely than narrow-winged birds to detect obstacles that create large eddies.

Which finding, if true, would most directly support the second research team's hypothesis?

A) A study using obstacles that created large eddies in foggy conditions found that the intermediate-winged kestrel (Falco tinnunculus) avoided more than half of the obstacles.

B) A study using obstacles that created large eddies in foggy conditions found that the falcon (Falco columbarius), which has relatively narrow wings, collided with more than half of the obstacles.

C) A study using obstacles that created large eddies in foggy conditions found that some specimens of the intermediate-winged kestrel (Falco tinnunculus) collided with obstacles more often than other specimens of the same bird did.

D) A study using obstacles that created large eddies in foggy conditions found that the narrow-winged falcon (Falco columbarius) collided with obstacles more often than the intermediate-winged kestrel (Falco tinnunculus) did.

12

Ranking of Environmental and Sociocultural Benefits of Community Parks

(scale of 1 to 25; 1 = highest)

Social ecological benefit	Park managers	Environ—mentalists	Local community
promotion of mental well-being	6	2	5
access to recreational space	4	10	3
preservation of natural habitats	23	24	18
improvement of air quality	7	5	6
support for local wildlife	2	8	9

Dr. Megan Cho, Dr. Louis Tan, and their team surveyed three groups of people in Portland, Oregon—park managers, environmentalists, and members of the local community—to compare their views on the benefits community parks provide. They asked each group to rate 25 benefits of community parks, with a conclusion that both environmentalists and the local community prioritize the promotion of mental well-being as a key benefit of community parks.

Which choice best describes data in the table that support the team's conclusion?

A) The improvement of air quality was ranked lower for the local community than it was for park managers.

B) The preservation of natural habitats was ranked higher for the local community than was the promotion of mental well-being.

C) The promotion of mental well-being was ranked higher for environmentalists than it was for the local community.

D) The promotion of mental well-being was ranked higher for environmentalists than were the other four benefits.

70

13

Text 1

The artist John Smith once argued that drawing is the most accessible of art forms to practice. While those who pursue other art forms—oil painting, sculpture, digital design—often need costly materials and large studios, drawing only requires a pencil and paper. Smith claimed that an artist could sketch on a park bench, in a coffee shop, or even on the margins of a notebook. Therefore, he believed people could create meaningful art without the need for significant financial resources.

Text 2

Any discussion of contemporary art must acknowledge the commercialization of the field. Although theoretically anyone can exhibit in popular galleries or publish in art magazines, many of those who do have formal training and considerable practice, which are time-intensive and costly. This financial barrier indirectly influences who can successfully enter the world of art.

Based on the texts, how would Smith (Text 1) most likely respond to the argument presented in Text 2?

A) By asserting that those artists who exhibit in renowned galleries are most likely to make a living solely from their artwork

B) By pointing out that people can create impactful art without the resources described by the author of Text 2

C) By suggesting that artists working in more commercially lucrative forms are unlikely to engage in drawing

D) By agreeing that most artists need to work other jobs to support the training requirements described in Text 2

14

The Beat Generation, which produced influential works like Jack Kerouac's novel *On the Road* and nonliterary expressions such as Allen Ginsberg's live readings, is often said to have ended by the 1960s. However, some scholars argue that the Beat Generation's spirit never truly disappeared, as its themes continue to resonate in contemporary art and music today. These scholars therefore suggest that _____

Which choice most logically completes the text?

A) if a cultural movement includes both literary and nonliterary expressions, then it is likely to have lasting impact.

B) if a cultural movement is highly experimental, then it is unlikely to sustain its influence for an extended period.

C) if the literary works of a cultural movement remain relevant, then the nonliterary works are less important.

D) if the influence of a cultural movement endures, then in some sense the movement itself persists.

15

Artists studying famous landscapes may look at paintings of natural wonders such as the Grand Canyon. A painting, however, cannot fully capture how a landscape changes with light and weather, or how it feels to stand at its edge. A painting of the Grand Canyon thus _____

Which choice most logically completes the text?

A) serves to exaggerate the landscape's dramatic depth.

B) misrepresents how the landscape appears to viewers who have never visited the Grand Canyon.

C) fails to convey the full impact of the landscape's scale and atmosphere.

D) conceals the signs of erosion that have shaped the landscape's features.

16

Handpicked, roasted, and ground to perfection, the coffee beans used by Brazilian-based artisan roaster Maria Costa are designed to inspire coffee enthusiasts to explore the deep flavors of the beverage _____ her meticulously crafted brews at the 2020 Coffee Culture Festival in São Paulo were no exception.

Which choice completes the text so that it conforms to the conventions of Standard English?

A) flavors;

B) flavors and to

C) flavors,

D) flavors

17

A renowned recipient of the Pulitzer Prize and the National Book Award, _____ known as narrative journalism when she pioneered a new storytelling technique that brought readers closer to real-life events.

Which choice completes the text so that it conforms to the conventions of Standard English?

A) the result of writer Joan Didion's expansion of journalistic storytelling was the introduction of a new narrative style

B) the introduction of a new narrative style by writer Joan Didion led to the evolution of journalistic storytelling

C) journalistic storytelling was expanded by writer Joan Didion who introduced a new narrative style

D) writer Joan Didion expanded journalistic storytelling and introduced a new narrative style

18

The Green Meadow Sanctuary is one of the 52 protected areas in the state's wildlife conservation system. The sanctuary, also referred to as Verdant Haven in the local dialect, was the subject of an article _____ in the State Gazette on August 5, 2020.

Which choice completes the text so that it conforms to the conventions of Standard English?

A) appearing

B) appears

C) has appeared

D) appeared

19

Chef Martin Lopez's passion for cooking started when he learned traditional recipes from his grandmother as a child, and he later developed unique culinary styles, creating signature dishes like "Spiced Avocado Tostadas" (2018) and "Heritage Mole" (2019). Yet he's best _____ especially after his 2021 cookbook Authentic Flavors became a bestseller internationally—as a chef.

Which choice completes the text so that it conforms to the conventions of Standard English?

A) known

B) known:

C) known—

D) known;

20

After extensive discussion, _____ finally reached an agreement: the committee would grant the 2022 Innovation Award to Dr. Emily Chen for her groundbreaking work in renewable energy solutions.

Which choice completes the text so that it conforms to the conventions of Standard English?

A) you

B) it

C) anyone

D) they

21

How did the term "serendipity" come into existence? Interestingly, _____. It first appeared in a letter by British author Horace Walpole.

Which choice completes the text so that it conforms to the conventions of Standard English?

A) it was coined by an author.

B) it was coined by an author?

C) wasn't it coined by an author.

D) was it coined by an author.

22

In the early 2000s, scientists discovered a new species of bacteria thriving in extreme environments, which they initially thought could only exist in hydrothermal vents deep in the ocean. _____ researchers would find similar bacteria in arctic ice sheets, but this discovery wouldn't come until years later.

Which choice completes the text with the most logical transition?

A) For example,

B) Eventually,

C) In other words,

D) Earlier,

23

The earliest known use of the word "alchemy" in English is credited to translations from Arabic texts in the 14th century. However, these texts were not originally written in English; _____ they were translated from Arabic, which was the dominant language of science during that era.

Which choice completes the text with the most logical transition?

A) as a result,

B) similarly,

C) rather,

D) finally,

24

The river Nile flows northward, making it one of the few major rivers in the world that flows in this direction. _____ the river Amazon flows primarily southward, following a different path across the continent.

Which choice completes the text with the most logical transition?

A) In reality,

B) Nevertheless,

C) Hence,

D) Next,

25

In a recent poll, respondents were asked to name cities they considered "iconic," defined as "well-known, historically significant, or visually striking." The survey compiled these responses into a ranked list and revealed that Paris and Rome both placed in the top ten. _____ no city surpassed New York in popularity.

Which choice completes the text with the most logical transition?

A) In other words,

B) As a result,

C) Still,

D) For example,

TEST 02

26

- Emily Carr was a Canadian artist who produced a significant number of paintings inspired by the natural landscape and Indigenous cultures.
- Her painting Forest Splendor was completed in 1931 and displayed in a gallery in 1950.
- Forest Splendor is composed of oil paint on canvas and measures 2,500 square inches in area.
- Her work Totem Spirit was completed in 1932 and displayed in a gallery in 1955.
- Totem Spirit is composed of oil paint and charcoal on canvas and measures 4,000 square inches in area.

Which choice most effectively uses information from the given sentences to emphasize how the two works are similar?

A) Created by artist Emily Carr in 1931 and 1932, respectively, both Forest Splendor and Totem Spirit use oil paint as a medium.

B) Artist Emily Carr completed Forest Splendor in 1931, and Totem Spirit followed in 1932.

C) Emily Carr's work Forest Splendor is composed of oil paint on canvas, while Totem Spirit is composed of oil paint and charcoal on canvas.

D) Between Emily Carr's works Totem Spirit and Forest Splendor, the former is the larger of the two.

27

While studying rocks, a student has taken the following notes:
- The Richter scale is a numerical scale used to measure the magnitude of earthquakes, with each unit increase representing a tenfold increase in magnitude.
- Earthquakes with larger magnitudes cause more severe shaking and damage than those with smaller magnitudes.
- The San Francisco earthquake of 1906 registered a magnitude of 7.9 on the Richter scale.
- The 2011 earthquake in Christchurch, New Zealand, registered a magnitude of 6.3 on the Richter scale.

The student wants to compare the magnitudes of the earthquakes in San Francisco and Christchurch. Which choice most effectively uses relevant information from the notes to accomplish this goal?

A) The San Francisco earthquake was stronger than the Christchurch earthquake, which is why it registered a higher magnitude on the Richter scale.

B) The Richter scale can be used to compare the severity of earthquakes based on their magnitude measurements.

C) An earthquake with a magnitude of 7.9, like the one in San Francisco, is stronger than one with a magnitude of 6.3, like the one in Christchurch.

D) The San Francisco earthquake registered a higher magnitude on the Richter scale, indicating it caused more severe shaking than the Christchurch earthquake.

Module 1 answer

1

Correct Answer: D) expressed

Explanation:

To "register" something in this context means to **show** it—in this case, to *express approval* through some discernible reaction (perhaps a nod, a look, or an internal acknowledgment that becomes outwardly visible). It implies **conveying** the approval somehow, not merely perceiving it.

Why not the others?
- **A) acknowledged** – This suggests a mental recognition without necessarily expressing it. But the context implies the elder's approval was *noticeable*, not just thought.
- **B) admired** – Admiring is a deeper emotional response than simply expressing approval. The elder might admire the youth, but the text doesn't provide that level of emotional depth—only a reaction to competence.
- **C) neglected** – Clearly the opposite of what happened. The elder did *not* ignore the youth; he noticed and responded.

2

Correct Answer: C) characteristic of

Explanation:

The phrase "cultural influences **characteristic of** the Southwestern United States" is idiomatic and precise. It means these influences are **typical or representative** of that region.

Why not the others?
- **A) unrelated to** – Opposite of what the sentence is trying to convey. The artifacts **are** relevant.
- **B) prohibitive in** – "Prohibitive" means discouraging or preventing something—makes no sense here.
- **D) unchanging in** – Doesn't fit the idea of "cultural influences"; culture evolves, and the sentence speaks of **representation**, not permanence.

3

Correct Answer: D) establish

📝 **Explanation:**

"To **establish** a meaningful impact" is a clear, formal, and idiomatic expression meaning "to make a lasting, effective contribution."

💬 **Why not the others?**

- **A) recognize** – Illogical: you *recognize* something that already exists. Doesn't fit with *making* impact.
- **B) disregard** – Inappropriate; the sentence wants to emphasize *creating* impact, not ignoring it.
- **C) restrain** – Again, this is about *building up* a global impact, not *holding it back*.

4

Correct Answer: D) It presents a possible reason⋯ that the text proceeds to challenge

📝 **Explanation:**

The author proposes a common-sense **assumption** (library hours cause usage differences), only to immediately **refute** it with evidence: Naples libraries are actually open more.

💬 **Why not the others?**

- **A) contrasting example** – Not a separate example, just a *hypothesis* being tested.
- **B) background info** – Not really; it's speculative reasoning, not setup.
- **C) transition to analysis** – Partly true, but too vague. The key function is **challenging a misconception.**

5

Correct Answer: C) explore common reasons why individuals are drawn to spend time in rural landscapes

📝 **Explanation:**

The passage is poetic and reflective, exploring **why** nature soothes us and why urban life feels foreign at times.

❓ Why not the others?

- **A) long for childhood** – No mention of childhood or nostalgia.
- **B) warn to appreciate urban settings** – The tone is *not* a warning, nor does it praise cities.
- **D) suggest people prefer cities** – Directly contradicted by the text's wistful longing for nature.

6

Correct Answer: D) captures this perfectly—it reflects the central **shift in understanding**: bats are more like dolphins and eagles in echolocation than previously thought.

❓ Why not the others?

- **A)** Incorrect—bats aren't said to have *more* advanced echolocation than dolphins or eagles, just that it is *similar*.
- **B)** Too narrow and misses the point—the devices are a means to the discovery, not the main idea.
- **C)** Misleading—Thompson's team wasn't the origin of the older assumption; the scientific community held that view. The team tested the assumption, not *changed their own minds* mid-study.

7

Correct Answer: B) captures this balance: the dominant association with the Indian Removal Act *obscures* other aspects of his presidency.

❓ Why not the others?

- **A)** True, but **too narrow**—the Indian Removal Act is a **detail**, not the **main point**.
- **C)** Unfounded in the text—nothing suggests Jackson's policies influenced later governance.
- **D)** Overstates the point. While his legacy is *heavily influenced* by his Native American policy, the text says his legacy is **"complex"**, not "primarily defined."

8

Correct Answer: B) is poetic and precise. The **"crowded avenues" (city)** are literally infused with **scented air (pine and earth)**—a metaphorical return to childhood. The simile *"like a memory of home"* links present with past, urban with rural.

❓ Why not the others?
- **A)** Sounds are described metaphorically ("shattering"), but it doesn't link city to countryside.
- **C)** Suggests nostalgia but doesn't reference city or nature—*too abstract*.
- **D)** Descriptive, but too literal. There's no metaphor or figurative link—just an observation about trees.

9

Correct Answer: C) provides direct **physiological evidence—lower blood pressure**—matching the stated metric of relaxation.

❓ Why not the others?
- **A)** Erratic readings = stress, not relaxation—this would undermine the claim.
- **B)** Preference ≠ physiological relaxation. You can like something without your body being more relaxed.
- **D)** Volume consistency is important scientifically, but doesn't **support** the claim—it's just **experimental control**.

10

Answer: A) surpassed the contribution made by education/health services but fell short of that made by technology.

📝 Why this is correct:
- Agriculture (**$12.45B**) is **greater than** Education/Health Services (**$10.32B**)
- But Agriculture is **less than** Technology (**$25.61B**) Hence, A captures this **dual comparison** with precision.

⟨?⟩ **Why the other choices fall short:**

• **B) exceeded the contribution made by both technology and education/health services.**

→ False. Agriculture **did not** exceed technology.

• **C) was greater than the contribution made by technology but equal to that made by education/health services.**

→ Double false! Agriculture is **less** than technology and **not equal** to education/health.

• **D) was lower than the contribution made by either education/health services or technology.**

→ Also false. Agriculture is **more** than education/health.

11

Answer: D) A study using obstacles that created large eddies in foggy conditions found that the narrow-winged falcon (Falco columbarius) collided with obstacles more often than the intermediate-winged kestrel (Falco tinnunculus) did.

📝 **Explanation:**

This answer **directly compares** the two bird types **under foggy conditions** with **large eddies**, exactly the situation in the hypothesis. It shows that **intermediate-winged birds detect (and thus avoid) obstacles better**, supporting the hypothesis perfectly.

⟨?⟩ **Why the other choices fail to provide the best support:**

• **A)** *Kestrel avoided more than half of the obstacles.*

We learn kestrels did well—but there's **no comparison** to narrow-winged birds. This is **partial support**, but not the strongest.

• **B)** *Narrow-winged falcon collided with more than half of the obstacles.*

Again, this shows **they did poorly**, but **no reference to intermediate-winged birds**. Partial, but insufficient.

• **C)** *Some kestrels collided more than others.*

This speaks only to **variation within one species**, not a comparison between wing types. Entirely unrelated to the hypothesis.

12

Answer: D)

 Why it supports the conclusion:
- Environmentalists gave "promotion of mental well-being" a **rank of 2**, which is their **highest priority** among the five listed benefits.
- This directly supports the idea that they **prioritize it**.
- The local community gave it a **5**, also among their **top rankings** (only "access to recreational space" was ranked higher, at 3).
So together, this confirms that both groups **value** mental well-being highly.

Why the other options fall short:
- **A)** *Air quality was ranked lower for the local community than for park managers.*
  - → True, but **not related to mental well-being**, which is the focus of the conclusion.
- **B)** *Natural habitats ranked higher than mental well-being for the local community.*
  - → False. Natural habitats = 18, mental well-being = 5. So mental well-being ranked **higher**.
- **C)** *Mental well-being ranked higher for environmentalists than for the local community.*
  - → Technically true (2 vs. 5), but this **only compares one group to another**, not to **other benefits**. It's weaker support than D.

13

Answer: B) By pointing out that people can create impactful art without the resources described by the author of Text 2

Why it's correct:
- **Text 1 (Smith's view):** Art, especially **drawing**, is **accessible** and does **not require expensive materials** or training.
- **Text 2** emphasizes that formal training and costs are **barriers** in the commercial art world. Smith would likely respond not by engaging in that system, but by reaffirming his belief that **art can thrive outside those systems**, with minimal resources.

Why not the others?
- **A)** Smith isn't concerned with making a living or the economics of art careers.
- **C)** He never suggests drawing is incompatible with other forms or industries.
- **D)** He **downplays the need for financial resources**, not agrees with the burden of them.

14

Answer: D) if the influence of a cultural movement endures, then in some sense the movement itself persists.

📝 **Why it's correct:**

• The text says: though the **era** of the Beats ended, their **themes live on** in contemporary art/music.
• So, the **"spirit"** of the movement endures.
• **D** captures that idea: if the **influence** lives on, the movement is **not truly gone**.

💬 **Why not the others?**

• **A)** True but not the main point of the paragraph—it's not a general claim about all movements.
• **B)** Opposite of the point—the passage claims **lasting influence** despite the experimental nature.
• **C)** Incorrect—it never argues that literary works diminish the value of nonliterary ones.

15

Answer: C) fails to convey the full impact of the landscape's scale and atmosphere.

📝 **Why it's correct:**

• The sentence sets up a contrast: a painting **cannot capture changes in light, weather, or emotional impact**.
• Thus, it **fails to fully convey** the **dynamic and immersive qualities** of the real place.

💬 **Why not the others?**

• **A)** Exaggeration isn't mentioned; the issue is limitation, not dramatization.
• **B)** Misrepresentation is too strong—nothing says the painting is inaccurate, just incomplete.
• **D)** Erosion isn't discussed at all—this introduces an unrelated idea.

16

Answer: A)

 Why the other choices are incorrect:

- **B) flavors and to** — ungrammatical and awkward. Attempts to turn the second clause into a phrase but fails.
- **C) flavors, —** A **comma between two independent clauses = comma splice**, which is a grammar error.
- **D) flavors —** No punctuation = run-on sentence.

17

Answer: D)

📝 **Explanation:**

This is a grammatically sound and **direct** continuation from the opening phrase. It makes Joan Didion the **clear subject** and maintains parallel structure.

A) Awkward, overly wordy, and the sentence lacks balance.

B) Passive voice and wordy.

C) "who introduced..." is a bit clunky, and overall the phrasing lacks elegance.

18

Correct Answer: A) appearing

📝 **Explanation:**

This is a **participial phrase** ("article appearing in...") modifying "article." It's concise, fluid, and grammatically correct.

B) *appears* — Tense mismatch (past main verb "was" vs. present "appears").

C) *has appeared* — Too complex and shifts focus.

D) *appeared* — Grammatically okay, but makes the sentence clunky and less fluid than **A**.

19

Answer: C)

 Explanation:

The dash sets off the **emphatic, explanatory clause**: "especially after..." It's stylish and grammatically correct, signaling that extra information is being added.

A) *known* — Needs punctuation after it.

B) *known:* — A colon would only be correct if what follows were a list or explanation directly tied to "known," but this is not quite the case.

D) *known;* — Semicolon improperly separates the sentence.

 20

Answer: D)

Explanation:

"They" correctly refers to the previously mentioned **group (the committee)**. This is the appropriate subject for a **plural verb** ("reached").

A) *you* — Incorrect subject; doesn't refer to the committee.

B) *it* — "Committee" is collective, but this usage suggests a non-human subject.

C) *anyone* — Too vague and singular; doesn't match the group context.

21

Answer: A

Explanation:

This is the only **complete declarative sentence** that fits the tone and punctuation of the passage. It follows the word "Interestingly" smoothly.

B) *it was coined by an author?* — That's a question, inappropriate with "Interestingly."

C) *wasn't it coined by an author.* — Inversion and punctuation are off; not declarative.

D) *was it coined by an author.* — Also a question, not a statement.

22

Answer: B)

 Why it's correct:

"Eventually" provides the most logical **temporal transition**: it signals that what was once thought impossible (bacteria living outside hydrothermal vents) was later proven otherwise.

A) For example – Signals an illustration, not a sequence.

C) In other words – Paraphrasing signal; not appropriate here.

D) Earlier – Implies a backward jump in time, which contradicts the "years later" in the second clause.

23

Answer: C)

Why it's correct:

"Rather" is used to **correct or contrast** a previous assumption. Here, it corrects the possible misconception that the texts were originally in English.

A) As a result – Implies consequence, not correction.

B) Similarly – Suggests comparison, which doesn't fit the contrast.

D) Finally – Implies sequence or culmination; not appropriate.

24

Answer: B)

Why it's correct:

"Nevertheless" signals **contrast**, which is key here: the Nile flows north, but **in contrast**, the Amazon flows south.

A) In reality – Adds emphasis, not contrast.

C) Hence – Indicates causality, not contradiction.

D) Next – Implies sequence, not opposition.

25

Answer: C)

 Why it's correct:

"Still" introduces a **counterpoint** or **unexpected fact**—despite other cities ranking highly, *New York surpassed them all.*

A) In other words – Restates, not contrasts.

B) As a result – Implies cause/effect, not contradiction.

D) For example – Signals elaboration, not contrast.

26

Correct Answer: A) Created by artist Emily Carr in 1931 and 1932, respectively, both Forest Splendor and Totem Spirit use oil paint as a medium.

 Why it's correct:

It clearly points out a **shared feature** (use of oil paint) and includes **chronological context**. This emphasizes similarity directly and effectively.

B) Just sequencing. No emphasis on **similarity**.

C) Focuses on a **difference**, not similarity.

D) Focuses on size—**contrast**, not similarity.

27

Correct Answer: C) An earthquake with a magnitude of 7.9, like the one in San Francisco, is stronger than one with a magnitude of 6.3, like the one in Christchurch.

Why it's correct:

This answer **directly compares** the two earthquakes by **explicitly referencing** their magnitudes and using accurate language ("stronger").

A) Explanation is vague and circular.

B) True but generic—doesn't **compare** the two events.

D) Adds interpretation ("caused more shaking") not directly drawn from notes.

Page Intentionally Left Blank

Module 2

Reading and Writing
27 Questions, 32 Minutes

DIRECTIONS

The questions in this section address a number of important reading and writing skills. Each questions includes one or more passages, which may include a table or graph. Read each passage and question carefully, and then choose the best answer to the question based on the passage(s).

All questions in this section are multiple-choice with four answer choices. Each question has a single best answer.

1

The Great Wall of China, stretching over 13,000 miles, is a remarkable structure that has stood for centuries, making it a _____ marvel of engineering.

A) sophisticated
B) conventional
C) inconsequential
D) monumental

2

The Great Wall of China—a series of fortifications made of stone, brick, tamped earth, wood, and other materials—was constructed along the northern borders of China to protect against invasions and raids. Although often described as simply a defensive structure, the Great Wall is actually _____, given that it symbolizes the ingenuity and strength of ancient Chinese civilization. It represents a lasting symbol of resilience that endures to this day.

Which choice completes the text with the most logical and precise word or phrase?

A) resourceful
B) intricate
C) unspoiled
D) evocative

3

Modern electric vehicles, like the Tesla Model S (introduced in 2012) and the Nissan Leaf (launched in 2010), are designed to reduce emissions and offer a quieter, smoother driving experience. These innovations aim to _____ a sense of environmental responsibility in drivers, even though some still argue about the environmental impact of battery production and disposal, creating mixed perceptions about their overall eco-friendliness.

Which choice completes the text with the most logical and precise word or phrase?

A) foster

B) limit

C) neutralize

D) deny

4

Scientific databases, such as the Protein Data Bank, are massive repositories of information on protein structures that can be utilized for empirical research to understand how _____ a particular protein is within various biological processes. For instance, one might hypothesize about the role of a specific enzyme, but only a comprehensive database analysis can confirm its recurring function across multiple species.

Which choice completes the text with the most logical and precise word or phrase?

A) pervasive

B) plausible

C) prominent

D) significant

5

The following text is adapted from Jane Doe's 1910 essay *Art and Society*.

The Tribune [an American newspaper], in response to various criticisms of the simplicity, form, and style of American architecture abroad, contends that the American approach is that each individual should feel free to build and design as they wish. However, society unceasingly attempts, not to make each individual's preferences the standard, but to cultivate a collective appreciation for what is universally elegant, functional, and meaningful, guiding individuals to recognize such values.

Which choice best describes the function of the underlined sentence in the text as a whole?

A) It implies that standards of design evolve over time.

B) It argues that Americans lack the refined aesthetic they ought to have.

C) It provides an example that reinforces the author's main argument.

D) It expresses a viewpoint the author opposes.

6

The mammal species *Sciurus niger* (the fox squirrel), which inhabits dense forests with thick tree cover, and *Tamias striatus* (the eastern chipmunk), which is more commonly found in open woodland or forest edges, share North American forest habitats along with *Buteo jamaicensis* (the red-tailed hawk), a predator that emits a high-pitched call as a warning to others of potential danger. Ecologist Jamie Lee and their team, studying the ecological community shared by these species, hypothesized that there is an inverse relationship between mammals' field of vision while foraging and their sensitivity to predator warning calls from neighboring species.

Which finding, if true, would most directly support Lee and team's hypothesis?

A) When Lee and team played *B. jamaicensis* alarm calls, *S. niger* and *T. striatus* displayed no reaction, whereas *B. jamaicensis* displayed predator-avoidance behavior.

B) Many local mammal species with foraging habits similar to those of *S. niger* displayed no reaction when Lee and team played *B. jamaicensis* alarm calls, whereas *S. niger* displayed predator-avoidance behavior.

C) Some individuals of *T. striatus* displayed predator-avoidance behavior when Lee and team played *B. jamaicensis* alarm calls, whereas nearly all did when *S. niger* alarm calls were played.

D) *T. striatus* displayed no reaction when Lee and team played *B. jamaicensis* alarm calls, whereas *S. niger* displayed predator-avoidance behavior in response to the calls.

7

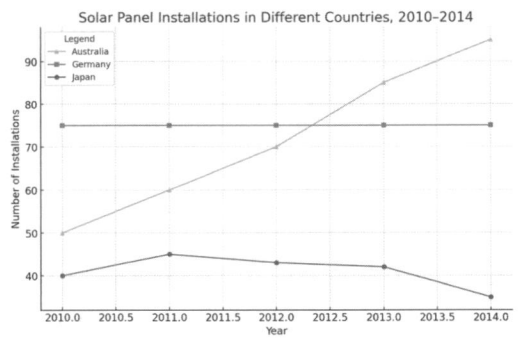

Solar Panel Installations in Different Countries, 2010-2014

Above is a report from an international organization that tracks the adoption of renewable energy technologies, such as solar panels, in different countries. From 2010 to 2014, the number of solar panel installations in many countries increased. However, there are also countries where the number decreased or remained unchanged; for example, _____

Question 7: Which choice most effectively uses data from the graph to complete the example?

A) *Australia was higher in 2014 than in 2010, whereas the number in Japan was higher in 2014 than in 2010.*

B) *Australia was higher in 2014 than in 2010, whereas the number in Germany was the same in 2014 as in 2010.*

C) *Germany was the same in 2014 as in 2010, but it had more solar installations than either Australia or Japan did in 2014.*

D) *Australia was lower in 2014 than in 2010, whereas the number in Germany was the same in 2014 as in 2010.*

8

Studies of the Effects Fertilizers vs. No Fertilizers on Crop Growth

Authors	Crop	Crop growth fertilizer (Kilograms per hectare)	Crop growth with no fertilizer (Kilograms per hectare)
Samir Patel and colleagues	corn	3,450	2,890
Laura Zhang and colleagues	potatoes	4,220	3,850
Michael O'Connor and colleagues	barley	5,130	4,780
Amina Yusuf and colleagues	carrots	3,120	3,550

Michael O'Connor and colleagues found that fertilizer application increased the yield of barley crops. However, some studies on other crops have found the opposite effect, for example _____

Which choice most effectively uses data from the table to complete the assertion?

A) *crop growths with fertilizer have ranged from 3,120 kilograms per hectare for carrots to 5,130 kilograms per hectare for barley.*

B) *Samir Patel and colleagues found a similar association in a study using corn.*

C) *Amina Yusuf and colleagues reported an even larger positive effect of no fertilizer on the yield of carrots.*

D) *a study using barley yielded 5,130 kilograms per hectare with fertilizer and only 4,780 kilograms per hectare without fertilizer.*

9

Population and Area Data for Various Regions in 2020

Region	Country	UN estimate	Reported region proper	Reported metropolitan	Metropolitan area (square Kilometers)
London	United Kingdom	9,304,000	4,488,000	14,327,000	8,382
Melbourne	Australia	5,078,000	2,123,000	5,356,000	9,993
Los Angeles	United States	10,127,000	3,976,000	13,214,000	12,559
Mexico City	Mexico	21,779,000	8,918,000	22,044,000	7,866

Population data can vary depending on which areas are counted. Typically, governments report one population count for the "region proper" (including only residents within strict boundaries) and another for the metropolitan area (including residents from adjacent localities). A journalist claims that UN population estimates likely include people outside the regions proper.

Which choice best describes data in the table that support the journalist's claim?

A) *All the region proper areas are below 10,000 square kilometers.*

B) *The metropolitan area of Melbourne is significantly larger than 4,000 square kilometers.*

C) *The reported region proper population of London is significantly larger than the reported region proper population of Los Angeles.*

D) *The UN estimated Mexico City's population to be 21,779,000, which is significantly larger than the reported population for the region proper.*

10

Desert Trails is a 1920 novel by Clara Henderson, originally written in English. In the novel, the town of Arroyo Grande is described as a captivating view for a group of travelers as they approach it from a distance: _____.

Which quotation from *Desert Trails* most effectively illustrates the claim?

A) "The desert was dressed in vibrant hues. Across its rugged peaks, the faint haze rested like a misty shroud on the land."

B) "They stepped into the narrow streets of Arroyo Grande as the town clock chimed, clear and lively, with a sound that echoed across the valley."

C) "Arroyo Grande appeared in the distance, glowing, bathed in the golden light, nestled among dense trees at the base of a towering, rugged cliff."

D) "All day they trudged through the arid landscape, up and down the dry, barren slopes, one after another, seemingly without end."

TEST 02

11

George Orwell's 1945 novella *Animal Farm* contains elements inspired by Orwell's political views and experiences: there are clear parallels between the events and characters in the novella and real-world political figures and ideologies. Consequently, *Animal Farm* is often described as an allegorical work. This characterization can be insightful, but it also introduces challenges in how the work is interpreted, as it might lead readers to think that Orwell merely allegorized historical events, which, in a creative domain where originality and artistic innovation are valued, can imply that _____.

Which choice most logically completes the text?

A) *Orwell should not have claimed that Animal Farm represents historical events.*

B) *the real-life inspirations for some characters in Animal Farm are difficult to trace.*

C) *Animal Farm is less of a literary accomplishment than it truly is.*

D) *critics debate whether Animal Farm displays more creativity than works lacking allegorical elements.*

12

Research has demonstrated that animal species with limited geographic habitats tend to exhibit lower behavioral diversity compared to species with wider distribution ranges. Based on these findings, scientists recently conducted experiments to assess how the behavioral diversity of various species of *Macropus*, a genus of marsupial found across Australia, might shift under altered habitat conditions. One of these species, *M. rufogriseus*, is typically found only in Tasmania. The researchers modeled what might occur if *M. rufogriseus* expanded into mainland Australian regions, and, in line with earlier research, the findings suggested that _____.

Which choice most logically completes the text?

A) other *Macropus* species could eventually inhabit Tasmania as well.

B) there was a progressive increase in the behavioral diversity of *Macropus* species in areas near Tasmania.

C) the behavioral diversity of *M. rufogriseus* increased over time.

D) *Macropus* species apart from *M. rufogriseus* would gradually become more prevalent in Tasmania.

13

Ancient myths surrounding the hero Heracles come from a variety of sources, including *Theocritus's Idylls*, composed around 275 BCE, and the *Library of Apollodorus* from the 1st or 2nd century CE. One of the most significant sources, *Diodorus Siculus's Historical Library*, was written in Greek in the 1st century BCE; some elements from it were later adapted by the Roman writer Seneca in *Hercules Furens* around 50 CE. However, while no source before 50 CE includes references to Heracles completing the Twelve Labors as a unified set, both *Hercules Furens* and the 3rd-century *Metamorphoses* by Ovid do. It can therefore be inferred that _____.

Which choice most logically completes the text?

A) Seneca did not use *Theocritus's Idylls* as a source for his version of Heracles's Twelve Labors.

B) Diodorus Siculus's accounts of Heracles in his *Historical Library* are more similar overall in content to those in *Apollodorus's Library* than they are to those in *Hercules Furens*.

C) Diodorus Siculus was unaware of the story of Heracles completing the Twelve Labors when composing his *Historical Library*, though historians know that such stories were available to him.

D) *Metamorphoses* is more historically accurate than *Historical Library* because *Apollodorus's Library* had not been written when Diodorus Siculus was writing his work.

14

The Study on Environmental Impact and Sustainability (EIS) seeks to examine long-term trends related to pollution and climate change by collecting and analyzing data from approximately 80,000 participants across various regions. As with most longitudinal studies, substantial funding is essential for EIS to gather the necessary data over timeframes and at intervals that ensure reliable conclusions. However, a simpler investigation, such as an ecology study focused solely on determining the average water consumption of households in a single city, is much less dependent on large amounts of funding because _____.

Which choice most logically completes the text?

A) *such studies are likely to be a lower priority for funding than EIS.*

B) *the ecology study is unlikely to be able to recruit 80,000 participants.*

C) *expanding the scope of such studies is unlikely to be feasible.*

D) *such studies are not attempting to monitor changes over extended periods.*

CONTINUE

15

In the late 18th century, colonial houses in New England were classified based on size and architectural complexity. The system took into account the number of rooms and stories each house had. "Grand" was the highest classification, while "modest" was the lowest, followed by unclassified homes. This classification influenced the size of a household: grand houses could accommodate between 15 and 20 family members and staff, while smaller houses accommodated fewer. Two of the colonial homes from this period were the Adams House (12 rooms and two stories) and the Phillips Estate (18 rooms and two stories). Of these two, only the Phillips Estate was classified as a grand house. It can therefore be concluded that _____.

Which choice most logically completes the text?

A) the Adams House could accommodate between 15 and 20 family members and staff.

B) all homes with at least 12 rooms were classified as grand houses.

C) the Phillips Estate required more than 20 staff members to operate effectively.

D) not all two-story houses were classified as grand houses.

16

The scientist Jane Goodall, along with others such as Dian Fossey and Biruté Galdikas, _____ widely known for the pioneering research on primate behavior, focusing on observing these animals in their natural habitats and advocating for their conservation.

Which choice completes the text so that it conforms to the conventions of Standard English?

A) has been

B) is

C) are

D) was

17

Today, the Nobel Prize is widely recognized as one of the most prestigious awards in the world, but when it was established in 1895, it was mainly intended to fulfill the vision of Alfred Nobel, who wanted to honor individuals who had made significant contributions to humanity in various fields. Over time, the prize has expanded _____ it now includes categories such as physics, chemistry, medicine, literature, peace, and economic sciences.

Which choice completes the text so that it conforms to the conventions of Standard English?

A) influence

B) influence,

C) influence, and

D) influence and

18

Artist Frida Kahlo's passion for painting developed when she was recovering from a serious accident in her teens, and she would go on to create an extensive collection of self-portraits that explored themes of identity, postcolonialism, and the human body. Yet she is best known as a surrealist painter, partly due to her _____ Portrait (1940), which became an iconic representation of Mexican culture.

Which choice completes the text so that it conforms to the conventions of Standard English?

A) painting (Mexican)

B) painting Mexican

C) painting: Mexican

D) painting, Mexican

19

Among Earth's forests, there are four main types: tropical, temperate, boreal, and montane. The Amazon Rainforest in South America is a tropical _____ it is one of the largest rainforests in the world, covering an area of about 5.5 million square kilometers.

Which choice completes the text so that it conforms to the conventions of Standard English?

A) forest, for example;

B) forest, for example,

C) forest; for example,

D) forest, for example

TEST 02

20

Architect Emma Sinclair is part of a committee responsible for evaluating new buildings to be added to the National Register of Architectural Landmarks, which includes the Thompson Library, constructed in 1924, and the Grandview Theater, built in 1931. Sinclair does not make these decisions alone, _____ nominations must receive approval from a panel of twelve other professionals.

Which choice completes the text so that it conforms to the conventions of Standard English?

A) however, all

B) however and all

C) however all

D) however. All

21

After learning about architect Julia Morgan, who designed over 700 buildings in California, the student found information about two other pioneers who worked in _____ Mary Colter known for her designs in the Southwest and Minoru Yamasaki who designed the original World Trade Center.

Which choice completes the text so that it conforms to the conventions of Standard English?

A) architecture.

B) architecture;

C) architecture

D) architecture,

22

The International Alliance for Cultural Cooperation (IACC) gathers comparative data on cultural exchange rates for its forty-three member nations. According to this data, in March 2023, an "event" of performances and exhibits valued at 200 euros (EUR) in France would have been valued at 85 EUR in another IACC member

_____

Which choice completes the text so that it conforms to the conventions of Standard English?

A) region Brazil.
B) region: Brazil.
C) region, Brazil.
D) region—Brazil.

23

"On Architecture," a study by Italian architect Renzo Rossi, addresses relatively simple building designs, while his work "The Foundations of Skyscrapers" tackles more complex structures. Regardless of the project's difficulty, Rossi always questions traditional design principles. _____ he evaluates each structure's purpose, irrespective of its complexity.

Which choice completes the text with the most logical transition?

A) For instance,
B) In that moment,
C) Indeed,
D) Conversely,

24

Though Baroque music was widely appreciated in seventeenth-century Europe, the style was rarely performed in royal courts until composer Johann Sebastian Bach popularized its intricate compositions. _____ his works include some of the first known uses of counterpoint techniques—such as in his "Brandenburg Concertos"—which earned him the title "master of harmony."

Which choice completes the text with the most logical transition?

A) Nevertheless,
B) That being said,
C) Furthermore,
D) Indeed,

25

While researching a topic, a student has taken the following notes:

- Alan Turing (1912–1954) was a mathematician and computer scientist born in London, England.
- He is widely regarded as one of the fathers of computer science.
- Turing developed the concept of a "Turing machine," a theoretical device that influenced modern computing.
- During World War II, he played a major role in breaking the German Enigma code, which was vital to the Allied war effort.
- Turing's contributions were recognized posthumously, and he is remembered as a pioneer in artificial intelligence.

The student wants to begin a narrative about Alan Turing's life. Which choice most effectively uses relevant information from the notes to accomplish this goal?

A) Alan Turing's story begins in London, England, in 1912.
B) Alan Turing made significant contributions to computer science, including his work on the "Turing machine" and his role in breaking the German Enigma code during World War II.
C) During World War II, Alan Turing helped decipher the German Enigma code, a critical achievement for the Allied forces.
D) Though his work was not fully recognized during his lifetime, Alan Turing is now celebrated as a foundational figure in computer science and artificial intelligence.

26

While conducting a research project, a student has taken the following notes:

- Dr. Robert Thompson is an environmental scientist.
- He coined the term "urbanflora" to describe plant species that thrive in urban environments.
- "Urbanflora" combines the words "urban" and "flora."
- His paper "City Gardens" discusses plants that adapt to city pollution.
- His study "Concrete Meadows" highlights hardy plants found in urban areas.

The student wants to provide an explanation and example of "urbanflora." Which choice most effectively uses relevant information from the notes to accomplish this goal?

A) The term "urbanflora," coined by environmental scientist Dr. Robert Thompson, is a combination of the words "urban" and "flora."

B) Dr. Robert Thompson uses the term "urbanflora," a combination of the words "urban" and "flora," to describe the plant species he studies that thrive in urban environments, such as those that adapt to city pollution.

C) Dr. Robert Thompson, who wrote "City Gardens," refers to the plant species he studies in urban settings as "urbanflora."

D) The subjects of "City Gardens" and "Concrete Meadows" are types of "urbanflora," a term that the papers' author, Dr. Robert Thompson, uses when describing plants in urban environments.

27

While researching a topic, a student has taken the following notes:

- The Scientists for Environmental Action (SEA) project aims to inspire aspiring environmental scientists by archiving and sharing information about pioneering environmental researchers.
- Dr. Maria Gomez is an environmental scientist included in SEA's Historic Researchers Directory.
- She was born in 1935 and conducted groundbreaking research on air pollution.

Which choice most effectively uses information from the given sentences to set up a discussion of Dr. Gomez's career for an audience already familiar with the SEA Project?

A) Dr. Maria Gomez is considered a renowned scientist included in SEA's Historic Researchers Directory.

B) Born in 1935, Dr. Maria Gomez made significant contributions to environmental science through her research on air pollution, as documented by the SEA project.

C) Among the many influential figures included in the SEA project is environmental scientist Dr. Maria Gomez.

D) The SEA project's Historic Researchers Directory highlights pioneering environmental scientists of the past, such as Dr. Maria Gomez (born 1935), to inspire new generations of environmental researchers.

Module 2 answer

Answer: D) monumental

📝 Why?

"Monumental" aligns with both the **literal scale** (13,000 miles!) and the **figurative awe** surrounding the Great Wall. It connotes both size and significance—making it a perfect fit.

💡 Others:

- **A)** Sophisticated – suggests complexity, but doesn't reflect scale or awe.
- **B)** Conventional – neutral and uninspiring; contradicts the uniqueness.
- **C)** Inconsequential – directly opposite of the intended meaning.

Answer: D)

📝 Explanation:

"Evocative" conveys the idea that the Wall **symbolizes** something beyond its physical structure—namely, the **ingenuity and resilience** of a civilization. It's about emotional and intellectual **resonance**.

💡 Others:

- **A)** Resourceful – describes a person, not a structure.
- **B)** Intricate – describes physical detail, not symbolic meaning.
- **C)** Unspoiled – has no relation to cultural symbolism.

3

Answer: A) foster

📝 Explanation:

"Foster" means to **encourage or promote**, which matches the intended message: electric vehicles **aim to inspire** environmentally responsible attitudes in drivers.

💡 Others:
- **B)** Limit – opposite of intent.
- **C)** Neutralize – suggests negating, not encouraging.
- **D)** Deny – irrelevant to inspiring responsibility.

4

Answer: A)

📝 Explanation:

The context is about how **common or widespread** a protein is across various biological processes and species. "Pervasive" fits this idea best.

💡 Others:
- **B)** Plausible – applies to hypotheses, not prevalence.
- **C)** Prominent – suggests fame or visibility, not spread.
- **D)** Significant – close, but too vague and general; not about **distribution**.

5

Answer: D) It expresses a viewpoint the author opposes.

📝 Explanation:

The Tribune's view supports **individual freedom in design**, but the **author's main argument** critiques that idea in favor of cultivating **shared standards** of elegance and function. Thus, the Tribune's claim is a **foil** for the author's rebuttal.

Others:

- **A)** No reference to evolving standards.
- **B)** Doesn't critique Americans broadly—just individualism in design.
- **C)** Not an example supporting the author's argument, but one being **challenged**.

6

Answer: D) *T. striatus* displayed no reaction when Lee and team played *B. jamaicensis* alarm calls, whereas *S. niger* displayed predator-avoidance behavior in response to the calls.

✎ Explanation:

This supports the hypothesis of an **inverse relationship** between **field of vision** and **sensitivity to alarm calls**:

- S. niger → denser forest → narrower vision → **relies more on audio** cues → reacts.
- T. striatus → open area → wider vision → **less reliant on audio** → doesn't react.

 Others:

- **A)** Irrelevant—hawks aren't the test subject in this hypothesis.
- **B)** Confuses control vs. variable—unclear comparison.
- **C)** Shows intra-species variation, but doesn't clearly contrast vision/sensitivity.

7

The correct answer is **B)** *Australia was higher in 2014 than in 2010, whereas the number in Germany was the same in 2014 as in 2010.*

✎ Why it's correct:

- It **contrasts** the **increase** in Australia with the **unchanged number** in Germany—perfectly fulfilling the "however" contrast structure.

⚲ Why the other choices fail:

- **A)** "…Japan was higher in 2014 than in 2010"
  → False! Japan **decreased**, not increased.

- **C)** *"···Germany had more installations than either Australia or Japan in 2014"*
  → Misleading. By 2014, **Australia (95)** had **more** than Germany (75).
- **D)** *"···Australia was lower in 2014 than in 2010"*
  → Completely false. Australia increased **significantly**.

8

The correct answer is **C)** *Amina Yusuf and colleagues reported an even larger positive effect of no fertilizer on the yield of carrots.*

📝 Explanation:

This is the only choice that highlights an **inverse effect**—fertilizer use **reduced** crop growth. It directly supports the prompt's contrast: "opposite effect."

💡 Why the other choices are incorrect:
- **A)** *"...crop growths with fertilizer have ranged from 3,120... to 5,130..."*
  → Just states a range. No **comparison** to "no fertilizer" yields = irrelevant.
- **B)** *"...Samir Patel and colleagues found a similar association..."*
  → False. Their corn study also showed a **positive effect** of fertilizer—not an **opposite** result.
- **D)** *"...barley yielded 5,130... and 4,780 without..."*
  → This is O'Connor's own study—**not** an opposite effect; in fact, it **supports** fertilizer use.

9

The correct answer is **D)** *The UN estimated Mexico City's population to be 21,779,000, which is significantly larger than the reported population for the region proper.*

📝 Why this supports the claim:
- **Mexico City's region proper** = 8,918,000
- **UN estimate** = 21,779,000
- That's a difference of nearly **13 million people**—a clear indication that the UN estimate must be including **areas beyond the region proper**, exactly as the journalist claims.

💡 **Why the other options fall short:**
- **A) All the region proper areas are below 10,000 square kilometers.**
  - → This talks about **area**, not **population**—irrelevant to the journalist's claim about **who is being counted**.
- **B) The metropolitan area of Melbourne is significantly larger than 4,000 square kilometers.**
  - → Also about **land area**, not population comparison. Doesn't relate to the **UN estimate** at all.
- **C) The reported region proper population of London is significantly larger than that of Los Angeles.**
  - → While it may be true, it doesn't support the **claim about UN estimates** including more people than the region proper.

10

Correct Answer: C)

 Why C is correct:
The question specifically asks for a **quotation that illustrates Arroyo Grande as a "captivating view" seen from a distance**.
Choice C is **the only one** that:
- Describes **Arroyo Grande** itself
- Places it **in the distance**
- Uses **visual imagery** ("glowing," "bathed in golden light," "nestled") that captures the "captivating" quality.

💡 **Why not the others?**
- **A)** Beautiful desert imagery, yes—but no **mention of Arroyo Grande**, nor is it framed as a **view from a distance**.
- **B)** Occurs **inside** the town. The travelers are already there, so it's not **from afar**.
- **D)** Describes the **journey**, not the **destination**, and focuses on hardship—not captivation.

11

The correct answer is **C)** *Animal Farm is less of a literary accomplishment than it truly is.*

📝 Why C is correct:

The passage warns that **labeling Animal Farm merely as allegory** may lead readers to **undervalue Orwell's artistic creativity**.

Thus, C best explains the **potential consequence**: it might be seen as **less of an original work** and more as a simple political echo.

💡 Why not the others?

- **A)** Misrepresents Orwell's intent; he didn't *claim* it was a literal representation—he acknowledged the allegory.
- **B)** Irrelevant to the claim—it's not about tracing characters, but **how people interpret Orwell's originality**.
- **D)** Introduces a **new debate** not present in the passage. The concern is about *devaluation*, not comparative creativity.

 12

Correct Answer: C)

📝 Why C is correct:

The passage is anchored in a **cause-effect chain**:

- **Limited habitat = less diversity**
- **Expanded habitat (via modeling) = ?**
- So, it logically follows that when **M. rufogriseus expands, its behavioral diversity increases**—this mirrors the initial research premise.

💡 Why not the others?

- **A)** Talks about *other* species moving into Tasmania—not relevant to the study or its modeling.
- **B)** Shifts focus to areas *near* Tasmania, whereas the experiment models M. rufogriseus in **mainland** regions.
- **D)** Again, shifts focus to *other species*, not the one under investigation.

TEST 02

107

13

Correct Answer: A)

📝 Why A is correct:

The inference rests on this: **No source before 50 CE** contains the **Twelve Labors as a unified set**, but Seneca's *Hercules Furens* does.

Thus, he must have used **later or different sources**—*not* Theocritus, whose work came **centuries earlier** and lacked that narrative structure.

💡 Why not the others?

- **B)** Makes an unsubstantiated comparison. The passage **doesn't compare** Diodorus and Apollodorus's similarity.
- **C)** Illogical—Diodorus wrote *before* 50 CE, when the unified Twelve Labors weren't yet codified. He wasn't "unaware," just writing **before the synthesis** emerged.
- **D)** Incorrect—Metamorphoses is **not** more "historically accurate" just because it was written later. The passage doesn't evaluate historical accuracy.

14

The correct answer is **D)** *such studies are not attempting to monitor changes over extended periods.*

📝 Why D is correct:

The contrast is between **EIS** (a long-term, data-intensive project) and a **simple ecology study**.
D highlights the **core difference: no long-term monitoring**, and therefore **less funding needed**.

💡 Why not the others?

- **A)** Irrelevant—doesn't explain *why* funding needs differ.
- **B)** True perhaps, but unrelated to funding logic.
- **C)** Talks about expansion feasibility, not **why** the smaller study doesn't need as much money.

15

Correct Answer: D)

📝 **Why D is correct:**

The passage notes the **Adams House has two stories and 12 rooms** but **is not** a grand house. Thus, **two stories alone are not sufficient**—that's the **logical conclusion**.

💡 **Why not the others?**

- **A)** False—Adams House wasn't classified as "grand," so it likely **didn't** house 15–20.
- **B)** Invalid—Adams House had 12 rooms and **wasn't** classified as grand. So not all homes with 12 rooms were grand.
- **C)** Unsupported—no info on staffing **needs** of Phillips Estate, only capacity.

16

Answer: B)

📝 **Explanation:**

The subject of the sentence is **"The scientist Jane Goodall"**, which is **singular**. The phrase "along with others···" is a **parenthetical** addition and does **not** make the subject plural.

💡 **Why the others fail:**

- **A) has been** → Incorrect tense. While possible grammatically, it suggests a focus on past recognition rather than present status.
- **C) are** → Plural verb does not match singular subject "Jane Goodall".
- **D) was** → Past tense; doesn't match the ongoing, present fame conveyed by "widely known".

17

Answer: C)

📝 **Why C is correct:**

The phrase "expanded influence, and" correctly uses **parallel structure** and **coordination**. The comma before "and" separates two **independent clauses**:

1. The prize has expanded influence

2. It now includes categories...

 Why the others fail:
- **A/B/D)** All omit proper punctuation or conjunctions needed between independent clauses, creating run-on sentences or comma splices.

18

Answer: B)

📝 **Why B is correct**:

Here, **"Mexican"** is part of the **title** of the painting—**"Mexican Portrait"**—and should directly follow "painting" as a **compound proper noun** without added punctuation.

 Why the others fail:
- **A)** Adds unnecessary parentheses—this would separate "Mexican" from the noun it modifies.
- **C)** The colon breaks the flow awkwardly; inappropriate unless "Mexican" were the start of a subtitle.
- **D)** Implies "painting" and "Mexican" are two separate descriptors, not a single title.

19

Answer: A)

📝 **Why A is correct**:

The **semicolon** properly separates two **independent clauses** while the phrase "for example" acts as an **interjection**.

It maintains clarity and formality, appropriate in explanatory writing.

 Why the others fail:
- **B/D)** Create comma splices—using only a comma between independent clauses.
- **C)** The comma after "for example" is unnecessary and creates awkward pacing.

20

Answer: D)

 Why D is correct:

The period after "however" signals a **strong separation** between two ideas, each a full sentence. "However" functions as a **conjunctive adverb**, and thus must be **preceded by a period or semicolon** when starting a new sentence.

💡 **Why the others fail**:
- **A)** Incorrect: needs a period or semicolon before "however".
- **B)** Awkward and incorrect coordination ("however and all" is not grammatical).
- **C)** Comma after "however" would imply a continuation, but "All nominations..." is an independent clause.

21

Answer: D)

Why D is correct:

"Mary Colter" is an **appositive**, renaming the "pioneers," and must be **set off by commas**. The phrase "who worked in architecture" is completed just before listing these names, so a comma is required.

💡 **Why the others fail**:
- **A/B/C)** Without the comma, the sentence becomes grammatically ambiguous and muddles the transition to the list.

22

Answer: A)

Why A is Correct:

This is a case involving **appositives**—nouns or noun phrases placed next to another noun to identify or explain it. Whether or not you need a comma depends on whether the appositive is **essential (restrictive)** or **nonessential (non-restrictive)** to the meaning of the sentence.

💡 **In this sentence:**

• **"Brazil"** is not being casually dropped into the sentence as extra information.

• Rather, **"Brazil" is identifying the specific IACC member region** being referred to.

That means **"IACC member region" is a restrictive modifier**: it narrows or defines what "Brazil" means in this context.

💡 **Why the Other Choices Are Incorrect:**

B) region: Brazil

> • A colon introduces **explanations, lists, or dramatic emphasis**, but here it **interrupts the natural flow**.
>
> • You wouldn't say "an IACC member region: Brazil" in casual or standard narrative prose.
>
> • It over-formalizes and **breaks the sentence's rhythm**.

C) region, Brazil

> • This treats **"Brazil" as nonessential**, implying it's **just extra detail** about the region.
>
> • That would be appropriate if you'd already established which region you meant, and "Brazil" were merely adding color.
>
> • But here, the **region is not identified until "Brazil" is mentioned**—so it's **essential**, and **no comma should be used**.

D) region—Brazil

> • The em dash is a **highly emphatic, interruptive punctuation mark**.
>
> • It suggests drama or a parenthetical aside.
>
> • This construction would **over-dramatize** what should be a **neutral comparison of valuation**.

23

Answer: C)

📝 **Why C is correct:**

"Indeed" is a **reinforcing transition**—it confirms and deepens the point just made:

He always questions traditional design principles → *Indeed, he evaluates purpose in every case.*

It emphasizes consistency and adds weight to the claim.

💡 **Why the others are wrong:**

• **A) For instance** — Introduces an **example**, but this is a **continuation**, not a specific instance.

• **B) In that moment** — Refers to a **specific time**, which is irrelevant here.

• **D) Conversely** — Implies **contrast**, but the sentence expresses **reinforcement**, not opposition.

24

Answer: D) Indeed,

 Why D is correct:

"Indeed" again serves as an **emphatic continuation**, underscoring the **importance of Bach's contributions**, especially after highlighting his impact in the previous sentence.

Bach popularized the style → Indeed, he pioneered specific techniques.

> **Why the others are wrong:**
> - **A) Nevertheless** — Implies contrast, but no contrast is being made.
> - **B) That being said** — Similar to "nevertheless"; implies **opposition** or concession.
> - **C) Furthermore** — Adds information, but "Indeed" is stronger for emphasizing historical significance.

25

Answer: A) Alan Turing's story begins in London, England, in 1912.

 Why A is correct:

It **establishes a biographical beginning**, suited to the narrative style requested. It anchors the reader in **time and place**, the most logical entry point into a person's life story.

> **Why the others are wrong:**
> - **B)** Too factual and compressed—better for a summary or academic profile.
> - **C)** Starts mid-career, not at the **beginning of a narrative**.
> - **D)** Reflects **legacy**, not an introductory tone.

26

Answer: B)

 Why B is correct:
- **Defines** the term clearly
- **Attributes** it correctly to Dr. Thompson

• **Provides an example** ("such as those that adapt to city pollution")
It satisfies all three components of the prompt.

💡 Why the others are wrong:
• **A)** Only gives the **definition**, no example.
• **C)** Introduces a paper but does **not define or exemplify** the term fully.
• **D)** Mentions titles and usage, but is **less direct** and lacks clarity of purpose.

Answer: C) Among the many influential figures included in the SEA project is environmental scientist Dr. Maria Gomez.

📝 Why C is correct:
• Efficiently connects Dr. Gomez to the **SEA project** (familiar context).
• Emphasizes her **status** as an "influential figure," leading naturally into a deeper discussion of her career.

💡 Why the others are wrong:
• **A)** Is a sentence fragment—not a complete thought.
• **B)** Good summary of her contributions, but **less focused** on SEA context.
• **D)** Over-explains the SEA project, which the audience already knows about (violates the prompt constraint).

TEST 3

Module 1

Reading and Writing
27 Questions, 32 Minutes

DIRECTIONS

The questions in this section address a number of important reading and writing skills. Each questions includes one or more passages, which may include a table or graph. Read each passage and question carefully, and then choose the best answer to the question based on the passage(s).

All questions in this section are multiple-choice with four answer choices. Each question has a single best answer.

1

Biologist Susan Clark noted that while well-established ecological systems, such as the rainforest, are recognized as such even as they adapt, there are more _____ ecosystems that, for instance, integrate aspects of both wetlands and forests to create something novel. The Everglades ecosystem arguably fits into this category, as it blurs the boundary between swamp and savannah.

Which choice completes the text with the most logical and precise word or phrase?

A) amorphous

B) neutral

C) fragmented

D) traditional

2

A critic at a recent film festival remarked that, although many directors produce remarkable films, in his opinion, no one has ever _____ Stanley Kubrick's work in 2001: A Space Odyssey. There is no greater achievement in science fiction cinema, according to the critic.

Which choice completes the text with the most logical and precise word or phrase?

A) convened

B) elevated

C) eclipsed

D) referenced

 CONTINUE

3

Though most rumors spread by gossip websites are quickly debunked, a few that should have been obvious were _____, such as the story about a famous actor secretly living in a remote village and the report of a tech company building a secret moon base. These stories persisted for years before finally being recognized as fabrications and corrected.

Which choice completes the text with the most logical and precise word or phrase?

A) spurious

B) mandatory

C) scrupulous

D) palpable

4

There are numerous well-documented cases of financial analysts making incorrect forecasts in stock markets. However, economist Jane Howard has argued that these forecast errors should not cause investors to _____ market analysis altogether. Market analysis is not just about predicting price changes; throughout investments, it guides where resources should be allocated most efficiently.

Which choice completes the text with the most logical and precise word or phrase?

A) distort

B) neglect

C) enact

D) supplement

5

Some animals, such as parrots (introduced to homes in the early 1900s) and dogs (domesticated thousands of years ago), exhibit human-like behaviors such as mimicking sounds or understanding basic commands, which help owners bond with them. While these traits can _____ feelings of companionship in people, animals that become too dependent on humans may lose some of their natural instincts, which can lead to behavioral issues in the long run.

Which choice completes the text with the most logical and precise word or phrase?

A) engender
B) repudiate
C) counterbalance
D) constrict

6

In 2020, Dr. Emma Grey and her team conducted a study concluding that urban air pollution has a significant effect on cognitive decline in elderly individuals. However, Grey and her team's study was conducted over a relatively short period of only 6 months. In a 2023 analysis of various researchers' conclusions on air pollution's effect on cognition, Dr. Peter Li and colleagues argue that such a short duration could lead to an overestimation of the impact, as cognitive decline often takes longer to manifest. This can result in exaggerated claims about the short-term effects of air pollution.

Which choice best describes the overall structure of the text?

A) It presents the result of a study, then raises a potential concern related to that result.
B) It describes a characteristic of a population, then explains why that characteristic is noteworthy.
C) It states a similarity between two scientific studies, then notes a difference between them.
D) It summarizes a problem that scientists are investigating, then provides a possible solution to that problem.

TEST 03

//// CONTINUE

7

The Silmarillion, first published in 1977, is a collection of mythopoeic stories by J.R.R. Tolkien. Although it is often regarded as a standalone work, it shares strong narrative connections with Tolkien's *The Lord of the Rings* trilogy. **Much like other prequels in major literary works, The Silmarillion ends rather abruptly, but with events that directly lead into the beginning of *The Fellowship of the Ring*.** As a result, the ending of *The Silmarillion* is only an issue if one regards the books as separate texts - creating the impression that both works should be read together as part of one grand narrative.

Which choice best describes the function of the underlined portion in the text as a whole?

A) It offers a detail that helps explain why it is not necessarily the case that a certain characteristic of *The Silmarillion* should be considered a flaw.

B) It presents a reason why *The Silmarillion* and *The Fellowship of the Ring* are considered two of Tolkien's most interconnected works.

C) It argues that *The Silmarillion* deserves to be viewed just as essential as *The Fellowship of the Ring* .

D) It demonstrates that those readers who most enjoy reading *The Fellowship of the Ring* will likely have appreciated *The Silmarillion* first.

8

Can apple trees grow in extreme cold environments? While you might assume that they cannot survive below-freezing temperatures, a recent study in Norway demonstrated that specific apple tree species are capable of thriving in cold environments when the trees are exposed to short periods of sunlight. In fact, some species performed even better in cold conditions: 40 percent of Arctic apple tree seeds sprouted when exposed to low temperatures, compared to just 10 percent that sprouted when planted in warmer environments.

According to the text, what percentage of Arctic apple tree seeds planted in cold environments sprouted?

A) 15 percent
B) 40 percent
C) 100 percent
D) 10 percent

9

Question: *In a speech about leadership given by Martin L. Scott in 2020, the speaker highlights the importance of leadership that inspires and empowers across diverse communities. Which of the following statements most effectively illustrates this concept?*

Options:

A) "Our cities, so worn and strained, / Need guidance, firm and just, / To mend the fractures of trust and hope." (from *"Leadership in Crisis"*)

B) "Let me be a leader for the people, no matter the color of their skin / Leading with courage and care: / To ignite passion and purpose / Wherever I may stand." (from *"Leader of Tomorrow"*)

C) "Bless our communities, / Where freedom finds its home, / And let us guide them with vision and strength." (from *"United We Lead"*)

D) "My mentor's words, my mentor's words, / They still echo in my mind; / A beacon of hope and wisdom, / Guiding me through." (from *"Mentor's Gift"*)

10

Table: Percentages of US Students Who Participate in Various Extracurricular Activities

Type of Activity	Age 10–14	Age 15–18	Age 19–22	Age 23–25
Sports	72%	80%	79%	76%
Music and Arts	68%	63%	56%	47%
Volunteer Work	63%	53%	58%	52%
Academic Clubs	65%	53%	51%	45%

A survey conducted in 2024 across US students found that over two-thirds of students between the ages of 10 and 25 participate in at least one extracurricular activity, while half of those who do participate engage in more than one. The survey asked students which activities they participated in, and the table presents the percentages for each type of activity, separated by age group.

Which choice best presents a conclusion about the extracurricular activity habits of US students that is best supported by the information in the text and the table?

A: The majority of US students who participate in sports also engage in additional extracurricular categories.

B: Across all US students, participation in extracurricular activities declines with age, regardless of the type of activity.

C: Students between the ages of 19 and 22 are more likely to engage in volunteer work and less likely to participate in sports than students between the ages of 15 and 18.

D: Students between the ages of 10 and 14 are more likely to participate in sports than students between the ages of 15 and 18.

TEST 03

11

The Explorers is a 1935 novel by Theodore Parker, originally written in English. In the novel, Parker depicts a group of adventurers who have gained a renewed sense of purpose and determination as they embark on the next leg of their exploration: _____

Which quotation from a translation of *The Explorers* most effectively illustrates the claim?

A: "The gentle breeze stirred once more. From deep within the valley, the rhythmic hum of the flowing river echoed through the peaceful and still night."

B: "All afternoon, [the adventurers] hiked across the rugged plains, over rocky ridges and through the thorny bushes, feet dragging behind them as the sun began to set in the distance. After hours, they finally saw a faint glimmer of light from a distant village."

C: "The adventurers stood tall, eyes focused on the path ahead. The air was crisp, filled with the earthy scent of pine trees, as they charged forward, leaving their mark on the untamed wilderness, as if the very land was theirs to claim."

D: "Before the last hill faded from view, Richard took a deep breath, knelt down on one knee, and gently placed his hand on the cool ground, his thoughts heavy with contemplation."

12

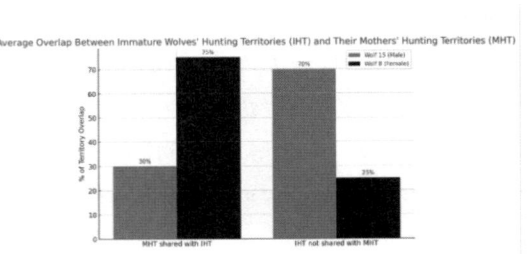

Average Overlap Between Immature Wolves' Hunting Territories (IHT) and Their Mothers' Hunting Territories (MHT)

Male wolves generally roam farther from their birth territory as they mature, while females tend to stay within or near their mother's territory. Sarah Winters and her team found that this behavior is reflected in the territorial overlap between immature wolves and their mothers, with females showing more overlap than males. For example, on average, Wolf 8's mother shared approximately _____.

Which choice most effectively uses data from the graph to complete the example?

A) 25% of its territory with Wolf 8's territory, whereas Wolf 15's mother shared approximately 60% of its territory with Wolf 15's territory.

B) 75% of its territory with Wolf 8's territory, whereas Wolf 15's mother shared approximately 60% of its territory with Wolf 15's territory.

C) 75% of its territory with Wolf 8's territory, whereas Wolf 15's mother shared approximately 30% of its territory with Wolf 15's territory.

D) 25% of its territory with Wolf 8's territory, whereas Wolf 15's mother shared approximately 30% of its territory with Wolf 15's territory.

13

Data Table: Top-Selling Book Genres in 2022 (U.S. Market)

Genre	Total Revenue	Average Price per Book	Award Won?
Fiction	$1,250,000,000	$12.50	No
Non-Fiction	$750,000,000	$15.00	No
Mystery/Thriller	$500,000,000	$10.00	No
Science Fiction	$4,400,000,000	$20.00	Yes

Many genres of books grow to be financially successful due to their widespread appeal, but some genres have more popularity due to their affordability. A market analyst claims that a genre's affordability can significantly influence its sales. However, recognition of an author or awards won can play a bigger role in sales figures. For example, _____.

Which choice most effectively uses data from the table to complete the example?

A) The average price per book for Fiction was $12.50, compared to $20.00 for Science Fiction.

B) Science Fiction earned more revenue than Non-Fiction, but Science Fiction had a higher average price per book.

C) both Non-Fiction and Fiction did not win awards, but Fiction sold more books.

D) Non-Fiction was not recognized by an award, but Fiction, which was not recognized, had higher revenue.

14

Mount Everest, the tallest mountain in the world, has seen a significant rise in the number of climbers attempting to reach its summit between 1953 and 2020. Despite the dangerous conditions, thousands of mountaineers have been successful in their expeditions. Interestingly, climbers using advanced oxygen equipment were more successful in reaching the summit than those who did not. Research has indicated that the use of supplemental oxygen reduces fatigue and improves overall performance in high-altitude conditions. This could suggest that climbers attempting to scale Mount Everest without oxygen assistance may have _____.

Which choice most logically completes the text?

A) been aware that their lack of oxygen equipment affected their own performance.

B) been influenced by the oxygen use of other climbers.

C) performed worse than they would have if they had used oxygen.

D) been unaffected by the challenges posed by high-altitude conditions.

TEST 03

CONTINUE

15

Australia has identified the eastern quokka as an endangered species that may face extinction due to habitat loss. However, biologists Jane Doe and John Smith have argued that terms like "endangered" and "thriving" are relative to the present environmental conditions. Shifts in land use or local ecosystems could either endanger a species further or provide new opportunities for its survival. These potential changes could create suitable living conditions in regions where the quokka currently struggles. In the case of Australia, these observations suggest that

_____.

Which choice most logically completes the text?

A) it's useful at present for the country to differentiate between endangered and thriving species in most situations but not in the case of the eastern quokka.

B) the country's classification of the eastern quokka as endangered may be valid now but might change in the future.

C) even if Australia's ecosystem doesn't undergo the transformations that biologists predict, the eastern quokka will likely remain threatened in the country.

D) the country once hosted a population of eastern quokkas that thrived, but they were eventually outcompeted by other native species.

16

Agriculture was essential to the Incan Empire, which thrived in the Andes Mountains from the 13th to the 16th century. The empire's people cultivated crops such as potatoes, maize, and quinoa, foods that _____ highly valued throughout the region.

Which choice completes the text so that it conforms to the conventions of Standard English?

A) has been

B) were

C) was

D) is

17

In her work as a sociologist, Dr. Sarah Johnson examines the role of traditional storytelling and folklore in indigenous communities of North America—specifically, how ancient legends and myths _____ as essential tools for passing down cultural values, history, and identity across generations.

Which choice completes the text so that it conforms to the conventions of Standard English?

A) is functioning

B) functions

C) has functioned

D) function

18

As a cognitive psychologist, Dr. Emma Lewis of Stanford University explores how individuals often rely on mental shortcuts that lead to flawed reasoning. Lewis's studies investigate phenomena that traditional psychological _____ assume that human reasoning is consistently logical—fail to account for.

Which choice completes the text so that it conforms to the conventions of Standard English?

A) models which -

B) models which

C) models- which

D) models, which

19

During the decades-long movement to secure the voting rights of women in the US, certain events were pivotal: the formation of the National Women's Party in _____ passage of the Nineteenth Amendment in 1920, which granted women the right to vote, is another such event.

Which choice completes the text so that it conforms to the conventions of Standard English?

A) 1916, for one, the

B) 1916, for one. The

C) 1916 for one, the

D) 1916. For one, the

20

A historian's record of Renaissance art in the 15th century, Giovanni Bellini's *Art Chronicle* is filled with detailed descriptions and commentary. Some of these appear as _____ "Masterpieces of the Time," Bellini catalogs his admiration for a golden fresco, an intricately carved marble statue, and vividly painted church murals.

Which choice completes the text so that it conforms to the conventions of Standard English?

A) lists in

B) lists, in

C) lists in:

D) lists: in

21

The Romance language family consists of several languages, including Spanish and Portuguese, which are spoken primarily in Spain and Brazil, _____ together accounting for a significant portion of the world's Romance language speakers, the Romance family continues to be a central focus for linguists like Dr. Marie Cohen.

Which choice completes the text so that it conforms to the conventions of Standard English?

A) respectively and

B) respectively,

C) respectively;

D) respectively

TEST 03

 CONTINUE

22

With some technological innovations, like the smartphone, engineers were able to produce a commercially viable version shortly after conceptualizing the idea—but this wasn't the case with all technologies. _____ the development process took several more years. The electric car, for example, was initially introduced in the early 1900s but didn't become widely used until the 21st century.

Which choice completes the text with the most logical transition?

A) Often,

B) Even so,

C) Similarly,

D) Furthermore,

23

Chlorophyll is a critical pigment in plants, responsible for absorbing light energy and enabling photosynthesis. It can also serve as a biomarker for photosynthetic efficiency in plants. _____ chlorophyll plays a dual role in energy absorption and as an indicator of plant health; in contrast, the presence of other pigments alone would not be sufficient for this purpose.

Which choice completes the text with the most logical transition?

A) In fact,

B) Moreover,

C) That is,

D) Nevertheless,

24

While preparing for a presentation, a student has made the following notes:

- The Great Pyramid of Giza is in Egypt.
- It was built as a tomb for the Pharaoh Khufu.
- The Mausoleum at Halicarnassus is in modern-day Turkey.
- It was built as a tomb for King Mausolus.
- Because the Pharaoh and the King were reputable, both are considered among the Seven Great Leaders of the Ancient World.

The student wants to emphasize a similarity between the two structures. Which choice most effectively uses relevant information from the notes to accomplish this goal?

A) Both the Pharaoh and the King were considered great leaders of the ancient world.

B) The Great Pyramid of Giza, which is a tomb, is in Egypt, not Turkey.

C) One tomb is in Egypt, and the other is in Turkey.

D) The Great Pyramid of Giza in Egypt, and the Mausoleum at Halicarnassus in Turkey, were both built as tombs for rulers.

25

- The Nobel Prize is an international set of awards given in various categories.
- The Physics category has been part of the Nobel Prizes since 1901.
- Marie Curie received the Nobel Prize in 1903 for Physics and again in 1911 for Chemistry.
- She was the first woman to win a Nobel Prize.
- Curie received two Nobel Prizes, one in each of two different fields, making her one of the few to achieve this.

Which choice most effectively uses information from the given sentences to emphasize the number of Nobel Prizes won by Curie?

A) A highly accomplished scientist with two Nobel Prizes to her name, Marie Curie made history in Physics and Chemistry.

B) During her career, Marie Curie was awarded two Nobel Prizes, one for Physics and another for Chemistry.

C) Physics, a field in which Marie Curie earned one of her Nobel Prizes, has been a category in the Nobel Prize awards since 1901.

D) Marie Curie received two Nobel Prizes, one of which was in Chemistry, which was introduced as a category in 1901.

26

- Pablo Picasso was a Spanish artist who created thousands of works, including paintings, sculptures, and drawings.
- His work *Guernica* was completed in 1937 and is considered one of his most famous pieces.
- *Guernica* is composed of oil on canvas and measures 11 feet by 25 feet in size.
- His painting *The Weeping Woman* was completed in the same year and is also highly regarded.
- *The Weeping Woman* is composed of oil on canvas and measures 2 feet by 1.5 feet in size.

Which choice most effectively uses information from the given sentences to emphasize how the two works are similar?

A) Between artist Pablo Picasso's works *Guernica* and *The Weeping Woman*, the former is much larger than the latter.

B) Composed by artist Pablo Picasso in 1937, both *Guernica* and *The Weeping Woman* use oil paint as a medium.

C) Artist Pablo Picasso completed *Guernica* in 1937, and *The Weeping Woman* followed in the same year.

D) Pablo Picasso's work *Guernica* is composed of oil on canvas, while *The Weeping Woman* is composed of oil on canvas but is significantly smaller.

27

- The Women in Science (WIS) project aims to inspire young female scientists by documenting and sharing information about the contributions of women in the sciences.
- Marie Curie is a prominent female scientist included in WIS's Historic Women in Science Directory.
- She was born in 1867 and died in 1934.

Which choice most effectively uses information from the given sentences to set up a discussion of Curie's career for an audience already familiar with the WIS project?

A) While Marie Curie is considered a pioneering scientist, there are many more such figures included in the WIS Historic Women in Science Directory.

B) Among the many influential figures included in the WIS project is the physicist and chemist Marie Curie.

C) Born in 1867, Marie Curie passed away in 1934, according to the WIS project.

D) The WIS project's Historic Women in Science Directory highlights female scientists of the past, such as Marie Curie (1867–1934), to inspire future generations of scientists.

Module 1 answer

1

Answer: A) amorphous

 Why *amorphous* is correct:

"amorphous" suggests something adaptable, without fixed form, able to shift and blend—perfect for describing ecosystems that integrate features of wetlands and forests. The Everglades are a real-world example of such an *in-between*, continuously shifting biome.

- **"amorphous"** mirrors the passage's emphasis on novelty and boundary-blurring. It evokes a sense of organic hybridity, where categories dissolve into one another.

  Why the others are wrong:
  - **B) neutral** – Neutral refers to emotional or political stance, not structural properties. An ecosystem isn't neutral between two types; it either integrates them or it doesn't.
  - **C) fragmented** – Fragmented implies broken apart, not blended. Fragmentation suggests disorder or loss, not the creative mixing the passage implies.
  - **D) traditional** – The passage is **contrasting** well-established (i.e., traditional) ecosystems with something different, not reinforcing the idea of tradition.

2

Answer: C)

 Why *eclipsed* is correct:

To "eclipse" something means to surpass or overshadow it. The critic's statement implies that *nothing* has surpassed Kubrick's film in greatness—thus, no one has *eclipsed* his work.

  Why the others are wrong:
  - **A) convened** – Means "gathered" or "assembled." Has nothing to do with artistic achievement or surpassing.
  - **B) elevated** – To elevate is to raise up, but the sentence implies comparison and superiority. Others *could* elevate his work, but that's not the point.
  - **D) referenced** – Referencing is neutral and common. It doesn't express greatness or lack thereof.

3

Answer: A)

📝 Why *spurious* is correct:

"Spurious" means false, illegitimate, or fabricated—precisely what these persistent rumors were. The examples (secret moon bases, hidden actors) are clearly *made up*, and the passage says they were later debunked.

💬 Why the others are wrong:

- **B)** *mandatory* – Means required. This is unrelated to rumors or truthfulness.
- **C)** *scrupulous* – Means morally exact or careful, the *opposite* of what false rumors are.
- **D)** *palpable* – Means easily perceived or felt; these rumors lasted long *despite* being unbelievable, so "palpable" doesn't fit.

4

Answer: B)

📝 Why *neglect* is correct:

"Neglect" fits the cautionary tone: don't *abandon* market analysis just because it's imperfect. The second sentence clarifies its usefulness beyond predictions.

💬 Why the others are wrong:

- **A)** *distort* – Means to twist or misrepresent, not ignore. Doesn't logically follow from the idea of *giving up* on analysis.
- **C)** *enact* – Means to make something law or carry it out. Not contextually related to dismissing analysis.
- **D)** *supplement* – Means to *add to*, which contradicts the idea of *abandoning* analysis.

5

Answer: A)

 Why *engender* is correct:

To "engender" means to give rise to or produce. Here, the sentence says animal traits like mimicking sounds *generate* emotional bonds in humans. It's a perfect semantic match.

 Why the others are wrong:

- **B) *repudiate*** – Means to reject or deny. This goes against the *positive bonding* described.
- **C) *counterbalance*** – Suggests balancing one thing with another, not *causing* something.
- **D) *constrict*** – Means to limit or tighten. Again, contrary to the feeling of emotional connection.

6

Answer: A) It presents the result of a study, then raises a potential concern related to that result.

Why A is correct:

- The first part discusses **Dr. Grey's 2020 study** and its conclusion: air pollution affects cognitive decline.
- The second part introduces **Dr. Li's critique**, highlighting that the short duration (6 months) may cause an **overestimation** of impact.
- This is classic structure: **present finding → raise concern**.

Why others are wrong:

- **B)** Focuses on population traits, which this passage doesn't.
- **C)** There's no explicit comparison between *two* studies' similarities—only a critique of one.
- **D)** No problem-solution dynamic is present. Li offers a caution, not a *solution*.

TEST 03

131

7 ....

Answer: A) It offers a detail that helps explain why it is not necessarily the case that a certain characteristic of *The Silmarillion* should be considered a flaw.

📝 Why A is correct:
- The passage says The Silmarillion ends abruptly.
- That could be seen as a flaw—but the underlined part explains *why it's not necessarily a flaw* if the two books are seen as a continuous story.
- It's a **justification**, softening what might be perceived as a criticism.

❓ Why others fail:
- **B)** Talks about narrative connections, but that's not the function of the *underlined portion*.
- **C)** Makes a value judgment (*deserves to be viewed...*) which the passage doesn't state.
- **D)** Makes assumptions about reader preference not supported in the text.

8 ....

Answer: B) 40 percent

📝 Why B is correct:
- Directly stated in the passage: *"40 percent of Arctic apple tree seeds sprouted when exposed to low temperatures."*
- This is a **data extraction** question—nothing to interpret, just to **read carefully**.

❓ Why the others are wrong:
- **A)** 15% is never mentioned.
- **C)** 100% is an exaggeration not supported.
- **D)** 10% refers to seeds in **warm environments**, not cold.

9

Answer: B)

📝 Why B is correct:

- This excerpt directly supports **inclusive, empowering leadership**, mirroring Scott's theme.
- It mentions diversity ("no matter the color...") and values ("courage and care").

❓ Why others don't match as closely:

- **A)** Is poetic and noble, but more about **city recovery** than leadership across *diverse communities*.
- **C)** Is too broad and vague; good leadership ideals, but less focused on **inclusivity**.
- **D)** Is about **mentorship**, not **inspiring diverse communities**.

10

Answer: C)

📝 Why C is correct:

- **Volunteer Work**: 19–22 = 58%, 15–18 = 53% → 19–22 more likely
- **Sports**: 19–22 = 79%, 15–18 = 80% → 19–22 slightly less likely
- This is a **comparative data inference**.

❓ Why others fall:

- **A)** May be true but isn't supported by *this* data.
- **B)** Incorrect: Volunteer work *increases* from 15–18 (53%) to 19–22 (58%) → not a universal decline.
- **D) Incorrect:** 10–14 (72%) vs. 15–18 (80%) → younger group is **less** likely in sports.

11

Answer: C)

📝 Why C is correct:

- The question asks for a quote that shows a **"renewed sense of purpose and determination."**
- Standing tall, focused eyes, charging forward—these are images of **purposeful resolve**.
- The phrase *"leaving their mark on the untamed wilderness"* evokes confidence and mission.

[?] **Why others mislead:**
- **A)** Peaceful night imagery—not about determination.
- **B)** Fatigue and light from a village show *relief*, not purpose.
- **D)** Focuses on **reflection**, not forward motion or renewal.

12

Answer: C)

[✎] **Why this is correct:**
- Matches the **75%** overlap for the female (Wolf 8), and **30%** for the male (Wolf 15).
- **Supports the pattern** mentioned in the paragraph: females show greater overlap with their mothers than males do.

[?] **Why the other choices fail:**
- **A)** 25% for Wolf 8? Incorrect. That's the *non-overlapping* portion.
- **B)** 75% is correct for Wolf 8, but **60%** for Wolf 15? No such figure appears—**misreads the graph.**
- **D)** 25% for Wolf 8 again reverses the values; that's **not** what was shared.

13

Correct Answer: B)

[✎] **Why B is correct:**
- The analyst's **main point** is that *awards and recognition* may outweigh affordability in driving sales.
- Science Fiction, despite being the **most expensive** genre per book ($20.00), **earned the most revenue** ($4.4B).
- It is also the **only genre with an award**, supporting the idea that **recognition, not affordability**, boosted its sales.

[?] **Why the others fall short:**
- **A)** Merely compares prices without addressing revenue or recognition.
- **C)** While accurate, it doesn't contrast the effects of **recognition vs. affordability**—the key focus.
- **D)** Repeats that both weren't recognized, which adds nothing new and misses the contrast the example is meant to highlight.

14

Answer: C)

 Why C is correct:

- The passage notes that oxygen **reduces fatigue** and **improves performance**.
- Thus, it's reasonable and **logically supported** to conclude that those who did **not** use oxygen would have had **better outcomes if they had**.
- This matches the cause-effect logic in the final sentence.

  Why the rest are misaligned:
  - **A)** Assumes self-awareness not mentioned in the text.
  - **B)** "Influenced by others" is speculative and unrelated to the core point.
  - **D)** Contradicts the claim that lack of oxygen **does** impair performance.

15

Answer: B) the country's classification of the eastern quokka as endangered may be valid now but might change in the future.

Why B is correct:

- The biologists argue that labels like "endangered" are **context-dependent** and can **shift** with environmental change.
- Thus, **current classification may be accurate**, but the **future could bring improvement**.
- This choice **faithfully reflects** the conditional tone of the final sentence and the evidence given.

  Why others don't work:
  - **A)** Suggests Australia should treat the quokka as an exception—not supported by the text.
  - **C)** Assumes a future where ecosystems don't change, contradicting the paragraph's conditional logic.
  - **D)** Introduces *historical competition*, a concept **not discussed** in the passage.

16

Answer: B) were

📝 **Why B is correct:**

• The sentence is in **past tense** ("was essential," "thrived"), so we must maintain that tense.
• "Foods that **were** highly valued..." is the grammatically correct and temporally consistent choice.

💬 **Why the others are incorrect:**

• A) *has been* – Present perfect tense; inconsistent with past narrative.
• C) *was* – Singular verb, but "foods" is plural.
• D) *is* – Present tense; contradicts the historical setting.

17

Answer: D)

📝 **Why D is correct:**

• Subject is **plural**: "legends and myths"
• Present tense is appropriate because it's a **general truth** being analyzed in a current academic context.

💬 **Why the others don't fit:**

• A) *is functioning* – Singular verb with plural subject.
• B) *functions* – Also singular.
• C) *has functioned* – Past perfect implies completed action, inconsistent with the current relevance described.

18

Answer: C)

📝 **Why C is correct:**

• The dash adds appropriate **emphasis** and separation before the nonrestrictive clause "which assume..."
• "Models" is the subject; "which" introduces a modifying clause that **further defines** these models.

136

Why others are incorrect:

- **A)** *models which - –* Misordered punctuation; dash should not come after "which".
- **B)** *models which –* Missing punctuation for a nonrestrictive clause.
- **D)** *models, which –* A comma works grammatically, but the **dash** adds stronger contrast, aligning with the sentence's tone.

19

Answer: B)

Why B is correct:

- "For one." functions as a parenthetical aside and must be set off with a **period** to avoid a run-on.
- "The passage⋯" then begins a new independent clause.

Why others fail:

- **A)** *1916, for one, the –* Creates a comma splice (run-on sentence).
- **C)** *1916 for one, the –* Missing comma before "for one".
- **D)** *1916. For one, the –* While grammatically possible, it subtly misemphasizes "For one" as the main subject rather than an aside.

20

Answer: D)

Why D is correct:

- Colon introduces a **clarifying example** or elaboration of the "lists."
- The prepositional phrase "in 'Masterpieces of the Time'" then logically follows.

Why others falter:

- **A)** *lists in –* Lacks punctuation for clarity.
- **B)** *lists, in –* Comma doesn't properly introduce a phrase that explains the "lists."
- **C)** *lists in: –* Illogical placement of colon; colon should come **after "lists"**, not "in."

137

21

Answer: C)

 Why C is correct:
- "Respectively" correctly matches Spanish with Spain and Portuguese with Brazil.
- **Semicolon** appropriately separates two **closely related independent clauses**.

  Why others are wrong:
  - **A)** *respectively and* – Makes the sentence a run-on.
  - **B)** *respectively,* – Creates a comma splice.
  - **D)** *respectively* – Without punctuation, the sentence becomes grammatically incorrect.

22

Answer: A)

 Why A is correct:
- "Often" logically introduces the idea that, **in many cases**, development takes longer.
- It sets up the contrast with the previous clause (smartphones were fast, others are not).

  Why others misfit:
  - **B)** *Even so,* – Implies a contradiction, not a general trend.
  - **C)** *Similarly,* – Suggests alignment, not contrast.
  - **D)** *Furthermore,* – Adds information but doesn't support the idea of contrasting examples.

23

Answer: C)

Why C is correct:
- "That is" **clarifies or rephrases** the previous idea, which is exactly what the sentence does: it explains chlorophyll's **two functions** in simpler terms.

Why others are not ideal:

- **A)** *In fact,* – Emphasizes truth but doesn't introduce an **explanatory restatement.**
- **B)** *Moreover,* – Adds information but doesn't clarify.
- **D)** *Nevertheless,* – Signals contrast, which is not present here.

24

Answer: D)

📝 **Why D is correct:**

- Directly highlights the **structural and functional similarity**: both are **tombs built for rulers.**
- Matches the goal of **emphasizing a similarity** between the two.
- Uses information from the notes effectively and succinctly.

 Why others fall short:

- **A)** Focuses on the *leaders* being great—not the **structures.**
- **B)** Makes a geographical distinction, not a similarity.
- **C)** Notes location contrast—accurate but **emphasizes difference**, not similarity.

25

Answer: B) During her career, Marie Curie was awarded two Nobel Prizes, one for Physics and another for Chemistry.

📝 **Why B is correct:**

- Clearly and **directly emphasizes the number** of prizes (two) and the **fields.**
- Chronologically accurate and grammatically clean.

Why others fall:

- **A)** Uses a broad phrase ("highly accomplished")—not as **precise** or focused on the **number of awards.**
- **C)** Shifts focus to Physics as a category, not Curie herself.
- **D)** Introduces unrelated detail about Chemistry category's introduction—**distracting** from the main point.

26 ....

Answer: B) Composed by artist Pablo Picasso in 1937, both *Guernica* and *The Weeping Woman* use oil paint as a medium.

 Why B is correct:
- Emphasizes **similarities** in:
  - **Date** (1937)
  - **Medium** (oil paint)
- These are the key similarities highlighted in the notes.

    ? **Why others don't match:**
- A) Emphasizes **size difference**, not similarity.
- C) Mentions **dates**, but lacks the comparison of **medium**—less complete.
- D) Introduces contrast (**"significantly smaller"**)—again, a difference, not similarity.

27 ....

Answer: B) Among the many influential figures included in the WIS project is the physicist and chemist Marie Curie.

 Why B is correct:
- Smoothly introduces Curie **within the context** of the WIS project.
- Sets the stage for a discussion of her **scientific career** by mentioning her roles clearly (physicist and chemist).
- A natural segue from the **project's mission to individual achievement**.

    ? **Why others miss:**
- A) Downplays Curie's importance by contrasting her with "many more." Not an ideal **lead-in** for focusing on her.
- C) Dry and overly focused on **birth/death dates**, not her role.
- D) Descriptive, but too **general**—reads like an overview rather than an **introduction to deeper discussion**.

Module 2

Reading and Writing
27 Questions, 32 Minutes

DIRECTIONS

The questions in this section address a number of important reading and writing skills. Each questions includes one or more passages, which may include a table or graph. Read each passage and question carefully, and then choose the best answer to the question based on the passage(s).

All questions in this section are multiple-choice with four answer choices. Each question has a single best answer.

1

Although our understanding of early human migration patterns across various continents was once _____, new findings from genetic data have provided us with a clearer view of how these populations spread and interacted over time.

Which choice completes the text with the most logical and precise word?

A) unparalleled

B) nebulous

C) complex

D) tangible

2

Databases such as the Global Species Database are extensive repositories of biological records that can be utilized for scientific investigations of how _____ a particular species is across various ecosystems. For example, one might estimate the distribution of a species, but only a thorough analysis of the database can confirm the actual spread of the species.

Which choice completes the text with the most logical and precise word?

A) credible

B) widespread

C) profound

D) authoritative

3

Artists like Frida Kahlo played a significant role in shaping Mexican art during the 20th century, particularly in the post-Revolutionary period. Creations from this era represent a/an _____ portion of what is recognized as the canon in Mexican art history, though earlier figures like José María Velasco should also be seen as essential contributors to the country's artistic legacy.

Which choice completes the text with the most logical and precise word?

A) overlooked

B) outsized

C) undefined

D) erratic

4

In the early 2000s, the value of certain vintage comic books increased significantly, which had the unexpected result of _____ interest: collectors who had not previously been interested in these books began purchasing them in large quantities, assuming the prices would continue to climb and the comics could be sold later for a substantial gain.

Which choice completes the text with the most logical and precise word?

A) exploiting

B) precipitating

C) monetizing

D) stabilizing

5

Text 1:

In separate studies, Dr. Anita Patel and Dr. Marcus Reed examined whether birds transfer seeds to one another using a common network of overlapping territories—a system involving shared nesting grounds. Patel and Reed excluded all alternative pathways by ensuring that birds from different nests were isolated from one another except through overlapping territories—a crucial step Dr. Simone Lee and her team's study did not take.

Text 2:

Patel and Reed took the necessary precautions of isolating nests (thereby excluding direct seed-sharing between nests). However, any experimental setup must ensure that overlapping territories are the only variable, but such overlapping regions might also allow environmental factors, like wind or rainfall, to distribute seeds. Therefore, Patel and Reed's experimental design cannot definitively determine whether any observed seed transfer occurred due to overlapping territories or another environmental factor.

Based on the texts, which choice best describes a point on which the author of Text 1 and the author of Text 2 would most likely agree?

A) Patel and Reed's study effectively excluded any explanation for seed transfer other than overlapping territories.

B) Excluding direct seed transfer between nests is sufficient to ensure that any observed seed transfer must involve overlapping territories.

C) Lee and colleagues' study was not designed in a way that would allow it to produce compelling evidence that seed transfer occurred via overlapping territories.

D) A barrier that prevents seed transfer exhaustively is necessary to evaluate seed transfer via overlapping territories.

6

The word "robot" is an example of a loanword—that is, a word that originated in one language and was later adopted by another. The term came to English indirectly from the Czech word *robotník*, which refers to a worker or laborer. The word was introduced to the world through the play *R.U.R.* (*Rossum's Universal Robots*), written by Czech playwright Karel Čapek. Similarly, the word "kiosk" has Turkish origins. The Turkish word *köşk* originally referred to a small pavilion or garden structure, but when borrowed into English, the meaning shifted to describe a small, stand-alone booth where goods or services are sold.

Which choice best states the main idea of the text?

A) Many English words with foreign origins first passed through other languages before entering English.

B) When borrowing from foreign languages, English adopted roughly as many words from Czech as from Turkish.

C) When English borrows words from foreign languages, the meanings often shift significantly from their original definitions.

D) The English words "robot" and "kiosk" are both examples of loanwords from foreign languages.

7

Dr. Anjali Mehta and her team studied a popular fitness tracking app used widely in India. The researchers found that when users received automatic reminders encouraging them to walk a minimum of 5,000 steps daily, the number of individuals meeting this goal significantly increased. Based on their findings, the researchers concluded that this and similar small app adjustments could promote healthier lifestyles and potentially reduce the risk of cardiovascular diseases in India by millions annually.

According to the text, which choice best describes a conclusion Mehta and her team drew from their study?

A) Rates of cardiovascular diseases in India are expected to increase in the near future.

B) Fitness tracking apps that encourage step goals are becoming more popular.

C) Users who understand how fitness tracking apps work are more likely to adopt healthier habits.

D) Small changes to how a fitness tracking app works can greatly promote healthier lifestyles.

8

The textile industry has long used mechanical methods to clean and soften large quantities of fabric. Recent advancements in ultrasonic cleaning were made through research in Japan on the treatment of cotton fibers. Ultrasonic cleaning is generally considered an improvement over more conventional mechanical cleaning methods: whereas traditional methods rely on physical agitation to remove debris and soften fibers, ultrasonic cleaning uses high-frequency sound waves to penetrate fabric at the microscopic level, reducing the time and energy required for industrial processing.

Based on the text, what is one disadvantage of some conventional mechanical cleaning methods?

A) They require more money than other methods do.

B) Their cleaning times are longer than those of other methods.

C) They are only effective on fabrics that are lightweight and small in size.

D) They are especially vulnerable to technological breakdowns.

9

Dr. Anil Kumar and colleagues have explored how urban migration patterns—a phenomenon that occurs when people relocate to cities in search of better opportunities—can result from economic conditions shared by different regions. Meanwhile, Dr. Priya Sharma and colleagues have investigated how migration can occur due to cultural or social factors unique to individual communities. However, the prevalence of migration driven by shared versus unique factors is still poorly understood. This motivated researchers Lisa Brown and Andrew Clarke to evaluate both types of migration drivers in a comprehensive study published in their 2022 report.

Which choice best states the main topic of the text?

A) Whether studies of migration patterns should focus on regions that share similar economic conditions.

B) How a particular study of migration relates to some other studies in the field.

C) What kinds of factors are most likely to drive migration in different regions.

D) Why migration patterns are particularly difficult for researchers to study.

10

The following text is from *The Rise of Augustus*, a historical novel published in 2024. The narrator is describing the influential politicians of the Roman Senate.

Lastly, bringing a sense of authority, was Senator Marcus Denter, whose countenance seemed sculpted for a marble statue, or perhaps a coin, and whose wide forehead gave the impression of immense intellect. However, it would have been tactless to ask for specific evidence of the achievements his decades in Roman politics had yielded. His recently circulated letters may have shed some light on his career, but since no concrete details were included until the fifth scroll, they could have been left in the archives.

Based on the text, which choice best describes Senator Marcus Denter?

A) He appears to be a figure of great importance, but his letters suggest some of his actions were morally questionable.

B) He has kept a humble persona despite years of effective service to the Roman state.

C) He has the look of a powerful man, but it is unclear whether he has done anything to justify that reputation.

D) He would be a well-known Roman hero if his contributions were not kept hidden.

TEST 03

11

Table: Monthly Average Tooth Lengths of Fossilized Shark Teeth

Period	Average High Temperature (℃)	Average Male Tooth Length (mm)	Average Female Tooth Length (mm)
Period A (Cool)	18	25.4	27.6
Period B (Moderate)	22	26.3	28.1
Period C (Warm)	27	29.8	31.2
Period D (Hot)	30	30.1	31.6

Paleontologists studying fossilized shark teeth across four geological periods have analyzed how tooth size correlates with prey size. The team measured the average tooth lengths for male and female sharks from fossil records spanning millions of years. The research findings indicate that variations in tooth size could reflect changes in prey availability and environmental conditions over time. For instance, the data suggest that sharks from warmer periods tended to have larger teeth, as is illustrated by the finding that _____.

Which choice most effectively uses data from the table to complete the assertion?

A) the average male tooth length was 25.4 mm during Period A but was 31.1 mm during Period D.

B) the average female tooth length was consistently larger than the male tooth length in all four periods in the table.

C) the average temperature was higher in Period C than in Period B.

D) the average female tooth length was larger in Period D than in Period A.

12

Some cosmetics contain microplastic beads, which can leach into waterways and soils via wastewater. In a 2018 study, Dr. Maria Gomez and colleagues found that microplastic beads accumulate in the bodies of freshwater snails (*Physa acuta*). While the bioaccumulation of microplastics may be inherently concerning, it has been hypothesized that microplastic bioaccumulation in invertebrates like *P. acuta* could serve as a valuable proxy, reducing the need for costly and invasive testing on vertebrate species—such as frogs (*Rana temporaria*), which are often used in regulatory compliance testing for microplastic bioaccumulation, as environmental protection standards currently mandate.

Which finding, if true, would most directly support the hypothesis presented in the text?

A) Microplastic concentrations in *P. acuta* tend to vary more from individual to individual than microplastic concentrations in *R. temporaria* when the species are exposed to similar levels of microplastics.

B) Compared with *R. temporaria*, *P. acuta* can tolerate significantly higher microplastic concentrations without showing adverse effects.

C) It is easier to detect low and harmless concentrations of microplastics in *P. acuta* than it is to detect high and harmful concentrations of microplastics in *R. temporaria*.

D) In comparable environments, *P. acuta* and *R. temporaria* display comparable rates of microplastic uptake.

13

Many baked goods, such as bagels and pretzels, gain their distinct texture and flavor from being baked; some are also dipped in alkaline solutions before baking. Food scientists Dr. Alice Shaw and Dr. Peter Mills studied the mass and moisture retention processes that occur when dough is treated with alkaline solutions, substances that become viscous or gel-like in water. During baking, water in the dough evaporates, leaving voids that flour (pure protein content) can fill. As the baking progresses, water from the inside moves toward the crust, provided the crust remains porous. However, alkaline solutions can create structures that limit the transfer of moisture out of the dough. Therefore, a dough baked without an alkaline treatment will likely _____ .

Which choice most logically completes the text?

A) have a more viscous crust when baking is completed than it would have if it were treated with an alkaline solution.

B) have a higher protein content than it would have if it were treated with an alkaline solution.

C) need to be baked at a lower temperature than it would need to be if it were treated with an alkaline solution.

D) require a different type of flour than it would need if it were treated with an alkaline solution.

14

Marine biologist Dr. Olivia Summers and her team analyzed the remains of a dolphin skeleton uncovered in 2015 at a coastal archaeological site near evidence of human activity (such as fish hooks) off the coast of Australia. Summers et al. concluded that the dolphin was a member of *Delphinus delphis*, a now extinct species closely related to modern dolphins, and carbon dating indicated the dolphin's presence at the site at the same time as human settlers. (In fact, the settlers may have intentionally buried the dolphin.) Moreover, while wild dolphins typically consume a diet of fish, isotopic analysis of the dolphin's teeth revealed that this dolphin's diet, like that of the humans, consisted partly of plant-based materials. Summers et al. thus concluded that _____ .

Which choice most logically completes the text?

A) the humans who lived at the same time as the dolphin likely consumed more plant matter than the dolphin did.

B) the dolphin had a diet more closely resembling that of modern dolphins than to that of humans.

C) the humans who lived at the same time as the dolphin used fishing nets similar to the hooks found at the site.

D) the dolphin may have been a domesticated animal for the people living near the coast at the same time.

CONTINUE

15

Environmental scientist Dr. Michelle Rivers and her team explored the impact of chemical runoff on aquatic life, as documented in a 2020 study of freshwater trout. Researchers performed a meta-analysis on studies that examined how chemical pollutants affect aquatic species and found that, in every study, key traits or behaviors of the organisms were visibly different between those exposed to pollution and those in a similar but unpolluted group. On average, studies of invertebrates demonstrated larger variations than studies of amphibians, but every category of aquatic species showed effects. There were also specific studies showing exceptionally large effects on certain species of invertebrates. Therefore, the meta-analysis suggests that _____.

Which choice most logically completes the text?

A) some studies of amphibians found larger impacts of chemical runoff than some studies of invertebrates did.

B) the differences that studies attribute to chemical runoff are likely to be more substantial for amphibians than for invertebrates.

C) the difference observed in the study conducted by Dr. Michelle Rivers was likely larger than the average difference in studies of freshwater trout included in the meta-analysis.

D) the studies in the meta-analysis that examined invertebrates were more likely than those that examined amphibians to determine whether the changes were detrimental.

16

Currently, the Netflix platform is celebrated as a leader in the entertainment industry, but when it first launched in 1997, it was little more than a mail-based DVD rental service; co-founders Reed Hastings and Marc Randolph wanted to capitalize on the declining popularity of traditional video stores by encouraging customers to rent movies online and have them delivered to their homes. Eventually, Netflix expanded its services and _____ its initial lineup of low-budget films was replaced with award-winning series from international creators, including *Money Heist* from Spain and *The Crown* from the UK.

Which choice completes the text so that it conforms to the conventions of Standard English?

A) influence and

B) influence,

C) influence, and

D) influence

17

Every year, the Pulitzer Prize in Fiction is awarded to a writer who has, in the words of the Pulitzer Board, "produced a distinguished work that deals with American life in an original _____ in 1953, for instance, judges honored Ernest Hemingway for *The Old Man and the Sea* due to its profound narrative on human resilience and the relationship between man and nature.

Which choice completes the text so that it conforms to the conventions of Standard English?

A) direction,"

B) direction" and,

C) direction";

D) direction"

18

After reading about Shirley Chisholm, who became the first Black woman to serve in the United States House of Representatives, the student discovered biographies of two other notable Black politicians who served in _____ Barbara Jordan of Texas and John Lewis of Georgia.

Which choice completes the text so that it conforms to the conventions of Standard English?

A) Congress

B) Congress.

C) Congress;

D) Congress:

19

Maria Sanchez's article on "plateau," a term used to describe a flat, elevated area of land, is one of many entries featured in *Geography Unfolded: A Guide to Global* _____ by Carl Davis and Laura Greene. The book provides an extensive vocabulary for describing various landforms found around the world.

Which choice completes the text so that it conforms to the conventions of Standard English?

A) Landscapes, edited

B) Landscapes edited

C) Landscapes. Edited

D) Landscapes and edited

20

Most major universities and colleges have had at least one woman serve as president. At Harvard University, for example, Drew Gilpin Faust became the first female president in 2007. In fact, the number of universities and colleges that have had only male presidents _____ almost every year.

Which choice completes the text so that it conforms to the conventions of Standard English?

A) shrinks

B) shrink

C) are shrinking

D) have been shrinking

TEST 03

21

In Canada, members of the House of Commons are elected using a first-past-the-post system. In this system, voters cast their ballots for individual candidates rather than political parties, and the candidate who receives the most votes in each riding wins a seat. _____, the number of seats a party holds in the House of Commons is directly related to the number of ridings it wins.

Which choice completes the text with the most logical transition?

A) second of all,

B) in fact,

C) by contrast,

D) accordingly,

22

Before the first highways were built in the United States, engineers cautioned against using different lane widths across various states. _____, state officials couldn't agree on a uniform standard. Thus, highways in Texas were constructed with wide lanes, while those in New York were built with narrower ones.

Which choice completes the text with the most logical transition?

A) For this reason,

B) In other words,

C) Similarly,

D) Nevertheless,

23

Harriet Tubman was an outspoken abolitionist whose home was a stop on the underground railroad (the network of people and places that enslaved people used to escape to freedom). _____ supporters of the railroad kept their involvement a secret to avoid detection. By and large, they were, like Tubman, vocal abolitionists.

Which choice completes the text with the most logical transition?

A) Occasionally,

B) For example,

C) Accordingly,

D) However,

24

The work of modern American artist John Doe often features references to other famous paintings and sculptures. Typically, these references are subtle and noticed only by the most observant of Doe's viewers. In his 2020 painting *Blue Reverie*, _____ Doe directly names a specific artwork—Pablo Picasso's *Guernica*—as the inspiration behind the piece.

Which choice completes the text with the most logical transition?

A) though,

B) fittingly,

C) similarly,

D) for example,

25

While studying a biology textbook, a student wrote down the following facts:

- Chromosomes are cellular structures that carry genetic information.
- Genes play a vital role in determining an organism's characteristics.
- Organisms of the same species typically share the same number of chromosomes.
- The house sparrow (*Passer domesticus*) and the blue jay (*Cyanocitta cristata*) are types of birds.
- The house sparrow has 40 chromosomes.
- The blue jay has 50 chromosomes.

The student wants to specify how many chromosomes the house sparrow has. Which choice most effectively uses relevant information from the notes to accomplish this goal?

A) The house sparrow's chromosomes contain genes, which are essential for determining an organism's traits.

B) The house sparrow (*Passer domesticus*) and the blue jay (*Cyanocitta cristata*) both have chromosomes, but the house sparrow has fewer than the blue jay does.

C) The house sparrow (*Passer domesticus*) has 40 chromosomes.

D) The blue jay, a species of bird, has fifty chromosomes.

26

While researching a topic, a student has taken the following notes:

- Emma Watkins was a painter and a member of the Art Nouveau movement.
- Her paintings combine elements of nature with geometric forms and flowing lines.
- Watkins' painting *The Garden Bloom* features vibrant floral designs.
- Watkins' painting *Urban Reverie* incorporates a mix of sharp angles and soft curves.

The student wants to emphasize a difference between the two paintings. Which choice most effectively uses relevant information from the notes to accomplish this goal?

A) *The Garden Bloom* and *Urban Reverie* are two paintings created by Watkins, an artist from the Art Nouveau movement.

B) In her two paintings *The Garden Bloom* and *Urban Reverie*, Watkins blends nature's beauty, such as floral designs, with geometric elements, like sharp angles and curves.

C) Watkins has different approaches to combining elements of nature with geometric designs, using both floral patterns and geometric forms in her works.

D) While both paintings incorporate geometric elements, *The Garden Bloom* does so by featuring vibrant floral designs, and *Urban Reverie* does so by using a combination of sharp angles and soft curves.

TEST 03

27

While researching a topic, a student has taken the following notes:

- The Geocentric Theory proposes that Earth is the center of the universe.
- This model was widely accepted until the 16th century.
- Observations of planetary motion by Galileo in 1610 showed that planets revolve around the Sun.
- These discoveries support the idea that the Heliocentric Theory is a more accurate representation of the solar system.
- More than a dozen astronomers provided evidence supporting the Heliocentric Theory.

The student wants to explain the implications of Galileo's discovery. Which choice most effectively uses relevant information from the notes to accomplish this goal?

A) It is the contention of the Geocentric Theory that Earth, not the Sun, is the center of the universe, a view widely accepted until the 16th century.

B) Galileo's observations of planetary motion in 1610 were among the early discoveries supporting the Heliocentric Theory.

C) The observations of planetary motion made by Galileo in 1610 should not be overlooked; they have important implications for the Geocentric Theory.

D) Contrary to the Geocentric Theory, Galileo's observations in 1610 showed that planets revolve around the Sun, providing crucial evidence for the Heliocentric Theory.

Module 2 answer

1

Answer: B)

📝 **Explanation:**

- "Once **nebulous**" = once **unclear or vague** — fits perfectly with "new findings··· provided a clearer view."
  - *Unparalleled* means unmatched (positive, illogical here).
  - *Complex* doesn't contrast cleanly with "clearer view."
  - *Tangible* means physically touchable—not relevant to knowledge clarity.

2

Answer: B) widespread.

📝 **Explanation:**

- Looking for a word to describe *how broadly a species exists* → **"widespread"** is exact.
  - *Credible* and *authoritative* relate to trustworthiness, not distribution.
  - *Profound* relates to depth or impact, not spatial extent.

3

Answer: B)

📝 **Explanation:**

- "Outsized" = disproportionately significant. Describes how post-Revolutionary art **dominates the canon**, despite earlier figures.
  - *Overlooked* would contradict the claim of major recognition.
  - *Undefined* or *erratic* don't match the context of *dominance* or *importance*.

Answer: B)

Explanation:

- "Precipitating interest" = causing interest suddenly → matches how price spikes led to collector interest.
  - *Exploiting* implies manipulation.
  - *Monetizing* = turning into profit, which is the effect, not the cause.
  - *Stabilizing* contradicts the idea of an increase.

Correct Answer: C)

Explanation:

- Both texts agree: **Lee's study lacked proper controls**, making its results weak.
  - A/B are **Text 1's views**, but Text 2 *disputes* the sufficiency.
  - D is **not mentioned** directly—Text 2 says "environmental factors might interfere," not that *only* an exhaustive barrier works.

6

Correct Answer: D)

Explanation:

- This is a **definition-and-examples** passage: robot (Czech), kiosk (Turkish) → both are **loanwords**.
  - A is too general; text focuses on **just two** words.
  - B introduces data about frequency not found in the text.
  - C suggests **semantic shift** is the main idea—it's a detail, not the core.

154

7

Correct Answer: D)

📝 **Explanation:**

- Main takeaway: **small app changes** (like step reminders) can promote **big health benefits**.
  - A/B/C are not directly supported or are tangential to the main conclusion.

8

Correct Answer: B)

📝 **Explanation:**

- Ultrasonic is "an improvement" because it reduces **time and energy** → suggesting conventional = **slower**.
  - A/D are **not mentioned**.
  - C is unsupported and overly specific.

9

Correct Answer: B)

📝 **Explanation:**

- The passage **relates a new study** (Brown & Clarke) to **previous ones** (Kumar and Sharma).
  - A/C describe content not fully explored.
  - D is too general—researchers do study migration, but *difficulty* is not the focus.

Answer: C) He has the look of a powerful man, but it is unclear whether he has done anything to justify that reputation.

 Explanation:

- The senator **looks important**, but narrator **questions his actual achievements** → uncertainty = key.
  - A suggests **moral flaws,** which are not mentioned.
  - B wrongly assumes **humility** or clear service.
  - D is overly flattering; **hidden contributions** aren't implied.

Correct Answer: D)

 Explanation:

- The prompt focuses on **temperature and tooth size** correlation → Period D vs. A (warm vs. cool) → **female tooth size increases**.
  - A: wrong value (31.1 mm not found); made-up number.
  - B: True, but doesn't **illustrate temperature effect**.
  - C: Irrelevant to tooth size correlation.

Correct Answer: D)

Explanation:

- Hypothesis: *P. acuta could substitute for R. temporaria.* So if **uptake rates are comparable**, it supports this idea.
  - A/C discuss **measurement precision**, not comparability.
  - B is about **tolerance**, which could *complicate* rather than support proxy use.

13

Answer: B)

📝 **Explanation:**

• Alkaline treatment **prevents moisture loss**, so without it = **more moisture loss → more protein remains →** **higher protein content** in final product.

  - A: viscous crust is a **property of the alkaline** version, not untreated dough.
  - C/D are **not discussed** at all.

14

Answer: D)

📝 **Explanation:**

• Diet and burial = strong clues of **domestication**.

  - A: Comparison of plant consumption is off-topic.
  - B: Contradicted—modern dolphins don't eat plants.
  - C: Fishing gear details aren't relevant here.

15

Answer: D)

📝 **Explanation:**

• **More likely... to determine whether the changes were detrimental"** implies these studies revealed more obvious or measurable impacts on invertebrates.

• The passage tells us:
  - Invertebrates had **larger average changes**.
  - Some species had **exceptionally large effects**.

• The logic follows: **If the changes are larger and more dramatic**, then it becomes **easier** to **detect whether** the changes were **harmful**.

• This doesn't mean the studies *intended* to measure harm—just that the **likelihood of being able to determine** the harm is greater in studies where **larger variations** were observed.

A) some studies of amphibians found larger impacts of chemical runoff than some studies of invertebrates did.

- At first glance this seems true: **"on average"** means overlap is possible.
- **BUT!** That's not what the conclusion is about.
- The sentence begins: **"Therefore, the meta-analysis suggests⋯"**
  - This is asking us for an **insight** or **conclusion**, not a statistical possibility.
- A is a **trivial statement**—technically true, but **not insightful**, and not a **logical endpoint** of the meta-analysis.
- The SAT does not reward stating the obvious when a more meaningful conclusion is available.
- **Weak, unimpactful, and not a strong completion of the passage's final sentence.**

B) the differences that studies attribute to chemical runoff are likely to be more substantial for amphibians than for invertebrates.

- Direct contradiction.
- The passage clearly states **invertebrates** had **larger variations on average**.
- B reverses the comparative relationship.
- Therefore, logically and factually **false**.

C) the difference observed in the study conducted by Dr. Michelle Rivers was likely larger than the average difference in studies of freshwater trout included in the meta-analysis.

- There is **no data** about the **size of the effect** in Dr. Rivers's own study.
- This is **pure speculation**.
- The passage only says she conducted a **study of freshwater trout**, which was one of many included.
- We **cannot infer** whether her results were above or below average.

 16

Answer: C)

📝 **Explanation:**

- The sentence is structured with **parallel verbs/actions** that happened after Netflix • expanded.
- The word **"and"** is needed to connect two related events:
  - → Netflix **expanded its services, and** its initial lineup **was replaced.**
- A comma **before** "and" is required because the two clauses on either side are **independent** (both have a subject and verb).

So:

➤ "Netflix expanded its services**, and** its lineup was replaced..."

💡 **Why Others Are Wrong:**

- **A) influence and** → missing comma between two independent clauses.
- **B) influence,** → no coordinating conjunction; it leaves a sentence fragment.
- **D) influence** → missing both comma and conjunction; structurally incorrect.

17

Answer: C)

📝 **Explanation:**

- The phrase **"in an original direction"** is a **quote**, and the sentence continues after it.
- When a **quote ends mid-sentence**, the **punctuation must match the sentence structure**, not the quote itself.
- Since the sentence continues after the quote, the **semicolon** is the proper choice to join two independent clauses.

Correct form:

"...in an original direction**;** in 1953, for instance..."

💡 **Why Others Are Wrong:**

- **A)** uses a comma **inside the quote** and no proper punctuation after—it's incomplete.
- **B)** has wrong word order and incorrect punctuation.
- **D)** ends the quote but provides no punctuation at all—sentence structure fails.

18

Answer: D)

📝 **Explanation:**

- The colon **introduces a list**, which is what follows: the **two politicians**.
- The sentence before the colon is a **complete clause** ("...served in Congress"), so the colon is properly used.
- This is the classic **"complete sentence : list"** structure.

Structure:

"...served in Congress: Barbara Jordan... and John Lewis..."

> 💡 **Why Others Are Wrong:**
> - **A) Congress** → lacks the punctuation needed to introduce the list.
> - **B) Congress.** → ends the sentence too early, cutting off the list improperly.
> - **C) Congress;** → semicolon joins independent clauses; doesn't introduce a list.

19

Answer: A)

 Explanation:

- This is an example of **appositive structure**: the noun phrase ("Landscapes") is **followed by a nonessential modifier** ("edited by Carl Davis…").
- **Comma needed** to set off the modifier.
- "Landscapes, edited by..." gives us the correct rhythm and clarity.

> 💡 **Why Others Are Wrong:**
> - **B) Landscapes edited** → lacks the comma, implying "Landscapes edited by Carl Davis" is the title. Unclear.
> - **C) Landscapes. Edited** → cuts sentence awkwardly in two; fragment results.
> - **D) Landscapes and edited** → grammatically confused; "and" incorrectly joins unrelated elements.

20

Answer: A)

 Explanation:

- The **subject** is **"the number"**, which is **singular**.
- The verb must agree: **"shrinks"** is singular.
- The action happens **regularly**, so the **simple present tense** is correct.

"The number... **shrinks** almost every year."

160

💡 **Why Others Are Wrong:**

- **B) shrink** → plural verb; doesn't agree with singular subject "number".
- **C) are shrinking** → progressive aspect not required; also plural subject-verb mismatch.
- **D) have been shrinking** → plural and past-perfect progressive—again, **doesn't match** singular subject.

21

Answer: D)

 Explanation:

- The second sentence **follows logically** from the first.
- If ridings determine seats, then it makes sense that the number of seats a party has is directly tied to how many ridings it wins.
- **"Accordingly"** means *as a logical consequence*—perfect fit.

    💡 **Incorrect Options:**

    - **A) second of all,** − informal and unrelated to the logic.
    - **B) in fact,** − emphasizes truth, but doesn't express logical consequence.
    - **C) by contrast,** − signals opposition, which is inappropriate here.

22

Answer: D)

 Explanation:

- Engineers **warned against** differing standards, **yet** states didn't agree—opposite outcome.
- **"Nevertheless"** is a **contrast transition**, perfect for this ironic situation.

    💡 **Incorrect Options:**

    - **A) For this reason,** − implies the second idea follows logically from the first, which is not true.
    - **B) In other words,** − signals restatement, not opposition.
    - **C) Similarly,** − implies alignment, but the ideas **contrast**.

23

Answer: A)

 Explanation:

- The contrast is **not total**—it's nuanced. While **most** kept things secret, Tubman was an exception.
- **"Occasionally"** suggests that **sometimes** people like Tubman were open, which aligns perfectly.

   💡 **Incorrect Options:**
   - **B) For example,** – wrongly implies Tubman is like the others, but she's actually **different**.
   - **C) Accordingly,** – implies logical flow, which isn't the case.
   - **D) However,** – too strong of a contrast; "occasionally" fits the subtle distinction better.

24

Answer: A)

 Explanation:

- The **surprise** is that Doe, usually subtle, is **direct** in this painting.
- **"Though"** signals that contrast **within the same sentence**, and comes at the start of the clause for soft opposition.

   💡 **Incorrect Options:**
   - **B) fittingly,** – doesn't make sense; direct naming is **not typical** for him.
   - **C) similarly,** – wrongly implies this is like his usual approach.
   - **D) for example,** – doesn't capture the **contrast** with the previous sentence.

25

Answer: C)

📝 **Explanation:**

- This sentence is **clear, direct**, and uses **scientific naming** properly.
- It accomplishes the exact goal: to **state how many chromosomes** the house sparrow has.

Incorrect Options:

- **A)** − too general; focuses on genes, not number of chromosomes.
- **B)** − introduces comparison, not necessary if the student just wants a clear fact.
- **D)** − focuses on blue jay, not house sparrow.

26

Correct Answer: D)

📝 **Explanation:**

- This option best **highlights the contrast** between the two.
- It **clearly distinguishes** how each painting uses geometry differently, aligning exactly with the student's goal.

   Others:
  - **A)** − general and factual; doesn't emphasize differences.
  - **B)** − too broad; emphasizes blend, not contrast.
  - **C)** − vague and doesn't clearly explain how the two works differ.

27

Correct Answer: D)

📝 **Explanation:**

- It clearly lays out the **conflict between theories** and how Galileo's work supported the newer model.
- It expresses the **implication** of his discovery: that the old model was **wrong**, and the new one **right**.

   Others:
  - **A)** − describes the Geocentric Theory but **doesn't explain Galileo's role**.
  - **B)** − factual but lacks explanation of **why it matters**.
  - **C)** − vague; doesn't **clearly connect** to the implication.

TEST 03

TEST 4

- Module 1

- Module 1 answers

- Module 2

- Module 2 answers

Module 1

Reading and Writing
27 Questions, 32 Minutes

1

"Refrigerators and other large kitchen appliances tend to use compressors that can't be easily replaced or repaired. Appliance expert Sarah Martinez suggests that when these internal parts break down, the machines are typically discarded, leading to environmental _____."

A) advice

B) damage

C) benefits

D) progress

2

The following text is adapted from Mark Twain's *The Adventures of Tom Sawyer*. Tom has been walking around after running away from home. It is nearing sunset.

Tom gazed at the field that had once appeared terrifying to him in a much softer light. Weeds, rocks, trenches, and other dangers to travelers were fading quickly, and a shimmering blanket of grass was covering the ground, which seemed too **fragile** to be disturbed by careless hands.

As used in the text, what does the word **fragile** most nearly mean?

A) Benevolent

B) Delicate

C) Precise

D) Empty

3

"Marie Curie, who was the first woman to win a Nobel Prize, and Katherine Johnson, whose calculations were critical to NASA's space missions, hold permanent spots in scientific history. Regardless of the achievements others may make later on, no one will ever _____ the status of these women as pioneers in their fields."

A) undermine
B) imply
C) extend
D) promote

4

"Whatever the initial reception of Mark Twain's *The Adventures of Tom Sawyer* and F. Scott Fitzgerald's *The Great Gatsby* when they first came out, both novels are now viewed as quite _____. In 2020, for example, literary scholars commended the former as 'a timeless masterpiece' and the latter as 'an intricate exploration of the American dream.'"

A) positively
B) critically
C) objectively
D) strangely

/// CONTINUE ➡

5

"To assess their theories about the climate of the Ice Age, climatologists must rely on _____ data. Only tangible sources—such as the ice core samples extracted from Greenland in 1989—can determine whether a hypothesis about Ice Age weather patterns holds up."

A) speculative
B) convenient
C) creative
D) measurable

6

"Jane Austen's novel *Pride and Prejudice* was first published in 1813. The book became widely successful and was later followed by other notable works. Austen's brother Henry, **who helped edit, publish, and promote her novels,** was instrumental in ensuring that her works reached a wider audience. Together, they envisioned bringing Austen's unique literary voice to the public. Since the publication of *Pride and Prejudice*, her novels have been studied and appreciated in academic circles worldwide."

Which choice best describes the function of the underlined portion in the text as a whole?

A) It highlights the significance of an organization involved in the publishing process.
B) It contrasts the actions of two individuals mentioned in the text.
C) It argues against a point made earlier in the passage.
D) It provides further background on a person central to the narrative.

TEST 04

/// CONTINUE

7

"Dr. Jane Smith and her team discovered that high wind speeds reduce the flight activities of hawks (*Buteo jamaicensis*), a behavior that can be explained by weighing the benefits against the costs: stronger winds may not allow hawks to improve hunting efficiency enough to compensate for the increased energy expenditure required for flying. While many other birds of prey adjust their behavior similarly, peregrine falcons (*Falco peregrinus*) exhibit the reverse trend, as their **dependence on aerial speed** leads to a different calculation of energy gain versus loss."

Which choice best describes the function of the reference to "dependence on aerial speed" in the text as a whole?

A) It emphasizes a feature of peregrine falcons that helps them to respond more effectively to wind speed changes than hawks and other birds of prey.

B) It identifies a characteristic of peregrine falcons that explains why they do not reduce flight activity under high wind speeds, unlike hawks and many other birds of prey.

C) It describes a behavioral pattern displayed by peregrine falcons that contrasts with the way they would typically be expected to respond to high wind speeds.

D) It presents a trait of peregrine falcons that supports the claim that hawks are not the only birds of prey whose flight activity is affected by high wind speeds.

9

Text 1:
George Orwell, author of *1984* and *Animal Farm*, is well-known despite his simplistic writing style. His narratives are straightforward; **his plots are basic and convey social messages rather than intricate storylines**. The fact that his work is still powerful, despite this, is a credit to his brilliant ability to provoke thought—even if readers engage only with his ideas, they will leave with much to reflect on.

Text 2:
Orwell is often critiqued for his simple style, but this criticism misses the point. His novels are designed not for literary complexity, but for conveying clear political messages. In works like *1984*, for example, the stark and direct plot serves to amplify the importance of the ideas he presents. His simplistic plots are not a flaw but a deliberate choice to serve his thematic goals.

Based on the texts, how would the author of Text 2 most likely respond to the description of Orwell's plots in the underlined portion of Text 1?

A) Orwell's narratives would have been more compelling if he had included more detailed storylines.

B) The simplicity of Orwell's plots is a hallmark of *1984* and *Animal Farm* but not of his other works.

C) The simplicity of Orwell's plots should not necessarily be viewed as a shortcoming in his writing.

D) Orwell's plots would have been more impactful if they had addressed fewer social messages.

9

"Birds use various objects as tools to complete tasks with more efficiency. Such tasks include nest building, finding food, and protecting themselves. It was once widely believed that only primates used tools. However, crows and other birds have shattered this myth, proving that tool use is not exclusive to primates. For example, crows use sticks to extract insects from tree bark, while parrots use leaves to clean themselves and shield their feathers from damage."

Which choice best states the main idea of the text?

A) Birds find it challenging to use objects as tools.

B) Unlike primates, crows are particularly skilled at using tools.

C) Contrary to earlier beliefs, primates aren't the only animals that use tools.

D) There are many misconceptions about tool use that scientists are beginning to question.

10

Table: Popular Arcade Games of the Ealrly 1990s

Title	Approximate number of units sold worldwide	Release year	Genre	Developer
Motal Kombat	7,000,000	1992	fighting	Midway
Street Fighter Ⅱ	6,300,000	1991	fighting	Capcom
Metal Slug	1,500,000	1996	action -shooter	SNK
Tekken	5,500,000	1994	fighting	Namco

A student is conducting research on the rise of arcade games in the early 1990s. The student wants to know the release year of the game *Street Fighter II*, developed by Capcom. The student finds that this game was released in _____.

A) 1990

B) 1991

C) 1994

D) 1992

TEST 04

CONTINUE

11

A psychology student is studying the effects of different learning methods on memory retention. In a 2020 experiment, a group of participants was asked to memorize a list of words using two methods: spaced repetition and massed practice. The student hypothesizes that participants using spaced repetition will remember more words in the long term, as this technique promotes better retention over time compared to massed practice.

Which finding, if true, would most directly support the student's hypothesis?

A) The participants who used spaced repetition remembered the highest number of words in the short term.

B) The participants who used spaced repetition recalled more words after a week than participants who used massed practice.

C) Psychologists today believe that massed practice leads to faster memorization of short lists of words.

D) Participants in the experiment reported enjoying spaced repetition more than massed practice.

12

Frankenstein is an 1818 novel by Mary Shelley. In the story, Dr. Victor Frankenstein creates a monster, which he soon begins to fear. The fear Victor experiences is evident when he says,

_____

Which quotation from **Frankenstein** most effectively illustrates the claim?_

A) "How [the creature] haunted my nightmares, I cannot describe. On nights when the wind howled through the trees and the moonlight filtered through my window, I saw him lurking in the shadows, his eyes glowing with malice."

B) "I recall [the creature] as if it were but a moment ago, standing at my door, towering over me with a look of sheer determination."

C) "[The creature] was a mute figure, always lingering at the edge of the woods or staring across the frozen lake, silent and still."

D) "During the time he existed, [the creature] made no changes to his appearance except when he patched his ragged clothes with scraps he found, though the tears in his fabric constantly plagued him."

13

Students in a psychology class investigated why individuals can differ in their ability to memorize complex information as they age. The students compared control participants and those who had a specific gene for cognitive function deactivated. Finding that participants with the gene Memp1 deactivated struggled more with memory tasks than did control participants, the students concluded that differences in memory ability among people are solely attributable to variations in the level of expression of **Memp1.**

Which finding, if true, would most directly weaken the students' conclusion?

A) Some control participants were very similar to the **Memp1** deactivated participants with regard to memory ability but showed a wide variety of levels of expression of **Memp1**.

B) The level of expression of **Memp1** does not appear to affect the functioning of any other cognitive abilities in people.

C) A sampling of people in various environments shows that individuals can differ from one another in the level of expression of **Memp1**.

D) The participants with **Memp1** deactivated were identical to the control participants except with regard to memory ability.

14

Peacocks are birds known for their extravagant tail feathers. Some males display large, colorful tail feathers with intricate patterns. Although they are known for this trait, some peacocks have much smaller or less colorful tails. Scientists in 2015 proposed that the large tail feathers help peacocks attract mates more effectively. However, zoologist Maria Silva disagrees. She argues that if the tail feathers serve such an important purpose, then it's most likely that

_____

Which choice most logically completes the text?

A) Some peacocks would avoid displaying their tails in certain environments.

B) More peacocks would have large, colorful tails.

C) Fewer bird species would evolve extravagant feathers.

D) Peacocks would become more aggressive over time.

CONTINUE

15

In Los Angeles, over 200 languages are spoken by its diverse population. In the neighborhood of Koreatown, one can find a high concentration of Korean speakers. Likewise, Little Tokyo has a large number of Japanese speakers, and the city's Thai Town is home to a significant number of Thai speakers. Immigrants from South Korea, Japan, and Thailand often settle in these neighborhoods, where their native languages are widely spoken and cultural ties are strong. It can therefore be inferred that _____.

Which choice most logically completes the text?

A) The concentration of languages spoken in a neighborhood can predict the economic success of that area within the city.

B) Languages spoken in a city are largely determined by historical trade patterns and international diplomacy.

C) Cultural diversity in a city often leads to fewer linguistic differences between immigrant groups and local populations.

D) Immigrants tend to settle in areas where their native language and culture are already established, creating ethnic enclaves within cities.

16

Highlighted in The Visionary Lens (2022) is a painting created in 1945 by Maria _____ "Abstract Dawn," Gonzalez's piece supports the exhibit's aim of celebrating the varied, groundbreaking, and often visually bold work of female artists from the 1930s through the 1960s.

Which choice completes the text so that it conforms to the conventions of Standard English?

A) Gonzalez. Titled

B) Gonzalez titled

C) Gonzalez, titled

D) Gonzalez and titled

17

Published in 1954, J.R.R. Tolkien's novel *The Fellowship of the Ring* is less widely known than his _____ it is still regarded by critics as a foundational work of modern fantasy literature.

Which choice completes the text so that it conforms to the conventions of Standard English?

A) *The Hobbit*, but

B) *The Hobbit*,

C) *The Hobbit*

D) *The Hobbit* but

18

On the other hand, the Great Barrier Reef, which _____ located off the coast of Queensland, Australia, experienced significant coral bleaching over the past decade, affecting nearly two-thirds of its coral population.

Which choice completes the text so that it conforms to the conventions of Standard English?

A) is
B) are
C) were
D) have been

19

When British explorers traveled to the South Pacific in the eighteenth century, they encountered new foods and customs from the Polynesian people. This is why many words for tropical fruits and plants come from _____ English word "banana" comes from the West African word *banema*, and "yam" is derived from the word *nyami*.

Which choice completes the text so that it conforms to the conventions of Standard English?

A) African. The
B) African (the
C) African the
D) African? The

20

The fact that many species of birds, including the red-tailed hawk (*Buteo jamaicensis*) and the American kestrel (*Falco sparverius*), are listed as protected under federal law emphasizes the need for conservation efforts that can prevent _____ from becoming threatened.

Which choice completes the text so that it conforms to the conventions of Standard English?

A) the bird
B) these birds
C) this bird's
D) these birds'

21

Diamonds form under extreme pressure and heat deep within the Earth's mantle, but in the lab, scientists can recreate similar conditions to grow synthetic diamonds at much faster rates. Geologist Dr. Samuel Turner, who studies the formation of natural and synthetic diamonds, _____ that these conditions allow for the creation of high-quality gemstones within weeks.

Which choice completes the text so that it conforms to the conventions of Standard English?

A) explains
B) are explaining
C) explain
D) have explained

TEST 04

22

While not the case with granite, some types of rock can undergo significant changes due to weathering. _____ limestone can dissolve slowly over time when exposed to acidic rainwater.

Which choice completes the text with the most logical transition?

A) For example,

B) Finally,

C) Conversely,

D) In any case,

23

Just as the state of California has a designated state flower, bird, and fish, it also has a state tree: the California redwood. The redwood is a fitting choice for state tree, in large part because it grows in abundance along the coast. _____ it serves as an essential habitat for many species of wildlife and helps combat climate change by absorbing large amounts of carbon dioxide.

Which choice completes the text with the most logical transition?

A) At that time,

B) Alternatively,

C) Conversely,

D) Moreover,

24

Approximately every few months, a powerful stream of molten lava erupts from the summit of Mount Etna, flowing rapidly down the mountain—a process that seems destructive to its surroundings. _____ as volcanologist Maria Lopez claims, "the volcano acts as a natural phenomenon that rejuvenates the landscape," allowing new vegetation to flourish in the nutrient-rich soil.

Which choice completes the text with the most logical transition?

A) Therefore,

B) Still,

C) Specifically,

D) In other words,

25

• Ancient ruins are often uncovered when large-scale excavations are conducted in historical regions.
• Examples of such discoveries include ancient cities and temples.
• Harrington is an ancient city found in modern-day Greece.
• Archaeologists have determined that it was inhabited more than 1,500 years ago.
• The city spans an area of approximately 3.2 square kilometers.

Which choice most effectively uses information from the given sentences to emphasize the size of the ancient city?

A) Long ago, a city now known as Harrington was inhabited by early civilizations.

B) Ancient cities, like Harrington in Greece, are discovered through large-scale excavations in historical regions.

C) Archaeologists have investigated the remains of Harrington, an ancient city covering 3.2 square kilometers in Greece.

D) When early civilizations settled in what is now Greece more than 1,500 years ago, they established Harrington, a massive city spanning 3.2 square kilometers.

TEST 04

//// CONTINUE ➡

26

While conducting research, a student has taken the following notes:

- "Climate Change and Marine Ecosystems" is a scientific article.
- It was written by marine biologist Dr. Susan Green.
- It was first published in the journal *Marine Biology Today* in 2010.
- The article is written from a scientific perspective.
- It focuses on the effects of rising ocean temperatures on coral reefs.

The student wants to indicate what the article focuses on. Which choice most effectively uses relevant information from the notes to accomplish this goal?

A) "Climate Change and Marine Ecosystems" focuses on the effects of rising ocean temperatures on coral reefs.

B) "Climate Change and Marine Ecosystems" was written by Dr. Susan Green.

C) "Climate Change and Marine Ecosystems" was published in *Marine Biology Today*.

D) "Climate Change and Marine Ecosystems" is written from a scientific perspective.

27

While researching a topic, a student has taken the following notes:

- The saguaro cactus is a species of plant.
- It can be found in the deserts of the southwestern United States.
- The saguaro cactus primarily absorbs water through its shallow roots.
- It has an average height of 12 meters.

The student wants to specify the average height of the saguaro cactus. Which choice most effectively uses relevant information from the notes to accomplish this goal?

A) The saguaro cactus is a plant that primarily absorbs water through its shallow roots.

B) One species of plant found in the southwestern United States primarily absorbs water through its roots.

C) The saguaro cactus can be found in the southwestern United States.

D) The saguaro cactus has an average height of 12 meters.

Module 1 answer

1

Answer: B) damage

 Why it's correct:

Machines discarded en masse strain landfills, leak chemicals, and harm ecosystems. The phrase "leading to environmental..." requires a noun reflecting *harm*, which "damage" precisely captures.

> **Why the others are wrong:**
> - **A) advice** – Illogical; advice is not a consequence of discarding machines.
> - **C) benefits** – Opposite in meaning. There is no *benefit* in environmental terms from discarding appliances.
> - **D) progress** – Again, discarding waste isn't *progress*. This would contradict the negative connotation.

2

Answer: B) Delicate

 Why it's correct:

"Fragile" here describes the landscape as soft, easily disrupted—a synonym for "delicate." The visual of a shimmering blanket of grass supports this interpretation.

> **Why the others are wrong:**
> - **A) benevolent** – Means kind or good-willed; not related to physical delicacy.
> - **C) precise** – Not relevant to something easily damaged.
> - **D) empty** – Not consistent with the imagery of grass covering the ground.

3

Answer: A)

 Why it's correct:

"Undermine" fits the idea that their historical status as pioneers is secure and cannot be lessened or weakened.

> **Why the others are wrong:**
> - **B) imply** − Makes no sense here; implying status isn't about challenging it.
> - **C) extend** − Extending status is ambiguous and doesn't match the idea of unchangeable historical significance.
> - **D) promote** − Promoting someone's status doesn't fit the contrast with "no one will ever⋯"

4

Answer: A) positively

 Why it's correct:

Both scholarly quotes praise the novels. The word "positively" matches the modern acclaim described.

> **Why the others are wrong:**
> - **B) critically** − Could imply either negative or neutral analysis, but context shows *praise* not critique.
> - **C) objectively** − This describes a tone, not necessarily *viewing with admiration*.
> - **D) strangely** − Illogical; nothing in the text supports this.

5

Answer: D)

 Why it's correct:

"Measurable" fits with "tangible sources" like ice cores. It signals objective, quantifiable evidence.

> **Why the others are wrong:**
> - **A) speculative** − Opposes the idea of relying on solid evidence.
> - **B) convenient** − Suggests ease, not scientific rigor.
> - **C) creative** − Irrelevant to data; doesn't belong in scientific context.

6

Answer: D) It provides further background on a person central to the narrative.

 Why it's correct:

The passage centers on Jane Austen; the underlined section adds context about her brother's supportive role.

 Why the others are wrong:

- **A) significance of an organization** – This is about a *person*, not an organization.
- **B) contrasts actions** – No comparison or opposition between Henry and Jane.
- **C) argues against a point** – There's no counterpoint being made here.

7

Answer: B) It identifies a characteristic of peregrine falcons that explains why they do not reduce flight activity under high wind speeds, unlike hawks and many other birds of prey.

 Why it's correct:

It directly explains why peregrine falcons behave differently from hawks. Their high-speed hunting style thrives in strong winds.

Why the others are wrong:

- **A) respond *more effectively*** – Not stated. Their response is *different*, not necessarily *better*.
- **C) contrasts with expected behavior** – It *doesn't* contradict what we expect of peregrines; it explains their known adaptation.
- **D) supports claim about hawks** – The falcons are a *counterexample*, not further support.

8

Answer: C) The simplicity of Orwell's plots should not necessarily be viewed as a shortcoming in his writing.

Why it's correct:

Text 2 supports the notion that Orwell's "simple" style serves a purpose. It refutes the idea that simplicity = weakness.

181

Why the others are wrong:

- **A) more detailed storylines** – Opposes Text 2's view.
- **B) only in 1984/Animal Farm** – Text 2 makes a general statement, not a book-specific one.
- **D) fewer social messages** – Again, this misses the core defense of using simple form to *enhance* social messaging.

9

Answer: C) Contrary to earlier beliefs, primates aren't the only animals that use tools.

 Why it's correct:

The entire paragraph dispels the *myth* that only primates use tools, with examples from bird species.

 Why the others are wrong:

- **A) challenging to use tools** – The opposite of what's shown; birds use tools effectively.
- **B) crows vs. primates** – Too narrow; parrots are also included.
- **D) scientists questioning misconceptions** – Overgeneralized and doesn't focus on *tool use specifically*.

10

Answer: B) 1991

📝 **Explanation:**

The student is looking for the **release year of *Street Fighter II***, which is listed in the table under the "Title" column. According to the table:

- **Title:** *Street Fighter II*
- **Developer:** Capcom
- **Release Year:** 1991

 Why the other choices are incorrect:

- **A) 1990** – This is before the actual release year listed in the table.
- **C) 1994** – This is the release year of *Tekken*, not *Street Fighter II*.
- **D) 1992** – This is the release year of *Mortal Kombat*, not *Street Fighter II*.

11 ....

The correct answer is **B)**.

 Why it's correct:

The student's hypothesis is specifically about **long-term retention**. Choice B addresses this directly by comparing memory *after a week*—supporting the idea that spaced repetition improves long-term memory.

Why the others are wrong:

- **A)** Only mentions **short-term** memory, which is not what the hypothesis is about.
- **C)** Speaks generally about psychologist opinions, not data from this experiment.
- **D)** Discusses *preference*, not *performance*. Enjoyment doesn't prove effectiveness.

12 ....

Answer: A)

 Why it's correct:

This quote directly expresses *haunting nightmares* and *malicious eyes*, which are classic markers of **fear**. The language conveys psychological terror and dread.

Why the others are wrong:

- **B)** Recollection and "determination" don't imply fear—more like tension or conflict.
- **C)** A *mute figure staring* might be eerie, but it lacks explicit evidence of Victor's fear.
- **D)** Focuses on the creature's **appearance and clothing**, not Victor's emotional reaction.

13 ....

Answer: A)

 Why it's correct:

If **control participants with normal Memp1** had **similar memory issues**, that *undermines* the idea that memory ability is solely caused by Memp1 expression. It suggests other factors must be at play.

TEST 04

183

🗩 **Why the others are wrong:**

- **B)** Talks about other cognitive functions—not relevant to the memory-based conclusion.
- **C)** Describes population variance, not contradicting the causal conclusion.
- **D)** Actually **supports** the conclusion—it highlights that memory is the only differing variable.

14

Answer: B)

📝 **Why it's correct:**

If large tails truly aided in reproduction, *natural selection* would favor them—so we'd expect most peacocks to have them. The fact that some don't suggests **they may not be essential** for mating success.

🗩 **Why the others are wrong:**

- **A)** Avoidance behavior doesn't address the mating hypothesis.
- **C)** Refers to other bird species—not peacocks—so it doesn't directly refute the hypothesis.
- **D)** Aggression isn't linked to tail function in mating here—irrelevant to the logic.

15

Answer: D)

📝 **Why it's correct:**

This directly summarizes the pattern described in the passage: *Koreatown, Little Tokyo, Thai Town.* These are examples of **ethnic enclaves** formed due to shared language and culture.

🗩 **Why the others are wrong:**

- **A)** Economic success isn't discussed at all.
- **B)** Mentions trade and diplomacy—concepts unrelated to residential patterns.
- **C)** Says linguistic differences decrease, which isn't implied anywhere.

16

Answer: A)

 Explanation:

The sentence is actually **two** clauses:

1. "Highlighted...Maria Gonzalez." → **Complete thought**

2. "Titled 'Abstract Dawn,' Gonzalez's piece..." → **Modifier + main clause**

A **period** is needed to separate them. "Titled" introduces a new clause and modifies "Gonzalez's piece."

⍰ **Why the others are wrong:**

- **B) Gonzalez titled** – Incorrect; makes the sentence grammatically jumbled and unclear.

- **C) Gonzalez, titled** – Comma splice. Can't just attach a modifier like that without a main clause.

- **D) Gonzalez and titled** – Illogical phrasing. "And titled" implies parallel structure, but there's no matching verb.

17

Answer: A)

 Why it's correct:

The sentence contrasts *two clauses*, so we need both a **comma** and the **conjunction** "but" to connect them properly.

⍰ **Why the others are wrong:**

- **B) The Hobbit,** – Missing the necessary conjunction for contrast.

- **C) The Hobbit** – Lacks both punctuation and conjunction.

- **D) The Hobbit but** – Missing the comma before "but," which is required when joining independent clauses.

18

Answer: A)

Why it's correct:

The subject "reef" is **singular**, so the singular verb "is" must be used.

🗨 **Why the others are wrong:**

- **B) are** – Plural verb; mismatches the singular subject.
- **C) were** – Past tense; the sentence is in present tense.
- **D) have been** – Plural, past perfect; doesn't match subject or tense.

19

Answer: A)

📝 **Why it's correct:**

This needs to be two sentences: the first ends with "African." Then the next begins with "The English word⋯"

🗨 **Why the others are wrong:**

- **B) African (the** – Incorrect punctuation and case.
- **C) African the** – Run-on sentence; missing punctuation.
- **D) African? The** – Question mark is inappropriate; this isn't a question.

20

Answer: B)

📝 **Why it's correct:**

"Birds" is plural in the context (red-tailed hawk **and** kestrel), and "these birds" maintains subject-verb agreement and makes the sentence flow.

🗨 **Why the others are wrong:**

- **A) the bird** – Singular; inconsistent with the plural subject.
- **C) this bird's** – Incorrect possessive and singular.
- **D) these birds'** – Possessive is unnecessary and ungrammatical here.

21

Answer: A)

📝 Why it's correct:

"Dr. Samuel Turner" is **singular**, present-tense subject, so "explains" matches in subject-verb agreement.

❓ Why the others are wrong:

- **B) are explaining** − Plural verb with singular subject.
- **C) explain** − Plural verb; doesn't match "Dr. Turner."
- **D) have explained** − Present perfect plural; doesn't match subject or desired tense.

22

Correct Answer: A)

📝 Why it's correct:

We are given a **general statement** (some rocks change) and then a **specific instance** (limestone dissolving). "For example" is the most logical transitional phrase to introduce such a specific illustration.

❓ Why the others are wrong:

- **B) Finally,** − Implies a concluding point, but we are in the middle of an idea.
- **C) Conversely,** − Suggests contrast, which is inappropriate here.
- **D) In any case,** − Vague and does not logically connect to the example.

23

Correct Answer: D)

📝 Why it's correct:

This sentence **adds an additional reason** to support why the redwood is fitting. "Moreover" signals an **additive** relationship between the two ideas.

Why the others are wrong:

- **A) At that time,** – Time-related; not relevant.
- **B) Alternatively,** – Suggests a different option, not relevant here.
- **C) Conversely,** – Suggests opposition, not logical addition.

24

Answer: B)

Why it's correct:

We have a **contrast** between the destructive appearance of lava and its *constructive ecological effect*. "Still" acknowledges this contradiction in a natural, fluid way.

 Why the others are wrong:

- **A) Therefore,** – Suggests causality, not contrast.
- **C) Specifically,** – Introduces examples, not contrasting ideas.
- **D) In other words,** – Rephrasing rather than contrasting.

25

Correct Answer: D)

Why it's correct:

This sentence emphasizes *both the historical significance* and the **size** ("massive city spanning 3.2 square kilometers"). It synthesizes key ideas into a coherent, focused message.

Why the others are wrong:

- **A)** Mentions history, not size.
- **B)** General, doesn't emphasize the city's dimensions.
- **C)** Closer, but "covering 3.2 km²" feels more clinical than "massive...spanning," which adds stronger emphasis.

26 ....

Correct Answer: A)

 Why it's correct:

This is a **direct and accurate summary** of the article's main subject, based on the student's notes.

? Why the others are wrong:

- **B)** Author detail; not the article's *focus*.
- **C)** Publication info; again, not content-related.
- **D)** Describes perspective, but doesn't say what the article is *about*.

27 ....

Correct Answer: D)

Why it's correct:

It directly answers the student's goal with a clear, factual sentence using the most relevant information from the notes.

? Why the others are wrong:

- **A)** Talks about water absorption—not relevant to the **goal** of average height.
- **B)** Vague and omits specific details.
- **C)** Geographical info, not height.

TEST 04

Module 2

Reading and Writing
27 Questions, 32 Minutes

DIRECTIONS

The questions in this section address a number of important reading and writing skills. Each questions includes one or more passages, which may include a table or graph. Read each passage and question carefully, and then choose the best answer to the question based on the passage(s).

All questions in this section are multiple-choice with four answer choices. Each question has a single best answer.

1

The release of Dr. Lee's research paper on climate change has sparked significant interest. Numerous scientists, environmentalists, and activists have _____ the paper, and it was awarded the Global Science Prize.

Which choice completes the text with the most logical and precise word or phrase?

A) criticized

B) dismissed

C) endorsed

D) misinterpreted

2

The following text is adapted from the memoirs of explorer James Carter.

"The trek through the dense Amazon forest, though short in length, was far from straightforward. It seemed as though the wilderness intended to place every **conceivable** challenge in the path of those who sought to traverse it."

As used in the text, what does the word 'conceivable' most nearly mean?

A) Possible

B) Regular

C) Visible

D) Simple

3

Mangrove swamps flourish along tropical coastlines. These ecosystems are crucial to many aquatic species. Strong tides and waves can make the shallow waters turbulent, offering limited protection for young fish and crustaceans. The dense mangrove roots reduce wave intensity. This results in a more _____ setting with gentler waters where marine life can thrive.

Which choice completes the text with the most logical and precise word or phrase?

A) unpredictable

B) tranquil

C) creative

D) hazardous

4

The newly discovered solar flare X2024 lasted for over 30 minutes, _____ for an event originating from a sunspot eruption. Solar flares from sunspot activity are usually over in less than 5 minutes.

Which choice completes the text with the most logical and precise word or phrase?

A) an occurrence

B) a delay

C) an anomaly

D) a phenomenon

CONTINUE

5

Coral polyps are small marine organisms that build colonies using calcium carbonate to form their protective skeletons. These structures are thought to be highly susceptible to changes in ocean acidity because calcium carbonate dissolves more readily in acidic waters. Dr. Sarah Wong and her team recently found that a mucous layer on coral exoskeletons helps reduce this dissolution under normal conditions. Interestingly, they also observed that, even when this layer was partially damaged, coral polyps still managed to repair the skeleton's internal framework.

Which choice best describes the main purpose of the text?

A) To advocate for more studies on the biological factors influencing coral polyp regeneration

B) To examine some of the ways ocean acidification has impacted coral reef formation

C) To discuss a study's findings on calcium carbonate's role in protecting coral polyps' exoskeletons

D) To present evidence suggesting that the concern about the effects of ocean acidification on coral structures might be unwarranted

6

London has high bicycle usage, but simply adopting a characteristic of London associated with bike-friendliness—such as its extensive network of bike lanes—may not be enough to encourage cycling in other cities. As cycling advocate Emma Green suggests, our understanding of what motivates individuals to ride bicycles remains incomplete: some research highlights convenience, other studies focus on perceived safety, and so on. However, cycling choices are influenced by a range of factors that differ depending on individual circumstances and needs.

Which choice best states the main purpose of the text?

A) To explore the impact of extensive bike lanes on a city's overall bike usage

B) To present a claim about how people's decision-making to cycle can be improved

C) To highlight the challenge of finding a consistent method to increase cycling in various cities

D) To explain the difficulties in comparing bike usage across cities with different infrastructures

6

The following passage is from the play A Forgotten Land, performed in 1845. The character Eliza has been living in a remote village with her mentor, Geoffrey, since she was a child. Geoffrey has suggested that Eliza may have little memory of her life before arriving at the village.

ELIZA: 'tis distant off,

More like a fleeting dream than a true memory

Of something my memory warrants. Did I not

Once have in my possession numerous women

that tended after me?

GEOFFREY: Indeed, thou hadst, Eliza, and more than that. But why

this stands out in thy mind? What else thou seest

From that shadowy past?

If thou remember ere from thou camest,

surely thou can recall how thou camest here.

In the text, what does Geoffrey most directly imply about Eliza and her memories?

A) Eliza's recollection is unclear because she is confusing a daydream from childhood with an actual event that took place.

B) Eliza's uncertainty about a specific memory from her early life before the village is affecting her ability to recall the journey that brought her to the village.

C) Eliza's memories of her childhood are tinged with sadness, reflecting her dissatisfaction with her current life in the village.

D) Eliza's ability to recall details from her past before arriving at the village suggests she may also be able to remember how she came to live in the village.

8

Text 1

A research group studying the coastal ecosystems of the Pacific Northwest has collaborated with 9 indigenous tribes in the region to investigate the long-term effects of climate change on local species. Their findings suggest that the Pacific herring (known as *ts'aqpa* in the native language) will likely be more negatively impacted than the bald eagle (*q'wil*a*), a result of rising sea temperatures over the next few decades. This joint research effort has fostered a strong working relationship between environmental institutions and tribal communities, improving the prospects for future collaborative environmental studies.

Text 2

Environmental agencies are increasingly working with indigenous communities to incorporate traditional knowledge into conservation strategies to address threats posed by climate change. This collaboration has strengthened ties between the agencies and the communities and has led to more successful conservation outcomes.

Based on the texts, both authors would most likely agree with which statement?

A) A collaborative research approach will help mitigate the effects of rising sea temperatures on species in the Pacific Northwest.

B) In the Pacific Northwest, conservation strategies focused on the Pacific herring are likely to be more successful than those focused on the bald eagle.

C) Conservation projects in the Pacific Northwest are likely to benefit from the collaboration between indigenous communities and environmental agencies.

D) It is more crucial to prioritize conservation of the Pacific herring over the bald eagle in the Pacific Northwest.

TEST 04

 CONTINUE

193

9

The following text is from a travel journal documenting a drive from a bustling city to the open desert:

"I sat back in the car, staring out at the fading city skyline behind us. Soon, the tall buildings gave way to vast expanses of land, and I saw the wide highway stretching endlessly ahead. As we moved further from the city, the road began to open up, no longer constricted by traffic or overpasses. The desert seemed to spread out in all directions, limitless and free, stretching as far as the eye could see. The air felt lighter, and the harsh sounds of the city were replaced by the quiet, peaceful hum of the wind."

Based on the text, which choice best expresses the narrator's characterization of the desert?

A) As the drive continued from the city into the desert, the landscape gradually became more rough.

B) The drive through the desert is mostly serene, but the wind picks up intensity briefly in certain areas.

C) The roads near the city are more congested and cramped than those in the desert.

D) The beauty of the desert is only surpassed by that of the city skyline.

10

The *Innovations in Science and Technology* (2024) exhibition at the Global Science Museum in Tokyo is dedicated to the work of 30 international scientists, including Maya Thompson, Raj Patel, and Lucas Feng. **Although the museum has hosted exhibitions focused entirely on scientists before, such as the Pioneers *in Robotics* event, the breadth of scientific fields covered in *Innovations in Science and Technology* distinguishes it from previous exhibits.**

Which finding, if true, would most directly support the underlined claim?

A) *Innovations in Science and Technology* and *Pioneers in Robotics* were curated to feature projects not originally developed at the Global Science Museum.

B) Thompson is a biologist, Patel is an engineer, and Feng is a physicist.

C) The Global Science Museum has a prestigious collection of scientific exhibits that include contributions from scientists worldwide, not just from Tokyo.

D) Patel is an international engineer, as were all of the scientists featured in *Pioneers in Robotics*.

11

Text 1

The demand for craft beer is increasing, and breweries are diversifying their offerings to cater to various consumer preferences. This trend is part of a broader shift towards a "craft economy," where consumers appreciate the uniqueness and quality of handcrafted products. To remain competitive, breweries need to focus on providing a distinctive customer experience, not just high-quality beer.

Text 2

Small breweries are becoming a significant part of the beverage industry. One reason for this growth is the rise of social media platforms that allow breweries to reach a wider audience and market their unique products directly to consumers. As consumer behavior shifts towards favoring local and artisanal goods, small breweries are increasingly relying on direct sales and social media presence to drive revenue.

Based on the texts, both authors would most likely agree with which statement?

A) Consumers are more interested in purchasing mass-produced beer than in craft beer.

B) Consumers' growing interest in unique and high-quality products is mostly confined to the beverage industry.

C) Changing consumer behaviors are leading to changes in the beverage industry.

D) The rising consumer demand for craft beer also generates higher demand for social media marketing.

12

Recent studies show that solar energy contributes significantly to powering small residential areas. Researchers are now investigating how dependent large urban areas are on solar power. In the first phase of their study, they covered some solar panels in certain urban areas, which resulted in those areas generating 40 to 90 percent less energy than those with uncovered panels. However, the researchers caution that this first phase did not indicate how much of the energy reduction was specifically due to the absence of solar panels.

Which finding, if true, would most directly support the researchers' claim?

A) Other energy sources, like wind turbines, also generate power for small residential areas, and some studies have allowed these sources to provide energy while excluding solar panels.

B) Other energy sources, like hydroelectric plants, also contribute to urban energy, and the shielding in the first phase of the study blocked their impact as well.

C) Solar panels are more commonly used to power large urban areas than small residential areas.

D) The shielding used in the first phase of the study did not affect the amount of sunlight the solar panels received.

TEST 04

195

13

Over 300 species of plants grow in the National Park, in addition to the numerous animals and insects that inhabit it—one can find rare orchids in the southern region, for example, or alpine flowers near the mountain peaks. Oak trees are the most common, covering 40% of the park, followed by pine trees at 25%. A botanist hypothesizes that a new variety of pine—differing from other pine species in some of its leaf shape, bark texture, and growth patterns—has developed in the park, partly due to its interaction with oak trees. Previous research shows that younger plants of non-dominant species are more likely to adapt features from the dominant species of a region than older plants. If the botanist's hypothesis is correct, it is therefore likely to be the case that _____.

Which choice most logically completes the text?

A) The proportion of younger pine trees that display unique characteristics specific to the park is higher in regions where many species coexist than in regions where oaks and pines dominate.

B) Both the number of plant species in the National Park and the number of varieties of each species will increase over time.

C) Oak trees in the National Park tend to have more adaptations borrowed from other plant species than from those of the same species in other regions.

D) Younger pine trees in the National Park would be more likely to exhibit characteristics specific to the park than older pine trees living in the same region would be.

14

A recent analysis by Jane Thompson and her team of ancient pottery shards found in a remote area of Greece reveals changes in their composition over time: while shards from around 300 BCE contain about 90% clay and 10% sand, shards from 250 BCE contain 70% clay and 30% sand, giving them a more granular texture that would have been noticeable. Because pottery with less than 80% clay was widely considered fragile and unsuitable for everyday use, Thompson et al. speculate that a decline in the quality of pottery occurred in the region around 250 BCE, which was likely reversed—despite economic pressures in the area—as a result of local potters' decision to _____.

Which choice most logically completes the text?

A) Keep the amount of clay in pottery consistent with that in shards from 250 BCE but make the pots smaller.

B) Announce that the percentage of clay in high-quality pottery would be increased to more than 80%.

C) Begin sourcing new types of sand not available to earlier potters.

D) Start producing larger pots with a ratio of clay to sand similar to that in shards from 250 BCE.

15

In 1950, French _____ official monument: the Eiffel Tower, which became one of the most iconic structures in the world.

Which choice completes the text so that it conforms to the conventions of Standard English?

A) officials designated the city

B) officials designated the city's

C) official's designated the city's

D) official's designated the city

16

Interest in renewable energy sources, the method by which sunlight, wind, and water are converted into usable electricity, is expanding because of innovative work by environmental engineers—many of whom, like solar energy expert Dr. Natalie Green, _____ this method to better understand how energy from natural resources can be harnessed more efficiently.

Which choice completes the text so that it conforms to the conventions of Standard English?

A) study

B) has studied

C) studies

D) is studying

17

If you had visited the museum in the summer of 1985, chances are you would have seen the _____ "Starry Night" by Vincent van Gogh. The painting is one of the most famous works in the world.

Which choice completes the text so that it conforms to the conventions of Standard English?

- A) painting:
- B) painting,
- C) painting;
- D) painting

18

Combining research from biology and chemistry, scientists working in the field of biochemistry explore a wide range of topics. Dr. Alice Wong of Harvard University studies cellular _____ other researchers investigate areas such as protein synthesis and enzyme regulation.

Which choice completes the text so that it conforms to the conventions of Standard English?

- A) energy production, for instance;
- B) energy production; for instance,
- C) energy production, for instance,
- D) energy production for instance;

TEST 04

CONTINUE

19

Dr. Julia Smith's research paper on "urban heat islands," a term that refers to areas within cities that are significantly warmer than surrounding rural areas, is included in the collection *Climate Change and the City*. The book wasn't written solely by _____ other experts, such as Brian Parker and Sarah Adams, also contributed chapters.

Which choice completes the text so that it conforms to the conventions of Standard English?

A) Smith, however;

B) Smith; however,

C) Smith. However,

D) Smith, however,

20

Recent archaeological excavations in the Nile Delta have led some researchers to propose that the region was once home to a complex trade network. This hypothesis _____ that certain artifacts, such as pottery and jewelry, were exchanged between distant cultures without interruption over several centuries, a claim that researchers Dr. Martin and Dr. Greene argue cannot be confirmed unless additional evidence is uncovered.

Which choice completes the text so that it conforms to the conventions of Standard English?

A) suggests

B) suggested

C) suggesting

D) has suggested

21

With his large-scale installation *Oceanic Dream*, Brazilian artist Marco Pereira succeeds in creating a surreal yet captivating experience. _____ when visitors enter the enormous gallery filled with glowing marine life sculptures, they are both awed and mystified—feeling as though they have stepped into a vibrant underwater world.

Which choice completes the text with the most logical transition?

A) Second,

B) Nevertheless,

C) Indeed,

D) Instead,

22

Hiking trails that include wooden bridges and handrails are known as eco-trails, named for their focus on minimizing environmental impact. As hiking these trails has evolved from a means of travel to a leisure activity, modern eco-trails are rarely constructed solely for transportation purposes. _____ modern routes are designed for recreational use, often showcasing beautiful landscapes or providing a peaceful walking experience.

Which choice completes the text with the most logical transition?

A) Nonetheless,

B) On the other hand,

C) Additionally,

D) More often,

TEST
04

CONTINUE

23

While researching a topic, a student has taken the following notes:

- Travel documentaries in the "slow documentary" genre consist of uninterrupted footage of natural landscapes and cultural events in real time.
- *Journey Across the Andes* is a Chilean slow documentary series.
- The 7-day-long program documented a trek across the Andes, from Argentina to Chile.
- It first aired in 2019.
- Slow documentaries have been called "hypnotic yet unengaging."
- American film critic Sarah Hill praises slow documentaries, writing that they offer "a deep and immersive form of travel from the comfort of home."

The student wants to use a quotation to refute the claim that slow documentaries are boring. Which choice most effectively uses relevant information from the notes to accomplish this goal?

A) While some have praised slow documentaries for offering "a deep and immersive form of travel from the comfort of home," others have called them "hypnotic yet unengaging."

B) Far from boring, slow documentaries can provide "a deep and immersive form of travel from the comfort of home," as Hill puts it, allowing viewers to experience the Andes trek in real time.

C) With broadcasts of uninterrupted natural landscapes, like the Andes trek, occurring in real time, slow documentaries just might be "hypnotic yet unengaging."

D) *Journey Across the Andes* can provide "a deep and immersive form of travel," as Hill puts it.

24

While researching a topic, a student has taken the following notes:

- DNA is the molecule that carries genetic information.
- Genes contain the instructions for determining an organism's characteristics.
- Different species typically have a different number of chromosomes.
- The house cat (*Felis catus*) and the Bengal tiger (*Panthera tigris tigris*) are species of felines.
- The house cat has thirty-eight chromosomes.
- The Bengal tiger has thirty chromosomes.

The student wants to specify how many chromosomes the house cat has. Which choice most effectively uses relevant information from the notes to accomplish this goal?

A) The house cat (*Felis catus*) and the Bengal tiger (*Panthera tigris tigris*) both have chromosomes, but the house cat has more than the Bengal tiger does.

B) The house cat (*Felis catus*) has thirty-eight chromosomes.

C) The house cat's chromosomes contain genes, which are crucial to determining the organism's characteristics.

D) The Bengal tiger, a species of felines, has thirty structures called chromosomes.

200

25

While researching fashion trends, a student has taken the following notes:

- At Paris and Milan Fashion Weeks, designers reveal their latest collections.
- Color experts publish reports on trending colors after each Fashion Week.
- A report on 2019 Paris Fashion Week highlighted the popularity of a warm shade of marigold yellow, soft and light in intensity.
- A report on 2022 Milan Fashion Week highlighted a striking emerald green shade that was bold in tone and deep in intensity.

Which choice most effectively uses information from the given sentences to describe a color that was popular at 2022 Milan Fashion Week?

A) Shades of warm marigold yellow and striking emerald green have both been featured in Fashion Week reports prepared by color experts.

B) Each Fashion Week, color experts compile reports on the popular colors worn by designers.

C) The color chosen by designers at 2022 Milan Fashion Week was a striking contrast to the warm, light marigold yellow that had been favored at 2019 Paris Fashion Week.

D) At 2022 Milan Fashion Week, many designer collections showcased a bold, deep shade of striking emerald green.

26

While researching a topic, a student has taken the following notes:

- The first International Congress on Mathematics was held in 1900.
- It brought together many of the world's leading mathematicians to discuss advancements in mathematics.
- The congress featured a debate between mathematicians David Hilbert and Henri Poincaré.
- Hilbert proposed that mathematical truths could be derived from a finite set of axioms, while Poincaré argued that mathematical intuition played a key role in discovery.
- Hilbert's position, later developed into formalism, became a central theory in mathematics.

The student wants to place Poincaré's argument within its historical context. Which choice most effectively uses relevant information from the notes to accomplish this goal?

A) During the early 20th century, Poincaré argued that mathematical intuition was essential for discovering truths, though Hilbert's formalist approach would eventually become more widely accepted.

B) The attendees of the 1900 International Congress on Mathematics were some of the most distinguished mathematicians of their time, including Poincaré, who challenged Hilbert's proposal.

C) In 1900, Hilbert and Poincaré engaged in a famous debate; Hilbert's position, later known as formalism, would go on to shape mathematical thinking for decades.

D) At the 1900 International Congress on Mathematics, Poincaré opposed the idea that mathematical truths could be derived solely from axioms.

TEST
04

201

27

While researching a topic, a student has taken the following notes:

- The Mohs scale of hardness ranks different types of wood based on their resistance to scratching.
- Woods with higher Mohs scale numbers are more resistant to scratches.
- Woods with lower Mohs scale numbers are more easily scratched by harder materials.
- Oak has a Mohs scale number of 6.
- Maple has a Mohs scale number of 5.
- Pine has a Mohs scale number of 2.

The student wants to make a generalization about different types of wood. Which choice most effectively uses relevant information from the notes to accomplish this goal?

A) Based on their Mohs scale numbers, oak (6) is harder than maple (5), and maple is harder than pine (2).

B) Oak can leave visible scratches on pine, which is why oak has a higher number than pine on the Mohs scale of hardness.

C) Any wood with a Mohs number of 6, like oak, can scratch wood with a Mohs number of 5, like maple.

D) The Mohs scale can be used to order oak, maple, and pine by their ability to resist scratching.

Module 2 answer

1

Answer: C) endorsed

 Why it's correct:

The context indicates **praise and recognition**: "sparked significant interest" and "awarded the Global Science Prize." The word *endorsed*—meaning "publicly approved or supported"—fits perfectly.

    💡 **Why the others are wrong:**
- **A) criticized** – Directly contradicts the tone of praise.
- **B) dismissed** – Suggests rejection, not celebration.
- **D) misinterpreted** – Irrelevant to the idea of the paper being *celebrated and awarded*.

2

Answer: A)

 Why it's correct:

"Conceivable" in this context means *every imaginable or possible challenge*. The wilderness is being portrayed as relentlessly difficult, not in any of the other senses.

    💡 **Why the others are wrong:**
- **B) regular** – Means frequent or expected; not about mental possibility.
- **C) visible** – Relates to sight, which is not implied.
- **D) simple** – Opposite of what's intended; challenges are complex.

3 ....

Answer: B)

📝 **Why it's correct:**

"Tranquil" means **calm and peaceful**, which contrasts the earlier mention of **turbulent** waters. The mangrove roots calm the waves—*tranquility* is the logical result.

💡 **Why the others are wrong:**
- **A) unpredictable** – Would contradict the calming effect.
- **C) creative** – Doesn't describe environmental conditions.
- **D) hazardous** – Contradicts the idea of *thriving* marine life.

4 ....

Answer: C) an anomaly

📝 **Why it's correct:**

Solar flares usually last under 5 minutes, so this unusually long one is *an anomaly*—something **deviating from the norm**.

💡 **Why the others are wrong:**
- **A) an occurrence** – Neutral and non-specific; lacks emphasis on *rarity*.
- **B) a delay** – Not accurate; it's not a delay, it's a duration issue.
- **D) a phenomenon** – Too vague and general; doesn't emphasize the *unusual* nature.

5 ....

Answer: D) To present evidence suggesting that the effects of ocean acidification on coral structures might be overstated

📝 **Why it's correct:**

The passage **acknowledges the concern** about acidification but presents findings that **reduce alarm**—coral polyps can still **repair internal damage**, even with a damaged mucous layer.

💡 **Why the others are wrong:**
- **A)** Mentions "advocacy" and "regeneration"—not the main focus.
- **B)** Discusses the impact of acidification generally, but doesn't match the **tone of reassurance** in the findings.
- **C)** Too narrow and incorrect—calcium carbonate isn't "protecting coral polyps," but forms their exoskeleton.

6

Answer: C) To highlight the challenge of finding a consistent method to increase cycling in various cities

 Why it's correct:

The text emphasizes that **bike infrastructure alone isn't enough**, and that **cycling motivations vary**, making consistency difficult.

💡 **Why the others are wrong:**
- **A)** Focuses only on one factor (bike lanes).
- **B)** The passage doesn't offer a method or solution.
- **D)** Though it mentions different cities, the **challenge isn't about comparing usage**—it's about applying solutions across contexts.

TEST 04

7

Answer: D) Eliza's ability to recall details from her past before arriving at the village suggests she may also be able to remember how she came to live in the village.

 Why it's correct:

Geoffrey says, *"If thou remember ere from thou camest, surely thou can recall how thou camest here."* →
A direct implication that one memory may unlock another.

💡 **Why the others are wrong:**
- **A)** No indication she's *confusing a dream.*
- **B)** Focuses on a specific memory; Geoffrey's interest is broader.
- **C)** No evidence of emotional tone or dissatisfaction.

8

Answer: C) Conservation projects in the Pacific Northwest are likely to benefit from the collaboration between indigenous communities and environmental agencies.

✍ Why it's correct:

This is a **shared theme** of both texts—mutual benefit, improved ties, and better outcomes.

◊ Why the others are wrong:

- **A)** Only Text 1 mentions the species; "mitigating effects" goes beyond both texts.
- **B)** Text 2 doesn't mention specific species.
- **D)** Prioritization between species is not discussed.

9

Answer: C)

✍ Why it's correct:

This is directly supported: "no longer constricted by traffic or overpasses... peaceful hum of the wind."

◊ Why the others are wrong:

- **A)** "Rough" isn't implied—the tone is positive.
- **B)** Wind's **intensity** isn't mentioned—just its *calm sound*.
- **D)** "City beauty > desert" is not the narrator's position.

10

The correct answer is **B)**

✍ Why it's correct:

This proves the *exhibit spans a wide range* of disciplines—biology, engineering, physics—supporting the claim of **breadth**.

💡 **Why the others are wrong:**
- **A)** Talks about the **origin of projects**, not scientific fields.
- **C)** General museum info—not relevant to *this exhibit*.
- **D)** Only about Patel and robotics—not comparative or broad.

Answer: C) Changing consumer behaviors are leading to changes in the beverage industry.

📝 **Why it's correct:**
- **Text 1** emphasizes the rise of the "craft economy" and the need for breweries to adjust experiences to meet **consumer preferences**.
- **Text 2** connects the **shift toward artisanal goods** and local products with breweries' increasing reliance on direct sales and social media.

Therefore: Both highlight how **consumer behavior** is **reshaping** the beverage industry—hence, C.

💡 **Why the others are wrong:**
- **A)** Directly contradicts both passages.
- **B)** Text 1 mentions this trend is part of a *broader craft economy*, so it's not *confined* to beverages.
- **D)** Only Text 2 mentions social media; Text 1 doesn't connect it to demand.

The correct answer is **B)**

📝 **Why it's correct:**
- If shielding also blocked **other energy sources**, then the drop in energy production **can't be attributed only to solar panels**—which directly supports the researchers' caution.

💡 **Why the others are wrong:**
- **A)** Talks about small residential areas, not urban centers.
- **C)** Irrelevant to the experimental finding—it's background info, not supportive of the claim.
- **D)** This would **weaken** the researchers' caution because it suggests the shielding was specific to solar panels.

TEST 04

13

The correct answer is **D)**

 Why it's correct:

- The hypothesis and prior research both point to **young, non-dominant plants (pines)** adapting traits from **dominant species (oaks)**.
- So if the hypothesis holds, **younger pines** will show those adaptations **more than older ones**.

  ◌ **Why the others are wrong:**
  - **A)** Adds variables (many species, regional variation) not discussed in the hypothesis.
  - **B)** Makes a broad prediction about **all plants**, which the passage doesn't support.
  - **C)** Reverses the relationship: the passage is about **pines adapting from oaks**, not the other way around.

14

The correct answer is **B)**

Why it's correct:

- This directly **reverses** the decline by returning to the clay threshold (>80%) that defines durability and quality.

  ◌ **Why the others are wrong:**
  - **A)** Keeps the suboptimal clay content and makes pots smaller—doesn't improve quality.
  - **C)** Introducing new sand types doesn't address **clay percentage**, which is the real issue.
  - **D)** Larger pots with poor material = even **worse** quality.

15

Answer: B)

📝 Why it's correct:

- "French officials" is the subject (plural noun).
- "designated" is the verb.
- "the city's official monument" is the object. Thus: *"French officials designated the city's official monument: the Eiffel Tower..."*

💡 Why the others are wrong:

- **A)** "the city" doesn't logically connect to "official monument" (would suggest the *entire city* is the monument).
- **C) & D)** "official's" is possessive singular—grammatically incorrect for this sentence.

16

Answer: A)

📝 Why it's correct:

The phrase "many of whom" is **plural**, so the verb must match: **"study."**

💡 Why the others are wrong:

- **B)** "has studied" is singular.
- **C)** "studies" is also singular.
- **D)** "is studying" is singular and present progressive—doesn't fit with the plural subject.

17

Answer: D)

📝 Why it's correct:

The sentence continues **smoothly** into the next clause: "The painting is one of the most famous..." So **no punctuation** is needed after "painting."

💡 **Why the others are wrong:**

- **A)** Colon (:) is used to introduce a list or explanation—not appropriate here.
- **B)** Comma is not needed; no separation required.
- **C)** Semicolon separates two full independent clauses—also incorrect here.

18

Answer: A)

📝 **Why it's correct:**

- "For instance" is a **parenthetical phrase** and needs to be surrounded properly.
- The **semicolon** is correct because it connects two independent clauses.

💡 **Why the others are wrong:**

- **B)** Reverses comma/semicolon placement.
- **C)** Needs semicolon before "for instance."
- **D)** Missing punctuation entirely.

19

Answer: A)

📝 **Why it's correct:**

- This is a compound sentence with **two independent clauses**, and "however" is functioning as a **conjunctive adverb**.
- So: "Smith, however; other experts also contributed..." is correct.

💡 **Why the others are wrong:**

- **B)** Wrong punctuation; semicolon **must** come before "however," not after "Smith."
- **C)** A period before "However" makes two **unrelated** clauses; loses the contrast.
- **D)** Missing semicolon to separate clauses.

20

Answer: A)

📝 Why it's correct:

- Present tense "suggests" matches the general tone and context of **current discussion** and ongoing research.

  #### 💡 Why the others are wrong:
  - **B)** "suggested" (past tense) implies the hypothesis is no longer held.
  - **C)** "suggesting" is a participle, not a main verb—sentence would be incomplete.
  - **D)** "has suggested" creates unnecessary perfect tense here.

21

The correct answer is **C)** "Indeed,".

📝 Why it's correct:

"Indeed" strengthens or reaffirms a previous claim. The sentence elaborates on how the artist *succeeds*, giving **supporting detail**.

  #### 💡 Why the others are wrong:
  - **A) Second,** – Implies a sequence not present here.
  - **B) Nevertheless,** – Suggests contrast, which is incorrect.
  - **D) Instead,** – Also suggests contrast or substitution, which doesn't fit.

22

The correct answer is **D)** "More often,".

📝 Why it's correct:

"More often" contrasts with "rarely" and logically continues the thought by showing **what is more typical now**.

Why the others are wrong:

- **A) Nonetheless,** – Suggests contradiction, which isn't appropriate here.
- **B) On the other hand,** – Suggests a counterpoint, but this is a **natural continuation**.
- **C) Additionally,** – Implies addition, not a contrast of frequency.

23

The correct answer is **B)**

📝 **Why it's correct:**

This directly **refutes** the idea that they're boring by using **Sarah Hill's positive quote** and applies it to a real example (the Andes trek).

 Why the others are wrong:

- **A)** Includes *both sides*, which doesn't fulfill the goal of refutation.
- **C)** Repeats the negative idea.
- **D)** Lacks clarity about how it refutes boredom—too vague.

24

The correct answer is **B)**

📝 **Why it's correct:**

This is a **precise, factual** statement directly using the notes to address the goal.

💡 **Why the others are wrong:**

- **A)** Compares to Bengal tiger unnecessarily—less direct.
- **C)** Talks about what chromosomes do, not how many there are.
- **D)** Focuses on Bengal tiger, not the house cat.

25

The correct answer is **D)**

 Why it's correct:

It clearly and **specifically summarizes** the 2022 Milan Fashion Week detail.

> **Why the others are wrong:**
> - **A)** Vague generalization—doesn't emphasize *2022 Milan*.
> - **B)** Too general; doesn't mention *specific color or year*.
> - **C)** Focuses too much on contrast with 2019, not 2022's color.

26

The correct answer is **A)**

 Why it's correct:

It situates Poincaré's views in **time** and contrasts them with Hilbert's future influence—providing **context and contrast**.

> **Why the others are wrong:**
> - **B)** Focuses on attendance, not Poincaré's *argument* in context.
> - **C)** Emphasizes **Hilbert**, not Poincaré.
> - **D)** Accurate but **too narrow**—lacks broader historical framing.

27

The correct answer is **D)**

 Why it's correct:

This is a **broad, organizing statement**—a proper generalization using the Mohs data.

> **Why the others are wrong:**
> - **A)** Too specific and itemized—not a **generalization**.
> - **B)** Focuses on application rather than overall pattern.
> - **C)** Incorrect overgeneralization—not all woods with higher Mohs scores can scratch others.

TEST 04

TEST 5

Module 1

Reading and Writing
27 Questions, 32 Minutes

DIRECTIONS

The questions in this section address a number of important reading and writing skills. Each questions includes one or more passages, which may include a table or graph. Read each passage and question carefully, and then choose the best answer to the question based on the passage(s).

All questions in this section are multiple-choice with four answer choices. Each question has a single best answer.

1

To enhance the development of sustainable farming techniques, a research team composed of both botanists and environmental scientists conducted an analysis of the soil restoration properties of cover crops. The team stated that the _____ expertise of these two fields led to a more innovative solution than efforts by experts in just one field could have produced.

Which choice completes the text with the most logical and precise word or phrase?

A) skepticism toward
B) exaggeration of
C) conflict between
D) integration of

2

The sunlight danced across the ocean waves, casting glittering streaks of gold upon the rolling blue expanse. Seagulls soared overhead, their cries blending with the gentle lapping of water against the rocks. The lighthouse stood as a sentinel, its bright beam a guide for passing ships. The vast sky was alive with hues of pink and orange, blending seamlessly into the horizon. The keeper gazed out, awed by the splendor of this breathtaking scene. The lighthouse keeper marveled at this remarkable **spectacle** of nature.

As used in the text, what does the word "spectacle" most nearly mean?

A) Reproduction
B) Obstruction
C) Ostentation
D) Display

3

Both peregrine falcons and hawks can identify prey from great distances, but the _____ of their vision varies significantly. Whereas hawks can clearly spot prey at moderate distances, peregrine falcons have the ability to perceive fine details even at extreme ranges, making them exceptional hunters in the sky.

Which choice completes the text with the most logical and precise word or phrase?

A) sharpness

B) toughness

C) collection

D) arrangement

4

Recent research conducted by Dr. Evelyn Carter and Dr. Michael Zhang explores the fascinating observation that while investigations into the effects of prolonged screen time on eye health are _____, studies on the impact of reduced screen usage during work hours remain scarce.

Which choice completes the text with the most logical and precise word or phrase?

A) plentiful

B) ambiguous

C) sporadic

D) introductory

5

The following text is adapted from Katherine Hill's 2015 novel *The Ancient Grove*. In the passage, the narrator, Clara, is visiting an old arboretum with her friend Daniel.

"The Hollow of Giants," Daniel said. He pointed to the massive oaks and sycamores surrounding us. "That's the name the locals gave it."
It wasn't much of a hollow anymore, since the trees had grown so densely that light barely filtered through. But the sight was still mesmerizing.
Between the trunks, **shrubs and vines twisted together like veins in a living organism,** forming a thick, unbroken tapestry. Scattered across the forest floor were ancient stumps, remnants of trees that must once have been towering giants in their own right.

Which choice best describes the function of the underlined portion of the text?

A) It creates an image to illustrate the intricate appearance of part of the arboretum.

B) It emphasizes that the narrator already knew the history of the arboretum.

C) It suggests that the narrator was expecting to see a meadow instead of a dense forest.

D) It specifies the exact time when the arboretum was last maintained.

6

Can corals survive in cooler waters? Can they thrive in conditions outside of their usual tropical habitats? You might think the answer to these questions is obviously no, but researchers in Australia recently showed that certain coral species can adapt to colder water temperatures if given enough time to adjust. In fact, some corals showed improved growth rates in these cooler conditions, with 25 percent of a specific coral species showing greater resilience compared to their counterparts in warmer waters.

Which choice best states the main purpose of the text?

A) To address long-standing questions about how coral habitats can be replicated in colder climates

B) To present a surprising finding about corals adapting to water temperatures outside their usual habitat

C) To discuss an unexpected result about the role of sunlight in coral survival under cooler conditions

D) To explain an important study of differences in ocean salinity and its impact on coral growth

CONTINUE

7

When people think of mammals that lay eggs, they typically think of the platypus, with its distinct bill and webbed feet. However, many other mammals that are less well-known also lay eggs. For instance, research indicates that the echidna, a spiny and burrowing creature, is another example of an egg-laying mammal.

Which choice best states the main purpose of the text?

A) To argue that only one type of mammal lays eggs
B) To explain why egg-laying mammals are rare
C) To point out the differences between egg-laying mammals and other mammals
D) To discuss the presence of egg-laying in certain types of mammals

8

Researchers Dr. Lisa Marshall, Eric Owens, and Priya Singh developed a machine learning model to analyze the distribution of public parks, recreational facilities, and green spaces in urban areas. Since defining a "public space" and its boundaries is often subjective, the team employed a spatial analysis algorithm to identify clusters of green areas within cities like Portland's downtown district. The model, which incorporates this algorithm, holds promise for optimizing the planning of urban public spaces.

Which choice best describes the overall structure of the text?

A) It describes how an algorithm can optimize the use of public spaces, discusses an example of its application, and suggests potential uses in other urban planning projects.
B) It introduces a research team's study of public spaces, describes an aspect of the study's methodology, and suggests a potential application of the team's research.
C) It summarizes trends in urban development, describes a potential challenge for city planners, and suggests a computational tool that can address that challenge.
D) It explains why city planners focus on improving public spaces, details a study that has addressed this question, and identifies one key finding.

9

Many believe that instrumental music, characterized by its slow pace and soothing melodies, contains some acoustic features that are universally calming to animals. In a study, Dr. Andrea Foster and her team played both a calming instrumental piece and a fast-paced classical piece to a group of shelter dogs. The researchers also measured the dogs' heart rates, as a reduced heart rate is considered a measure of relaxation. They claim that the instrumental music did indeed relax the dogs.

Which finding, if true, would most directly support Dr. Foster and her team's claim?

A) The heart rates of the dogs in the study were more irregular during the instrumental music than during the classical music.

B) The dogs' heart rates were significantly lower during the instrumental music than during the classical music.

C) Owners of the dogs in the study preferred the instrumental music over the classical music when asked which they would play to calm their pets.

D) Both the instrumental and classical music pieces were performed by the same orchestra.

10

Millions of Metric Tons of Wheat Procuced in 1995 and 2020

Country	1995	2020
Canada	21.4	35.2
China	101.2	134.3
Australia	19.1	25.9
Argentina	11.8	19.7

While doing research for a paper about global agriculture, a student finds information about wheat production in different countries in 1995 and 2020. The student notes that China produced 101.2 million metric tons of wheat in 1995 and _____.

Which choice most effectively uses data from the table to complete the statement?

A) 35.2 million metric tons of wheat in 2020.

B) 134.3 million metric tons of wheat in 2020.

C) 19.7 million metric tons of wheat in 2020.

D) 25.9 million metric tons of wheat in 2020.

TEST
05

//// CONTINUE

11

Hawaii is a remote group of islands in the Pacific Ocean. Indigenous people there began cultivating taro plants about 1,500 years ago. Taro plants were originally domesticated much earlier in both Southeast Asia and Polynesia. So, were taro plants brought to Hawaii from Southeast Asia or Polynesia? Ancient trade routes connected Hawaii with Polynesia but not with Southeast Asia. **Therefore, taro plants in Hawaii probably came from Polynesia and descended from Polynesian taro plants.**

Which finding, if true, would most directly weaken the underlined claim?

A) Taro plants are depicted in ancient Hawaiian carvings alongside images of Polynesian canoes.

B) Modern varieties of taro don't match descriptions of taro plants in ancient texts from Hawaii, Polynesia, or Southeast Asia.

C) The taro plant population of ancient Polynesia was much larger than the taro plant population of ancient Southeast Asia.

D) Ancient taro plants in Hawaii were genetically less similar to taro plants in Polynesia than to ancient taro plants in Southeast Asia.

12

Observing Feeding Habits by Immature Lions

Individual	Region	Sex	Total number of observation events recorded	Proportion of observation events directed at adults from a different pride
A	Savanna	female	2	0.00
B	Grassland	female	7	0.29
C	Savanna	male	25	0.70
D	Grassland	male	2	1.00

One way that immature lions learn hunting techniques is by closely observing older lions during their feeding behaviors. Since male lions often leave the pride of their birth upon reaching maturity and females do not, researchers hypothesized that it is more advantageous for immature males than females to focus on observing lions from different prides. This should result in sex-specific differences in observation behavior.

Which choice best describes data from the table that support the researchers' hypothesis?

A) The proportion of observation events directed at adults from a different pride ranged from a low of 0.00 to a high of 1.00.

B) Individual D directed a higher proportion of observation events at adults from a different pride than did individual C, and individual B directed a higher proportion than individual A.

C) Individual A and individual B directed a lower proportion of observation events at adults from different prides than did individual C and individual D.

D) Individual C had the highest total number of observation events recorded at 25.

13

Almost all works of historical fiction contain references to clothing, including descriptions of garments worn by characters. In a 2022 study, Jennifer Lee, Arjun Patel, and Sofia Mendes claim that an observable pattern in such references reflects a shift in fashion trends prompted by the Industrial Revolution in the late nineteenth century. The researchers drew this conclusion from an analysis of more than 30,000 novels spanning multiple centuries and regions, using software to recognize and tally both specific clothing references—such as "silk cravat" or "cotton dress"—and implied ones, such as descriptions of textile types typically associated with specific time periods.

Which finding from the study, if true, would most directly support the researchers' conclusion?

A) Novels published after the year 1850 include references to synthetic fabrics, such as polyester, less frequently than novels published before 1850.

B) Novels published after 1880 contain significantly more references to clothing associated with fashion trends than do novels from earlier periods.

C) References to clothing made from wool and silk occur with roughly the same frequency in novels published before and after the Industrial Revolution.

D) Among novels published in the late nineteenth century, references to machine-produced garments become steadily more common as publication dates approach 1900.

14

As exemplified by Maori songs about fishing techniques and Hawaiian songs about planting taro, ecological knowledge can be transmitted in Indigenous songs, and in some cases, this knowledge is preserved only in this way. Keoni Maka'ala, a knowledge keeper for the Native Hawaiian people, collaborated with ethnobotanist Dr. Leilani Akamu to share songs referencing traditional taro terraces that the people implemented in the past to sustain their communities. Drawing on archaeological evidence as well, Akamu et al. determined that the prevalence of the practice described in the songs corresponded with greater taro yield and quality despite increased harvesting pressure—a finding that demonstrates that _____.

Which choice most logically completes the text?

A) representation of practical applications of agricultural knowledge is the defining characteristic of the music of certain Indigenous peoples.

B) effective methods for the cultivation of staple crops are among the agricultural knowledge preserved in Indigenous songs.

C) the Native Hawaiian people likely would not have detailed their cultivation of taro terraces in songs if their efforts had not produced significantly better harvests.

D) the taro cultivated on traditional terraces by Native Hawaiian people in the past likely were a different variety than the taro cultivated in those areas today.

TEST 05

223

15

A group of marine biologists recently began a long-term study of the effects of various conservation efforts on the leatherback sea turtle (*Dermochelys coriacea*). The species population is currently estimated to be around 35,000 worldwide. However, accurately counting these turtles is challenging due to their extensive migration patterns, which makes it difficult to determine whether the population is growing, shrinking, or remaining stable. The study may thus _____.

Which choice most logically completes the text?

A) cause other conservationists to adopt a new methodology for estimating global populations.

B) risk making inaccurate conclusions about the effectiveness of different conservation strategies.

C) benefit from including additional marine species beyond the leatherback sea turtle.

D) fail to consider less-documented migration patterns of the leatherback sea turtle.

16

Writing in Braille, Louis Braille developed a tactile system using dots such as the cell, a unit of _____ and the pattern, a unit of syntax. The cell, for instance, is represented by a grid of raised dots that can be felt with a fingertip.

Which choice completes the text so that it conforms to the conventions of Standard English?

A) text; the figure; a unit of meaning;

B) text the figure, a unit of meaning

C) text; the figure; a unit of meaning;

D) text, the figure; a unit of meaning,

17

Included in Breaking Boundaries, a 2023 international art exhibition in Paris, was the work of designer Emma Walker, who is best known for her innovative installations that _____ natural elements with urban structures. Her work is praised for redefining sustainable architecture and challenges conventional ideas of space, ecology, and design.

Which choice completes the text so that it conforms to the conventions of Standard English?

A) blend—

B) blend,

C) blend:

D) blend

18

Utilizing a dynamic interplay of light and shadow, Tokyo-based photographer Kaito Sato creates evocative compositions, wherein elements of traditional Japanese aesthetics, modern minimalism, and natural landscapes converge. The Tokyo Art Space _____ his work in a solo exhibition that ran in late 2023.

Which choice completes the text so that it conforms to the conventions of Standard English?

A) features

B) has been featured

C) featured

D) will feature

20

The human eye contains the iris, a muscular structure that controls the size of the pupil and is attached to the _____ this structure regulates the amount of light entering the eye.

Which choice completes the text so that it conforms to the conventions of Standard English?

A) lens,

B) lens;

C) lens

D) lens that

19

While the giant panda can be found in mountainous regions like the Qinling Mountains and the Minshan Mountains in China, more than 70 percent of this endangered species is located in Sichuan Province. There, conservationist Li Mei is on the front lines of restoration efforts that—through habitat protection and bamboo reforestation_____ aim to increase the panda population and secure its survival.

Which choice completes the text so that it conforms to the conventions of Standard English?

A) study,

B) study—

C) study:

D) study

21

The unconventional approach to music theory with which Johann Sebastian Bach composed is manifested in the German composer's "inventions," his term for the two-part contrapuntal compositions in which he explored many of his _____ among these inventions was the famous C major invention, a cornerstone of Baroque keyboard repertoire.

Which choice completes the text so that it conforms to the conventions of Standard English?

A) ideas: and

B) ideas;

C) ideas and

D) ideas,

225

22

Marie Curie moved to Paris in 1891 to pursue an education in science. Little is known of her early days as a student there, but by 1898 she had begun her groundbreaking research on radioactivity. _____, in 1903, she and her husband, Pierre Curie, would be awarded the Nobel Prize in Physics, a milestone in her illustrious career.

Which choice completes the text with the most logical transition?

A) In other words,

B) Conversely,

C) Thus,

D) Later,

23

Air pollution caused by nitrogen dioxide is harmful to both human health and ecosystems, but the plant species Tillandsia usneoides (Spanish moss), not only thrives in areas with high nitrogen dioxide but also helps mitigate the pollutant. As a natural air purifier, Tillandsia usneoides absorbs significant amounts of nitrogen dioxide from the air and safely converts it into organic compounds; _____ nitrogen dioxide levels in polluted areas decrease.

Which choice completes the text with the most logical transition?

A) specifically,

B) nevertheless,

C) in addition,

D) accordingly,

CONTINUE

24

While researching a topic, a student has taken the following notes:

- **A protostar** is a dense region of gas and dust that forms in a nebula, the birthplace of stars.
- Over time, gravity causes the protostar to collapse further, eventually igniting nuclear fusion to form a star.
- This process is believed to take millions of years and is part of the stellar life cycle.
- Protostars have been observed in regions like the **Orion Nebula**.
- The protostar **IRAS 16293-2422** is located about 400 light-years away from Earth.
- The protostar **HL Tau** is about one million years old.

The student wants to specify when HL Tau formed. Which choice most effectively uses relevant information from the notes to accomplish this goal?

A) HL Tau is a protostar, a dense region of gas and dust that forms in a nebula.

B) The protostar HL Tau formed about one million years ago.

C) HL Tau is located in the Orion Nebula, a region known for the birth of protostars.

D) Over millions of years, gravity causes protostars to collapse and form stars.

25

While researching a topic, a student has taken the following notes:

- **Solaris** is a city in the state of **Nevada**, United States.
- Cities are local governmental entities responsible for providing essential services to their residents.
- One service they provide is waste management.
- Solaris's population was 75,432 in 2021.
- Nevada has 16 counties.

The student wants to provide an example of a public service that Solaris is responsible for. Which choice most effectively uses relevant information from the notes to accomplish this goal?

A) Solaris is one of many cities in Nevada providing essential services to their communities.

B) Solaris—a local governmental entity in the state of Nevada—provides essential services to its residents.

C) As a city, Solaris is responsible for providing waste management to its residents.

D) In 2021, the city of Solaris had a population of 75,432.

TEST 05

CONTINUE

26

While researching a topic, a student has taken the following notes:

- **Willow Creek Shelter** is an ancient cliff dwelling located in **northern Arizona**.
- It was built into a recessed cliff face and inhabited from approximately **1250–1300 CE**.
- The recessed cliff provided shade from the hot desert sun.
- **Mesa Verde** is an ancient cliff dwelling located in southwestern Colorado.
- It was built in an open area and inhabited from approximately **1200–1275 CE**.
- This open terrain allowed for easier access to farmland.

The student wants to explain an advantage of the Willow Creek Shelter dwelling site. Which choice most effectively uses relevant information from the notes to accomplish this goal?

A) The location of Willow Creek Shelter, an ancient cliff dwelling in northern Arizona, provided an advantage to its inhabitants.

B) Located in northern Arizona, Willow Creek Shelter is an ancient cliff dwelling that was inhabited from approximately 1250–1300 CE.

C) The open terrain surrounding Willow Creek Shelter allowed for easier access to farmland.

D) Since it was built into a recessed cliff face, Willow Creek Shelter was naturally shaded from the hot desert sun.

27

While researching a topic, a student has taken the following notes:

- In a 2020 study, researchers Jane Doe, Michael Smith, and Emily White sought to explore the effects of freezing temperatures on the germination of **Sunflower (Helianthus annuus)** seeds.
- The researchers tested 100 **Sunflower** seeds that had been exposed to freezing temperatures for 48 hours.
- Of these, 85 seeds (85%) germinated.
- As a control, the researchers tested 100 **Sunflower** seeds that had not been exposed to freezing temperatures.
- Of these, 92 seeds (92%) germinated.

The student wants to describe the study's research methodology. Which choice most effectively uses relevant information from the notes to accomplish this goal?

A) In the study, a lower percentage of Sunflower seeds exposed to freezing temperatures germinated compared to those that had not been exposed.

B) The team of researchers tested the germination of 100 Sunflower seeds that had been exposed to freezing temperatures and 100 Sunflower seeds that had not been exposed.

C) Jane Doe et al. wanted to explore the effects of freezing temperatures on Sunflower seed germination.

D) Research by Jane Doe et al. revealed that 85% of the Sunflower seeds exposed to freezing temperatures germinated.

Module 1 answer

1

Correct Answer: D) *integration of*

 Why it's correct:

"Integration of" means **combining different elements into a unified whole**, which fits the idea of two scientific fields **collaborating** to produce innovation.

Why the others are wrong:
- **A) skepticism toward** – Implies doubt, which contradicts the positive tone of innovation.
- **B) exaggeration of** – Implies dishonesty or overstatement; irrelevant here.
- **C) conflict between** – Suggests disagreement, not collaboration.

2

Correct Answer: D) Display

Why it's correct:

"Spectacle" here refers to a **visually striking scene**—a "display" of nature's beauty.

Why the others are wrong:
- **A) Reproduction** – Irrelevant; nothing is being reproduced.
- **B) Obstruction** – Negative connotation, inconsistent with tone.
- **C) Ostentation** – Implies showiness or vanity, which doesn't fit the reverent mood.

3

Correct Answer: A) sharpness

Why it's correct:

"Sharpness" refers to **clarity of vision,** which is the focus of comparison between falcons and hawks.

🔲 **Why the others are wrong:**

- **B) Toughness** – Refers to strength, not visual acuity.
- **C) Collection** – Doesn't relate to how vision functions.
- **D) Arrangement** – Too vague and not relevant to clarity.

4

Correct Answer: A) plentiful

📝 **Why it's correct:**

"Plentiful" accurately contrasts with **"scarce"**, and implies **many studies** exist on screen usage effects.

🔲 **Why the others are wrong:**

- **B) Ambiguous** – Refers to unclear meaning, not quantity.
- **C) Sporadic** – Would not contrast sharply with "scarce."
- **D) Introductory** – Would imply the research is new, not abundant.

5

Correct Answer: A) It creates an image to illustrate the intricate appearance of part of the arboretum.

📝 **Why it's correct:**

This sentence employs **vivid visual imagery** ("twisted together like veins...") to depict the **complex interweaving of plant life**—a classic example of descriptive imagery.

🔲 **Why the others are wrong:**

- **B)** There's no mention of the narrator's prior knowledge.
- **C)** No textual evidence suggests Clara expected a meadow.
- **D)** No time is referenced regarding maintenance.

6

Correct Answer: B) To present a surprising finding about corals adapting to water temperatures outside their usual habitat

 Why it's correct:

The word "surprising" fits the **tone shift** after "you might think···" and the content reflects coral **adapting outside tropical habitats**, which is the focus.

Why the others are wrong:
- **A)** No mention of **replicating habitats**, just observation of coral adaptation.
- **C)** The passage **doesn't mention sunlight** at all.
- **D) Salinity** is irrelevant—only temperature is discussed.

7

Correct Answer: D) To discuss the presence of egg-laying in certain types of mammals

 Why it's correct:

The passage **broadens** understanding of egg-laying mammals and gives **examples**.

Why the others are wrong:
- **A)** False—text directly says **multiple mammals** lay eggs.
- **B)** Doesn't explain *why* they are rare, only that **they exist**.
- **C)** Doesn't **contrast** them with other mammals.

8

Correct Answer: B) It introduces a research team's study of public spaces, describes an aspect of the study's methodology, and suggests a potential application of the team's research.

Why it's correct:

It follows this **exact flow**: introduction → methodology → application.

TEST
05

?⃞ **Why the others are wrong:**

- **A)** Doesn't highlight the **introduction of the research team.**
- **C)** No mention of **trends** in urban development.
- **D)** The passage never says **why** planners focus on public spaces—it just describes the study.

9

Correct Answer: B) The dogs' heart rates were significantly lower during the instrumental music than during the classical music.

✎ **Why it's correct:**

A **lower heart rate** = more relaxed. This directly **confirms** the research claim.

?⃞ **Why the others are wrong:**

- **A)** Irregular heart rates ≠ relaxation—this could imply **stress**.
- **C)** Owner preference doesn't reflect **the dogs' physiological responses**.
- **D)** The orchestra used doesn't impact the **dogs' reactions**—irrelevant detail.

10

Correct Answer: B) 134.3 million metric tons of wheat in 2020.

✎ **Explanation:**

The table presents data on wheat production in millions of metric tons for the years **1995** and **2020** across four countries.

The question specifically refers to **China**, which according to the table:

- Produced **101.2 million metric tons** in **1995**
- Produced **134.3 million metric tons** in **2020**

Thus, the correct completion of the sentence is:

*The student notes that China produced 101.2 million metric tons of wheat in 1995 and **134.3 million metric tons of wheat in 2020.***

?⃞ **Why the other choices are incorrect:**

- **A)** 35.2 million metric tons – refers to **Canada** in 2020.
- **C)** 19.7 million metric tons – refers to **Argentina** in 2020.
- **D)** 25.9 million metric tons – refers to **Australia** in 2020.

11

Correct Answer: D) Ancient taro plants in Hawaii were genetically less similar to taro plants in Polynesia than to ancient taro plants in Southeast Asia.

📝 **Explanation:**

This claim is based on the **assumption** that ancient trade routes linked Hawaii to Polynesia, not Southeast Asia, so Polynesia is the more likely source.

To **weaken** this claim, we need **evidence that contradicts the idea** that Hawaiian taro came from Polynesia. **Genetic evidence** is particularly strong because it traces actual biological relationships between plants.

• **D provides this exact contradiction**: If ancient Hawaiian taro is **genetically closer to Southeast Asian taro** than Polynesian taro, it challenges the conclusion that it came from Polynesia. This implies that the trade route assumption might be incomplete or inaccurate.

   ❓ **Why the other choices are wrong:**

     • **A)** Supports the claim: Ancient carvings associating taro with Polynesian canoes **reinforce** the Polynesian origin.

     • **B)** Is irrelevant: Mismatches with *modern varieties* and ancient *descriptions* don't say anything about the genetic lineage or origin.

     • **C)** Also supports the claim indirectly: A **larger Polynesian population** of taro would make it **more likely** that taro came from there, not less.

12

Correct Answer: C) Individual A and individual B directed a lower proportion of observation events at adults from different prides than did individual C and individual D.

📝 **Explanation:**

The **researchers' hypothesis** is:

*It is more advantageous for immature males than females to observe lions from different prides, so **males should more often direct observations at lions from other prides.***

To **support** this hypothesis, we need data that shows **male lions (C and D)** have a **higher proportion of observations** directed at adults from **different prides** than female lions (A and B).

• **Females (A and B)** have proportions **0.00 and 0.29**

• **Males (C and D)** have proportions **0.70 and 1.00**

This **clear sex-based difference** in behavior supports the hypothesis.

233

⟨?⟩ Why the other choices are wrong:

- **A)** States a range (0.00 to 1.00), but doesn't relate this to **sex-specific patterns**.
- **B)** Makes individual comparisons but doesn't clearly tie the pattern to **male vs. female**.
- **D)** Refers only to the **total number** of observation events—not the **proportion** directed at other prides, which is the relevant variable for the hypothesis.

Correct Answer: D) Among novels published in the late nineteenth century, references to machine-produced garments become steadily more common as publication dates approach 1900.

✏ Why it's correct:

The researchers are connecting **clothing references** in fiction to the **rise of industrialized fashion**. An **increase in mentions of machine-made garments** directly supports the idea that **the Industrial Revolution influenced fashion**, which was then **reflected in literature**.

⟨?⟩ Why the others are wrong:

- **A)** Polyester was **not** widely used in the 1800s; it's a **20th-century fabric**, making this misleading.
- **B)** "Fashion trends" is too vague and doesn't tie directly to **industrialization**.
- **C)** Saying frequencies of silk and wool stayed the same does **nothing to support the shift** they're talking about.

14

Correct Answer: C) the Native Hawaiian people likely would not have detailed their cultivation of taro terraces in songs if their efforts had not produced significantly better harvests.

✏ Why it's correct:

This logically connects the **preservation of agricultural knowledge in songs** to the **success of the farming method**. If the method **wasn't effective**, it's unlikely it would have been **memorized and passed down**.

Why the others are wrong:

- **A)** Overgeneralizes—goes beyond what the text supports.
- **B)** Plausible, but **too broad**; it doesn't tie in the **connection between effectiveness and preservation**.
- **D)** Speculates about **variety**, not relevance of the method or the songs.

15

Correct Answer: B) risk making inaccurate conclusions about the effectiveness of different conservation strategies.

Explanation:

The inability to track turtle populations accurately means that **any conclusions about conservation impact** may be **flawed or uncertain**. This risk is exactly what the sentence is warning about.

Why the others are wrong:

- **A)** There's no mention of creating new methodologies—only **difficulty** in drawing conclusions.
- **C)** Expanding to other species is **beside the point**—the issue is **population tracking**.
- **D)** "Failing to consider migration patterns" is already mentioned, but the key consequence of that is the **inaccuracy in conclusions**, which **B** captures best.

16

Answer: C)

Why it's correct:

This sentence uses **parallel apposition**:

- "the cell, a unit of text;"
- "the figure, a unit of meaning;"
- "and the pattern, a unit of syntax."

 Why the others are wrong:

- **A)** Misuses punctuation by mixing a semicolon with a semicolon **and** a comma.
- **B)** Missing needed punctuation to separate and clarify the elements.
- **D)** Punctuates inconsistently.

TEST 05

17

Answer: D)

 Why it's correct:

The clause needs a **simple present verb** to match "installations that blend..."
The sentence is in **present tense**, and the verb is part of a **restrictive relative clause**.

> **Why the others are wrong:**

- **A, B, C)** All introduce punctuation that unnecessarily interrupts the flow of the sentence. No break is needed between "that" and "blend."

18

Answer: C)

Why it's correct:

The event is in the **past**: it "ran in late 2023," so the past tense **"featured"** is appropriate.

> **Why the others are wrong:**

- **A) features** – Present tense doesn't match.
- **B) has been featured** – Passive and doesn't match the direct subject "Tokyo Art Space."
- **D) will feature** – Future tense, but the event already occurred.

19

Answer: B)

Why it's correct:

The em dash sets off the parenthetical "through habitat protection..."
So the **main clause continues after the dash**: "efforts...aim to increase..."

> **Why the others are wrong:**

- **A), C), D)** Lack proper punctuation to separate the modifying phrase, causing confusion.

236

20

Answer: B)

 Why it's correct:

This connects **two independent clauses**, so a **semicolon** is required.

 Why the others are wrong:

- **A, C)** A comma or no punctuation creates a **comma splice or run-on sentence**.
- **D)** Incorrect structure; "that" creates a relative clause which does not match the grammar of the rest of the sentence.

21

Answer: B)

 Why it's correct:

Two **independent clauses** again. "He explored many of his ideas" and "Among these inventions was..." → Use a **semicolon**.

 Why the others are wrong:

- **A, D)** Misuse punctuation and create comma splices.
- **C)** Lacks a proper break between independent clauses.

22

Answer: D)

 Why it's correct:

"Later" fits the **chronological progression** from 1891 → 1898 → 1903. It indicates **time passing** before the Nobel Prize.

 Why the others are wrong:

- **A) In other words,** – Used for restating, not sequencing.
- **B) Conversely,** – Suggests contrast; not logical here.
- **C) Thus,** – Suggests cause-and-effect, which doesn't apply to the timeline.

23

Answer: D)

 Why it's correct:

"Accordingly" signals **logical consequence**—because Tillandsia absorbs the pollutant, levels **decrease**.

Why the others are wrong:

- **A) Specifically,** – Would narrow focus, not show a result.
- **B) Nevertheless,** – Suggests contradiction.
- **C) In addition,** – Adds information, not a cause-effect link.

24

Answer: B)

 Why it's correct:

This directly states the **timing**, matching the note:

"HL Tau is about one million years old."

Why the others are wrong:

- **A)** Defines what a protostar is—not the time HL Tau formed.
- **C)** Introduces incorrect info—HL Tau is **not** located in Orion.
- **D)** Describes the general process, not HL Tau specifically.

25

Answer: C)

 Why it's correct:

Waste management is a **concrete example** of a city service and is explicitly noted.

Why the others are wrong:

- **A, B)** General and vague—no **specific service** is mentioned.
- **D)** Provides a population stat, not a service.

26 ....

Correct Answer: D) Since it was built into a recessed cliff face, Willow Creek Shelter was naturally shaded from the hot desert sun.

 Why it's correct:

This clearly **uses relevant info**: recessed cliff = **natural shade** = environmental advantage.

   Why the others are wrong:
   • **A)** Too vague—doesn't explain what the advantage is.
   • **B)** Factual, but doesn't specify the advantage.
   • **C)** False—**Mesa Verde**, not Willow Creek, had open terrain.

27 ....

Correct Answer: B) The team of researchers tested the germination of 100 Sunflower seeds that had been exposed to freezing temperatures and 100 Sunflower seeds that had not been exposed.

Why it's correct:

This captures the **experimental and control groups**, providing a **complete and accurate** description of the method.

   Why the others are wrong:
   • **A)** Focuses on results, not method.
   • **C)** States the **research question**, not the method.
   • **D)** Also focuses on results, not how the test was conducted.

TEST 05

Page Intentionally Left Blank

Module 2

Reading and Writing
27 Questions, 32 Minutes

DIRECTIONS

The questions in this section address a number of important reading and writing skills. Each questions includes one or more passages, which may include a table or graph. Read each passage and question carefully, and then choose the best answer to the question based on the passage(s).

All questions in this section are multiple-choice with four answer choices. Each question has a single best answer.

1

Despite significant advancements in renewable energy, early implementations of solar power systems in the 2000s struggled with inefficiencies due to limited technological innovations. Engineers would later _____ this limitation after the development of advanced photovoltaic materials and more efficient energy storage systems.

Which choice completes the text with the most logical and precise word or phrase?

A) confirm

B) assume

C) classify

D) alleviate

2

One prevalent theory about the extinction of dinosaurs, the "asteroid impact hypothesis," proposes that a massive asteroid struck Earth, releasing debris that drastically altered the climate. Until recently, this asteroid was _____, but geologists now claim to have uncovered fragments of the impact site in the Chicxulub crater in Mexico.

Which choice completes the text with the most logical and precise word or phrase?

A) desultory

B) notional

C) veritable

D) spurious

3

Scientific journals with specialized focuses became a crucial part of academic publishing in the late 20th century. While some researchers praised this trend, arguing that such journals promoted in-depth exploration of niche topics, less _____ critics contended that this approach created silos of knowledge and hindered interdisciplinary collaboration.

Which choice completes the text with the most logical and precise word or phrase?

A) recalcitrant

B) earnest

C) sanguine

D) misanthropic

4

Cultural transmission involves the passing of traditions and practices from one generation to the next within a society; cross-cultural exchange, on the other hand, involves the sharing of ideas and customs between distinct societies. *While cross-cultural exchange is common among neighboring regions, such as the diffusion of Greek and Roman architectural styles, it has been less frequently observed between geographically distant societies.* However, recent findings suggest that cross-cultural exchange may have played a significant role in the spread of ancient technologies across continents.

Which choice best states the function of the underlined sentence in the text as a whole?

A) It explains why a traditional assumption about a cultural process is incorrect.

B) It argues that two cultural phenomena are more interconnected than they may initially appear to be.

C) It contrasts the frequency with which a cultural phenomenon has been observed in two different contexts.

D) It highlights a distinction between the mechanisms underlying two types of cultural interactions.

5

During the Renaissance period, which spanned the 14th to 17th centuries, art was primarily commissioned by wealthy patrons who sought to display their power and taste. The first publicly accessible art galleries were established in the late 16th century and were soon followed by exhibitions sponsored by European monarchs. As art historian Maria Rosetti observes, however, these two traditions are not as distinct as they appear, as both private patrons and royal sponsors used art as a means of showcasing their influence, albeit on different scales.

Which choice best states the main purpose of the text?

A) To challenge the idea that private art patronage diminished during the Renaissance

B) To argue that European monarchs held excessive control over artistic developments

C) To provide a brief summary of public access to art during the Renaissance period

D) To emphasize the fundamental similarity between private and royal art sponsorship during the Renaissance

6

The following text is from Elizabeth Browning's 1844 poem "Serenity."

My heart aches softly, and my dreams do yearn
For twilight's glow and calm where shadows turn.
Carry me forth, ye winds, to quiet fields,
Just let me rest far from the rush of time,
Where whispers of the breeze are nature's shields,
Which mingled with the stars that gently climb,
Draw me toward the tender arms of night,
To cradle me in peaceful, glowing light.

Which choice best states the main purpose of the text?

A) To justify the speaker's hesitation about seeking solace in nature's embrace

B) To contrast the chaos of the speaker's waking life with the tranquility of resting in twilight

C) To illustrate the growing intensity of the speaker's desire to escape ongoing hardship in the quiet of the evening

D) To convey the speaker's longing for the evening's serenity to bring emotional comfort

TEST
05

CONTINUE

7

Text 1:

In parts of Europe, the gray wolf is a significant predator of red deer. Researcher L. Andersson and colleagues found that when gray wolves were temporarily removed from specific regions, red deer populations increased noticeably. This finding highlights a foundational ecological *principle*: predators help regulate the population size of their prey species.

Text 2:

M. Thompson and colleagues conducted a study in northern Canada, where grizzly bears were excluded from areas where they commonly hunted caribou. The exclusion did not result in a significant rise in caribou population numbers. Many other predator-prey studies report population increases in prey species, but these studies often focus on smaller animals like hares and fish, which reproduce quickly, rather than larger, slower-reproducing animals like caribou. This difference may explain the discrepancy in the findings.

Based on the texts, the author of Text 2 would most likely agree with which statement about the "principle" mentioned in Text 1?

A) It is plausible, but many of the studies that support it have methodological flaws.

B) It has been challenged by some studies, but the findings of those studies have not been widely accepted.

C) It may be true for some predators but only because those predators share certain behavioral traits.

D) It has some evidential support, but it should not be regarded as universally applicable.

8

Many authors associated with the modernist literary movement, which emerged in the early 20th century, follow the stylistic model popularized by James Joyce: stream-of-consciousness narration, fragmented structure, and experimental language. Yet the movement is far from monolithic. Virginia Woolf, for example, incorporates a more lyrical and introspective tone into the modernist framework. This stylistic diversity is further encouraged by literary journals of the time, which sought to highlight a variety of modernist approaches while maintaining a unified focus on innovation.

Which statement about Virginia Woolf is best supported by the text?

A) While some of her works adhere to the stylistic model of James Joyce, others reject it outright.

B) Her writing diverges from the typical modernist style but doesn't abandon its core principles.

C) She developed her distinctive style without being influenced by other modernist authors of her era.

D) Her inclusion in literary journals inspired other modernist writers to experiment with style.

9

Marine biologist Elena Ramos and colleagues conducted a study of how water temperature and coral color relate to coral feeding behavior, which wouldn't have been possible without data gathered by local divers and other amateur marine enthusiasts in the region. Considering over five years' worth of data, the researchers found that blue corals were observed to attract small fish more frequently than other coral types, and that corals exhibited higher feeding activity in warmer waters compared to cooler waters.

According to the text, which factors seemed to be linked to the behavior of corals in Elena Ramos and colleagues' study?

A) Water temperature but not coral color
B) Coral color but not water temperature
C) Both coral color and water temperature
D) Neither coral color nor water temperature

10

Nineteenth-century scientist Charles Darwin is renowned for his metaphor of the "tree of life," which he putatively used to represent the interconnectedness of all species through evolution. Note "putatively": as historian Emily Richards has argued, Darwin included this metaphor only briefly in his work *On the Origin of Species* to illustrate a specific idea about speciation. It was largely overlooked until some twentieth-century biologists eager to secure an intellectual pedigree elevated it to a fully-established paradigm.

Which choice best states the main idea of the text?

A) Twentieth-century biologists expanded the significance of Darwin's tree of life metaphor beyond its intended use, though it is still useful for understanding the evolutionary interconnection.
B) Darwin's metaphor of the tree of life has been understood as an overarching representation of evolution, but it was originally intended to highlight a specific aspect of speciation.
C) The prominence of Darwin's metaphor of the tree of life stems less from its role in Darwin's work and more from the emphasis placed on it by later biologists for their own ends.
D) The tree of life metaphor reflects Darwin's nuanced understanding of evolutionary processes but was underutilized during his time and only later recognized for its scientific potential.

11

"*Nature's Harmony* is a 1920 essay by Charlotte Alden. In the essay, the author explains how calming nature can be for those seeking peace, writing _____.

Which quotation from *Nature's Harmony* most effectively illustrates the claim?

A) "Do not shy away from the modest reflections of a daydreaming, even though they may lack the grandeur of vivid psychotherapy."

B) "Home welcomes everyone, regardless of status or appearance, holding an unchanging charm that touches both heart and mind alike."

C) "Gentle are the whispers of the breeze! They soothe like a balm and renew the weary soul, as if carrying the blessings of a serene haven."

D) "Now, my reader, hear this: What has been lost cannot be regained. We cannot undo the harm inflicted by carelessness on this fragile world."

12

"Ancient Mars is thought to have undergone a shift from a smooth, unchanging crust to a fractured, dynamic surface regime, in which surface layers interacted with the subsurface. Researchers studied the timing of this transition, hypothesizing that fractures allowed subsurface and surface material to mix. Analyzing mineral data from rocks ranging from 300 million to 4 billion years old, the researchers estimated that the transition occurred around 3.5 billion years ago."

Which finding, if true, would most directly support the researchers' conclusion?

A) Subsurface rocks older than 3.5 billion years display significantly more mineral variety than surface rocks of the same age.

B) There is a clear correlation between the age of surface rocks and their mineral similarity to subsurface rocks, with the correlation strengthening notably at around 3.5 billion years ago.

C) Subsurface rocks younger than 3.5 billion years contain minerals that are absent in older subsurface rocks but present in older surface rocks.

D) Among rocks predating 3.5 billion years, most are subsurface-origin, but this trend reverses for rocks younger than 3.5 billion years.

13

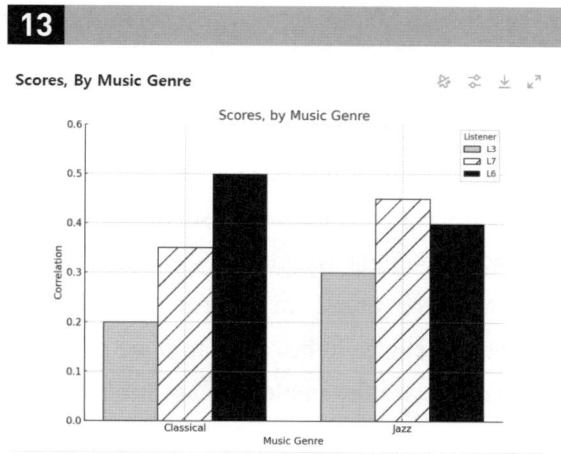

Scores, By Music Genre

Neuroscientist Mira Takahashi and colleagues developed a computational model to predict how much a person will enjoy a particular music genre on a scale from 1 (not at all) to 5 (very much). They then recruited participants to use the same scale to rate several music genres and calculated the correlation between the ratings predicted by the model and those reported by the participants. Assuming Listener L6 gave equal ratings to the classical and jazz genres, the data in the graph indicate the model predicted that _____.

Which choice most effectively uses data from the graph to complete the example?

A) Listener L6 would derive more enjoyment from classical music than from jazz music.

B) Listener L6's rating for classical and jazz music would equal one another.

C) Listener L6 would derive less enjoyment from classical music than from jazz music.

D) Listener L6's ratings for classical and jazz music would differ from one another.

14

For its 1986 performance piece *Urban Noise*, the experimental theater group Echo taped members Laura Rivera and Marcus Lopez to a crowded urban plaza in New York City. The performance is evidently a commentary on the cacophony of urban life, but many critics focus on Rivera and the challenges faced by women in public spaces, which is understandable but leaves the presence of Lopez, a male collaborator, unexplained. We should instead consider that in 1986, the performance art world's recognition of minority artists was (and had long been) dominated by Eurocentric themes, leaving non-Western artists—like Echo's members—struggling to gain visibility; attending to this context opens an interpretation that accounts for all the evidence, allowing us to conclude that _____.

Which choice most logically completes the text?

A) the main subject of *Urban Noise* is minority artists' experience of being doubly marginalized by cultural erasure and the prioritization of Eurocentric narratives.

B) while Rivera's presence in *Urban Noise* represents the challenges women faced in urban spaces, Lopez's presence represents non-Western artists' frustration at their lack of recognition in the performance art world.

C) *Urban Noise* is best understood not as a critique of the challenges women face in urban spaces but rather as a critique of the exclusionary practices of the performance art establishment.

D) *Urban Noise* is a reflection on the limiting aesthetic frameworks placed on minority artists in general rather than on the challenges women face in urban spaces specifically.

CONTINUE

15

Marine biologists Julia S. Park and Timothy L. Greene studied the behavior of coral reef fish, specifically butterflyfish and damselfish, both of which have been observed in natural reefs as well as artificial aquarium settings, to understand how environmental factors influence their interactions. Aquarium studies are helpful because they allow for control of key variables, but butterflyfish behavior is strongly influenced by the complexity of their surroundings. Therefore, it's not altogether surprising that when Park and Greene reviewed studies of butterflyfish, they found that _____.

Which choice most logically completes the text?

A) aquarium-raised fish and wild reef fish exhibited very similar interaction patterns.

B) baseline aggression levels were higher in aquarium-raised butterflyfish than in wild reef butterflyfish.

C) significant differences in interaction patterns were found for both aquarium-raised butterflyfish and wild butterflyfish.

D) aggression levels were higher in wild damselfish than in aquarium-raised damselfish.

16

Despite the fact that what is now known as the Richter scale was first conceptualized by Kiyoo Wadati, the scale is named after the twentieth-century American seismologist Charles Richter. One might assume cases like this, where a scientific tool or system is not named after the original developer, to be _____ they are counted among a litany of examples of misattribution in scientific history.

Which choice completes the text so that it conforms to the conventions of Standard English?

A) rare on the contrary,

B) rare, on the contrary;

C) rare, on the contrary,

D) rare; on the contrary,

17

Featured in *Visionaries of the Natural World: Celebrating Environmental Art*, a 2022 group exhibition at the National Museum of Ecology in Portland, Oregon, was the work of artist Kevin Thompson, who is best known for his sculptures that blend depictions of endangered animals with elements of their natural habitats. His work challenges conventional understandings of ecology, conservation, sustainability, and _____ he is celebrated for pushing the boundaries of environmental art.

Which choice completes the text so that it conforms to the conventions of Standard English?

A) preservation,

B) preservation, and

C) preservation and

D) preservation

18

Marie Zhang is a poet from Shanghai, China, who has garnered critical acclaim for her lyrical works. Writers in other creative genres, such as prose and theater, are less frequently acknowledged on the global stage, but many are still well _____ Ling Wei, for example, is a highly regarded playwright from Beijing.

Which choice completes the text so that it conforms to the conventions of Standard English?

A) known

B) known:

C) known and

D) known,

19

Recent observations of Glacier 12—a remote ice formation in Antarctica—have revealed that its bluish tint likely results from the compression of snow over centuries, forming dense ice crystals. Such findings are ultimately _____ the blue coloration may instead be caused by reflections of the sky or the absorption of light wavelengths, rather than the physical properties of the ice itself.

Which choice completes the text so that it conforms to the conventions of Standard English?

A) speculative, though

B) speculative, though,

C) speculative; though

D) speculative, though;

20

In the essay "Memorable Landscapes" from John Ruskin's *Modern Painters*, the author marvels at the interplay of sunlight on mountain peaks, the glint of a distant lake, and the softness of autumn foliage. So perceptive a critic is Ruskin, an advocate for natural beauty, that his vivid descriptions of nineteenth-century landscapes _____ readers even today.

Which choice completes the text so that it conforms to the conventions of Standard English?

A) has fascinated

B) fascinates

C) fascinate

D) is fascinating

21

The present-day city of Kyoto, Japan, was the capital of the Heian period and served as the political and cultural hub of the Japanese empire, one of many historical capitals across Japan's history. Each of these capitals _____ established along geographical or ceremonial lines: Kyoto, for example, was chosen due to its proximity to natural water sources and sacred mountains.

Which choice completes the text so that it conforms to the conventions of Standard English?

A) have been

B) are

C) were

D) was

22

When, in 2010, a group of environmental scientists decided they wanted to create a global campaign to reduce plastic waste, one of their primary goals was to raise awareness about the harmful effects of plastic on marine ecosystems. _____ they launched the initiative Clean Oceans, which focuses on educating communities about sustainable alternatives to single-use plastics.

Which choice completes the text with the most logical transition?

A) In summary,

B) In other words,

C) For example,

D) To that end,

23

The metric system, a standardized method of measurement introduced in 1795, was originally based on calculations derived from the Earth's meridian. _____ as years went by, adjustments were made to increase its precision, yet the system's fundamental units remained consistent; it wasn't until the 20th century that definitions of these units were refined to be based on universal constants like the speed of light.

Which choice completes the text with the most logical transition?

A) Granted,

B) Again and again,

C) Specifically,

D) To that end,

24

Notes:

- Maria Santos is a Brazilian climate scientist.
- Climate scientists study atmospheric and environmental patterns.
- Greenhouse gases are one of the primary contributors to climate change.
- Carbon dioxide emissions were identified as a significant greenhouse gas in the late 20th century.
- Santos is known for her work on modeling carbon dioxide absorption in tropical rainforests.

The student wants to provide an example of a climate scientist whose research focuses on carbon dioxide. Which choice most effectively uses relevant information from the notes to accomplish this goal?

A) The research done on carbon dioxide absorption in rainforests exemplifies the work climate scientists do to advance our understanding of greenhouse gases.

B) By studying carbon dioxide in tropical rainforests—to name just one example—climate scientists can learn more about greenhouse gases.

C) Climate scientist Maria Santos is known for her work on modeling carbon dioxide absorption in tropical rainforests.

D) Carbon dioxide is a major greenhouse gas that climate scientists are still trying to understand.

TEST 05

 CONTINUE

25

Notes:

- *Whispering Waves* is a 2010 installation by American artist Sarah Thompson.
- It consists of blue LED lights arranged in patterns to mimic ocean waves.
- *Electric Pulse* is a 2018 installation by Canadian artist Daniel Cho.
- It consists of red LED lights that flash in rhythmic sequences resembling a heartbeat.
- LED lights became widely used in art installations in the early 2000s.
- LED lights are valued for their energy efficiency and versatility in artistic expression.

The student wants to emphasize a difference between the two installations. Which choice most effectively uses relevant information from the notes to accomplish this goal?

A) While the installations share a common material, one mimics ocean waves while the other is designed to evoke a heartbeat.

B) Representing ocean waves in *Whispering Waves* (2010) and rhythmic heartbeats in *Electric Pulse* (2018), LED lights have a variety of artistic applications.

C) American artist Sarah Thompson's and Canadian artist Daniel Cho's installations highlight the versatility of LED lights in modern art.

D) Thompson's installation was created in 2010 and Cho's in 2018, both well after the widespread adoption of LED lights in art.

26

Notes:

- Historical analysis and thematic analysis are two approaches to literature.
- Historical analysis examines how the time period in which a text was written influences its themes and characters.
- Such an analysis of Charles Dickens's *Oliver Twist* might consider how the novel reflects the socioeconomic conditions of Victorian England.
- Thematic analysis focuses on identifying and interpreting the recurring themes within a text.
- Such an analysis of *A Tale of Two Cities* might consider how themes of sacrifice and redemption are central to its narrative.

The student wants to present historical analysis to an audience unfamiliar with the concept. Which choice most effectively uses relevant information from the notes to accomplish this goal?

A) An approach to literature, historical analysis examines how the time period in which a text was written influences its themes and characters.

B) A thematic analysis of *A Tale of Two Cities* might consider how themes of sacrifice and redemption are central to its narrative.

C) Thematic analysis differs from historic analysis in that thematic analysis focuses on identifying the recurring themes in a text.

D) *Oliver Twist* reflects the socioeconomic conditions of Victorian England, as historical analysis might reveal.

27

While researching a topic, a student has taken the following notes:

- There are more than 1,000 National Parks worldwide.
- Yellowstone National Park is a 2.2-million-acre area in the United States.
- Yellowstone is home to various endangered species, including the gray wolf and grizzly bear.
- Banff National Park is a 2,564-square-mile area in Canada.
- Banff was created to protect mountain ecosystems, including glaciers, forests, and diverse wildlife.

The student wants to provide an overview of the National Park program. Which choice most effectively uses relevant information from the notes to accomplish this goal?

A) Over 1,000 National Parks worldwide protect endangered ecosystems and species.

B) Canada's Banff National Park was established to protect mountain ecosystems.

C) Both Yellowstone and Banff National Parks were created to preserve diverse wildlife.

D) Yellowstone, one of the world's largest National Parks, covers 2.2 million acres in the United States.

Module 2 answer

Answer: D)

📝 **Explanation:**

The sentence describes how early solar power systems struggled with *inefficiencies*. Then, it states that engineers *later* did something **after** improved photovoltaic materials and energy storage systems were developed. The logic is that those advancements **reduced or eased** the prior limitations.

• **D) alleviate** means to **lessen or relieve** something negative — in this case, the inefficiencies. It is the only choice that logically and precisely describes how engineers **solved or improved** the problem.

💡 **Why the others are wrong:**

• **A) confirm** — Engineers would not confirm a limitation after new technology; they'd address it. Confirming implies **verifying**, which doesn't fit the context of overcoming inefficiencies.

• **B) assume** — To assume a limitation is to **take it as true without proof**, which is not only vague but contradictory in this context. They already knew about the inefficiencies; they didn't assume them after solving them.

• **C) classify** — Classifying a limitation is a **categorizing action**, not a **problem-solving** one. It does not imply any progress or improvement.

2

Answer: B)

📝 **Explanation:**

The sentence sets up a contrast: **Until recently**, the asteroid was *X*, but now physical **fragments** have been found. The implication is that the asteroid was previously **hypothetical or speculative**, but has now become grounded in physical evidence.

• **B) notional** means **based on theory or idea rather than physical reality** — perfectly matching the idea that the asteroid impact was *only a theory* before recent evidence emerged.

💡 **Why the others are wrong:**

- **A) desultory** — means *lacking a plan, purpose, or enthusiasm*. This doesn't make sense when referring to a physical object like an asteroid. It doesn't fit semantically.
- **C) veritable** — means *true or real*. That's the **opposite** of what the sentence is saying *before* the new evidence.
- **D) spurious** — means *false or fake*. This is too strong and implies **deception**, not **lack of evidence**. Also, the hypothesis wasn't considered false, just unproven.

 3

Answer: C)

📝 **Explanation:**

The structure of the sentence contrasts two types of responses: one group **praised** the rise of niche journals, while the **less [something]** critics **contended** that it caused knowledge silos. We need a word that describes the critics' **less positive or optimistic** outlook.

- **C) sanguine** means **optimistic or hopeful**. The *less sanguine* critics, then, are those who are **more doubtful or critical**, which fits perfectly with their concerns about siloing knowledge.

💡 **Why the others are wrong:**

- **A) recalcitrant** — means **stubbornly uncooperative**. That's a **behavioral** description, not one of attitude or outlook. Too extreme and off-tone.
- **B) earnest** — means **sincere and serious**. "Less earnest" critics would be **flippant or unserious**, which doesn't match the tone of **thoughtful critique** in the sentence.
- **D) misanthropic** — means **hating humanity**. That's far too strong and totally off-base. The critics aren't anti-human, just concerned about knowledge fragmentation.

 4

Answer: C) It contrasts the frequency with which a cultural phenomenon has been observed in two different contexts.

📝 **Explanation:**

The underlined sentence compares **how often** cross-cultural exchange is observed:

- **"common among neighboring regions"** vs. **"less frequently observed between geographically distant societies"**. This is a clear **contrast in frequency** across **two contexts**.

Why the others are wrong:

- **A) incorrect assumption** — The sentence **doesn't refute** a belief; it simply describes patterns.
- **B) interconnectedness** — No argument is made that the two phenomena (cultural transmission and cross-cultural exchange) are **interconnected**.
- **D) mechanism distinction** — That would be relevant if the sentence explained **how** each process works. It doesn't — it only talks about **how often** it happens.

5

Answer: D) To emphasize the fundamental similarity between private and royal art sponsorship during the Renaissance

Explanation:

The entire passage sets up a seeming **difference** (private vs. royal art sponsorship) and then **undermines** that difference in the final sentence:

- "...**not as distinct as they appear**... both... used art as a means of showcasing their influence."

The main idea is to **emphasize similarity**, especially in motive, even if scale differs.

 Why the others are wrong:

- **A) private patronage diminished** — The text doesn't address **diminishing** patronage; it's about comparing motivations.
- **B) monarchs had excessive control** — No such **criticism** is made. It's neutral in tone.
- **C) summary of public access** — While public galleries are mentioned, the **main focus** is not public access but **motivations of sponsorship**.

6

Answer: D) To convey the speaker's longing for the evening's serenity to bring emotional comfort

Explanation:

The poem is a **lyrical meditation** on yearning for peace and respite. Phrases like **"My heart aches softly," "just let me rest," "cradle me in peaceful, glowing light"** show the speaker's **emotional vulnerability** and **desire for soothing calm** found in nature and night.

- **D)** captures this perfectly — it frames the poem's essence: **longing for serenity** and **emotional comfort**.

💡 **Why the others are wrong:**

- **A)** suggests *hesitation*, but there is none in the poem. The speaker is fully embracing the idea of rest in nature.
- **B)** mentions a **contrast** with the "chaos" of life, but the poem **doesn't depict chaos** directly. It implies tiredness, but not conflict.
- **C)** refers to "growing intensity" and "ongoing hardship," but the tone is more **gentle yearning** than *escalating urgency*.

7

Answer: D) It has some evidential support, but it should not be regarded as universally applicable.

 Explanation:

Text 1 supports the ecological **principle** that predators regulate prey. Text 2 **questions** this by offering an exception (grizzly bears and caribou), suggesting that **this principle might not hold for all species**, especially slow-reproducing ones.

- **D)** reflects this nuance: the principle works in **some cases**, but **not universally**.

💡 **Why the others are wrong:**

- **A)** implies *methodological flaws*, which Text 2 doesn't suggest. It questions **applicability**, not rigor.
- **B)** wrongly implies the **challenging studies are unaccepted**; but Text 2 **legitimizes** its study.
- **C)** speculates about *behavioral traits*, which is **not stated** or supported in the text

---

8

Answer: B) Her writing diverges from the typical modernist style but doesn't abandon its core principles.

 Explanation:

The text says that Woolf **uses a different tone** — lyrical and introspective — yet still operates **within the modernist framework**, which is unified by **innovation**.

- **B)** neatly balances **divergence in style** with **loyalty to modernist ideals**.

💡 **Why the others are wrong:**

- **A)** falsely suggests she **rejected** Joyce's model outright. The text only says she offers a different **version** of modernism.

TEST 05

257

- **C)** incorrectly claims she was *uninfluenced* by others. No such claim is made.
- **D)** invents a causal relationship (her inclusion inspired others), which the text **never implies**.

9

Answer: C) Both coral color and water temperature

📝 **Explanation:**

The text says:

- **Blue corals attracted small fish more frequently** → showing that **color** affects feeding.
- **Feeding activity was higher in warmer waters** → showing that **temperature** affects feeding.
- **C)** is correct because both variables are **linked to coral behavior**.

  💡 **Why the others are wrong:**
  - **A)** ignores the coral color effect.
  - **B)** ignores the water temperature effect.
  - **D)** contradicts the evidence outright — both variables **do** affect behavior.

10

Answer: C) The prominence of Darwin's metaphor of the tree of life stems less from its role in Darwin's work and more from the emphasis placed on it by later biologists seeking to popularize evolutionary theory.

📝 **Explanation:**

The passage emphasizes that Darwin **barely used** the metaphor and that its fame came from **20th-century biologists** who **elevated** it. Emily Richards even notes it was **largely overlooked** until later.

- **C)** correctly focuses on the **discrepancy between its original minor use** and its **later prominence** due to others.

  💡 **Why the others are wrong:**
  - **A)** suggests it's still "useful," which is **beside the point**. The text emphasizes **misplaced prominence**, not practical value.
  - **B)** overly softens the discrepancy — it says Darwin "intended to highlight a specific aspect," but doesn't capture the idea that the metaphor was **overblown later**.

- **D)** inaccurately portrays Darwin's use as "nuanced" and "underutilized," while the passage frames it as **brief and overlooked**, not subtle and profound.

 11

Correct Answer: C) "Gentle are the whispers of the breeze! They soothe like a balm and renew the weary soul, as if carrying the blessings of a serene haven."

📝 Explanation:

The question asks which quote **best illustrates** the essay's claim that **nature is calming and brings peace**.
- **C)** directly conveys **soothing**, **balm-like**, and **serene** effects of nature. A perfect match.

  ### 💡 Why the others are wrong:
  - **A)** is too abstract and dismissive — "daydreaming" and "lack of grandeur" don't show *calm*.
  - **B)** is about **home**, not **nature**.
  - **D)** is about **irreversible harm** and **loss**, which is **antithetical** to calming peace.

12

Correct Answer: B) There is a clear correlation between the age of surface rocks and their mineral similarity to subsurface rocks, with the correlation strengthening notably at around 3.5 billion years ago.

📝 Explanation:

The hypothesis is that **mixing began around 3.5 billion years ago**. The strongest support would show that **before** that point, minerals in surface and subsurface rocks were **distinct**, and **after**, they began to **resemble** each other.
- **B)** provides exactly that: a **correlation** starting at 3.5 billion years ago.

  ### 💡 Why the others are wrong:
  - **A)** confuses the timeline — mineral variety in subsurface rocks doesn't prove mixing.
  - **C)** offers some **mineral cross-over**, but doesn't address **correlation at 3.5 billion years** — it's less direct.
  - **D)** speaks of **which rocks are more common**, not **whether minerals mixed**, so it's too indirect.

13

Correct Answer: D)

 Explanation:

Listener L6 gave **equal ratings** to classical and jazz.

This means:

- Any **difference in correlation** cannot be due to L6's ratings, since they are **identical**.
- Therefore, the **model's predictions** must have been **different**, because if the model had predicted the same ratings as L6 gave, the correlation would have been equally strong for both genres.
- **A) Listener L6 would derive more enjoyment from classical music than from jazz music.**

  ✗ *Incorrect*: The **actual enjoyment** (ratings) from L6 are stated to be **equal**.
- **B) Listener L6's rating for classical and jazz music would equal one another.**

  ✗ *Incorrect in this context*: Yes, this is **true**, but it was **given** in the question — it doesn't make use of the graph to **complete the inference**.
- **C) Listener L6 would derive less enjoyment from classical music than from jazz music.**

  ✗ *Incorrect*: Same issue as A) but reversed. Again, **actual ratings are equal**, so this contradicts the premise.

The key is the **model's prediction**: since the correlation is **higher for classical** than jazz, and the actual ratings are **equal**, this means the **model's predicted ratings were not equal** — they **differed**.

In other words: If L6's ratings were identical for both genres, but the model matched better with classical than jazz, then **the model must have predicted different ratings**, not the participant. Thus, the model **predicted that L6's ratings would differ** — even though they didn't.

- **D)** is therefore correct: the model predicted that Listener L6's ratings would **differ**, even though they were actually the same.

14

Correct Answer: B) while Rivera's presence in *Urban Noise* represents the challenges women faced in urban spaces, Lopez's presence represents non-Western artists' frustration at their lack of recognition in the performance art world.

 Explanation:

- **B)** is correct because it explicitly ties:
  - Rivera → gendered reading (which critics already focus on)

260

- Lopez → cultural erasure of minority artists, **thereby including both performers** in a unified interpretive frame.

💡 **Why the others are incorrect:**

- **A)** is too **broad and general**, turning the work into a critique of **cultural marginalization only**, leaving out **Rivera's gendered role**. But the prompt insists both gender and cultural identity are significant.

- **C)** goes **too far** by **rejecting the gender reading entirely**, which the text never does. It criticizes **overemphasis**, not **invalidity**.

- **D)** again dismisses the **specific reading of gender** too completely. The passage suggests an **inclusive interpretation**, not a replacement.

Correct Answer: C) significant differences in interaction patterns were found for both aquarium-raised butterflyfish and wild butterflyfish.

📝 **Explanation:**

We are told that:

- Aquarium studies are **helpful** for variable control.
- **But** butterflyfish behavior is **strongly influenced by the complexity** of surroundings.
- Therefore, it's **not surprising** that Park and Greene **found something specific** when reviewing aquarium vs. wild studies.

This implies: the artificial aquarium environment, being **less complex**, likely **altered behavior**, especially in butterflyfish, whose behavior is **sensitive to environmental structure**.

- **C)** makes the most logical completion: differences in **interaction patterns** were found between wild and aquarium settings. This aligns with the idea that **environmental complexity matters**.

💡 **Why the others are incorrect:**

- **A)** contradicts expectations. If aquarium and wild fish showed **very similar behavior**, it **would be surprising**, given the earlier setup.

- **B)** focuses narrowly on **aggression**, which is **not mentioned** in the context of butterflyfish (only "interaction patterns" broadly).

- **D)** shifts to **damselfish**, while the prompt's final focus is clearly on **butterflyfish** — making it irrelevant as a conclusion to the paragraph.

16

Correct Answer: D)

 Why D) is correct:

- The sentence is making a **contrast**: although you might expect such naming to be rare, it's actually **common**.
- **"On the contrary"** is a **transitional phrase** introducing that contrast and must be **set off properly**.

  💡 **Correct punctuation rule:**
  - Use a **semicolon** before **"on the contrary"** when it links two independent clauses.
  "…to be rare; on the contrary, they are counted…"

  💡 **Why the others are wrong:**
  - **A)** lacks punctuation after "rare," creating a run-on.
  - **B)** uses a semicolon, but places it **after** the transition instead of before.
  - **C)** uses a **comma**, which is incorrect between two independent clauses.

17

Correct Answer: B) preservation, and

 Why B) is correct:

- This sentence contains a list: **"ecology, conservation, sustainability, and preservation"**.
- The **Oxford comma** (before "and") is standard in formal writing.
- The final clause **"he is celebrated…"** is a **complete independent clause**, so it must be **preceded by a comma** to avoid a comma splice or fused sentence.

  "…sustainability, and preservation, he is celebrated…"

  💡 **Why the others are wrong:**
  - **A)** lacks both the Oxford comma **and** the comma before "he," causing a run-on.
  - **C)** omits the comma before "he," again causing a comma splice.
  - **D)** lacks both the "and" (breaking the parallelism) and the needed punctuation.

18

Correct Answer: B)

 Why B) is correct:

- The colon is used here to **introduce an example**: "Ling Wei, for example…"
- The phrase before the colon is a **complete sentence**, making it grammatically correct.

  "…*many are still well known: Ling Wei, for example…*"

  Why the others are wrong:

  - **A)** just ends the clause without a clear signal of an example.
  - **C)** adds "and," breaking the logical structure—this isn't a compound sentence.
  - **D)** misuses a comma, making the sentence grammatically jarring.

19

Correct Answer: D)

 Why D) is correct:

- The clause structure is: **Main clause, interjection (though), independent clause**.
- The semicolon properly separates **two independent clauses**, and "though" acts as a **concessive connector**, set off by commas/semicolon.

  "*Such findings are ultimately speculative, though; the blue coloration may instead be caused…*"

  Why the others are wrong:

  - **A)** ends with a weak comma between two clauses—comma splice.
  - **B)** places a comma after "though," but lacks proper separation between full clauses.
  - **C)** uses a **semicolon before "though"**, but lacks follow-up punctuation.

20

Correct Answer: C)

 Why C) is correct:

- The subject is **"descriptions"** (plural), not "Ruskin."
- The verb must agree: **descriptions…fascinate**.

  "*…descriptions…fascinate readers even today.*"

💡 **Why the others are wrong:**
- **A)** *has fascinated* → past perfect, unnecessary here.
- **B)** *fascinates* → incorrect subject-verb agreement (singular).
- **D)** *is fascinating* → wrong structure; "descriptions are fascinating" would work, but it alters the sentence.

 21

Correct Answer: D)

📝 **Why D) is correct:**
- Subject: **Each of these capitals** is **singular** ("each" is singular even if the noun that follows is plural).
- Verb must match: **"Each···was established···"**

  "Each of these capitals was established···"

  💡 **Why the others are wrong:**
  - **A)** *have been* → plural
  - **B)** *are* → present tense and plural
  - **C)** *were* → past tense but still plural

 22

Correct Answer: D)

📝 **Explanation:**
- The sentence explains the **goal** (*raise awareness about plastic's harm*) and then moves to describe an **action taken to fulfill that goal** (*launching Clean Oceans*).
- **"To that end"** is the perfect transition: it signals **purpose** or **intentional consequence**.

  "···one of their primary goals was ··· To that end, they launched the initiative ···"

  💡 **Why others are wrong:**
  - **A) In summary,** – Used to **conclude** an argument, not introduce an action.
  - **B) In other words,** – Used to **restate** or paraphrase, which is not happening here.
  - **C) For example,** – Doesn't fit, because the launching of Clean Oceans is not **just an example**, but a **result of the goal**.

23

Correct Answer: A) Granted,

 Why A) is correct:

- The sentence admits a **concession**: yes, the original metric system had limitations.
- **"Granted"** introduces a clause that acknowledges a truth, often followed by a **contrast** or clarification—exactly what's happening here.

  "Granted, adjustments were made ⋯ yet the system's fundamental units remained ⋯"

  Why others are wrong:

  - **B) Again and again,** – Suggests **repetition**, which is not the focus.
  - **C) Specifically,** – Would indicate **elaboration**, but the sentence offers a **contrast**, not a specification.
  - **D) To that end,** – Implies purpose, which is **not** the relationship here.

24

Correct Answer: C) Climate scientist Maria Santos is known for her work on modeling carbon dioxide absorption in tropical rainforests.

 Why C) is correct:

- The question asks for a **specific example** of a climate scientist focused on **carbon dioxide**.
- **Only C)** directly mentions Maria Santos **by name**, **her specialty (carbon dioxide modeling)**, and her **research context (tropical rainforests)**.

  "Climate scientist Maria Santos is known for her work on modeling carbon dioxide absorption in tropical rainforests."

  Why others fall short:

  - **A)** and **B)** are **general** statements — they don't name Santos.
  - **D)** mentions carbon dioxide but is also **too general** and lacks the personal example.

TEST 05

265

25

Correct Answer: A) While the installations share a common material, one mimics ocean waves while the other is designed to evoke a heartbeat.

Why A) is correct:

- The question asks for a sentence that **emphasizes the difference** between **two installations**.
- **A)** does so **clearly** and **directly**, contrasting their **artistic representations** (waves vs. heartbeat).

  "While the installations share a common material, one mimics ocean waves while the other is designed to evoke a heartbeat."

  #### Why others don't work:
  - **B)** highlights LED versatility, not the difference between **these two** works.
  - **C)** is about **artists**, not installations.
  - **D)** mentions years of creation but not **differences in artistic intent**.

26

Correct Answer: A) An approach to literature, historical analysis examines how the time period in which a text was written influences its themes and characters.

Why A) is correct:

- The question asks for an **introduction** of historical analysis to an audience **unfamiliar with the concept**.
- **A)** does just that: defines historical analysis in clear, introductory terms.

  "An approach to literature, historical analysis examines how the time period in which a text was written influences its themes and characters."

  #### Why others don't meet the goal:
  - **B)** focuses on thematic analysis instead.
  - **C)** compares thematic vs. historical analysis but doesn't explain **what historical analysis is**.
  - **D)** is an example, not an explanation — it's fine support, but not suitable as an introduction.

27

Answer: A)

✍ Why A) is correct:

• The question asks for an **overview** — a **broad, general summary** of National Parks.
• **A)** is the only choice that:
  - Mentions the **global scale**
  - Emphasizes **protection of ecosystems and species**

  "Over 1,000 National Parks worldwide protect endangered ecosystems and species."

💡 Why others fall short:

• **B)** is specific to **Banff**, not an overview.
• **C)** compares two parks, but still too **narrow**.
• **D)** focuses only on **Yellowstone**, not the broader concept of National Parks.

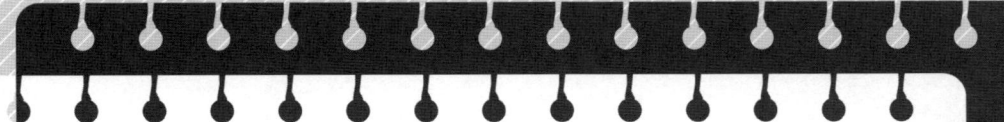

TEST 6

- Module 1

- Module 1 answers

- Module 2

- Module 2 answers

Module 1

Reading and Writing
27 Questions, 32 Minutes

1

The following text is from a fictional story about a young artist reflecting on her craft.

As she worked late into the night, carefully **contemplating** the colors she would use in her next painting, she thought about the emotions she wanted to evoke. For her, the choice of colors was more than just an artistic decision; it was a means to connect deeply with her audience.

As used in the text, what does the word "contemplating" most nearly mean?

A) Debating

B) Considering

C) Disregarding

D) Hoping for

2

Renowned chef Maria Lopez is celebrated for her innovative recipes that combine flavors from various cuisines, from Mediterranean herbs to Asian spices. These creations are highly praised, ensuring that Lopez receives widespread _____ for her culinary talents.

Which choice completes the text with the most logical and precise word or phrase?

A) criticism

B) acclaim

C) empathy

D) instruction

3

Often, the Academy Award for Best Director is presented to a single individual, such as Kathryn Bigelow in 2010. But occasionally, the Academy chooses to honor collaborative efforts, in which case, the award is given _____. For example, in 2007, Joel and Ethan Coen were jointly recognized for their work on the film *No Country for Old Men*.

Which choice completes the text with the most logical and precise word or phrase?

A) **retroactively**

B) **collectively**

C) **symbolically**

D) **unintentionally**

4

I am the sea, I am it, the waves
Of which each crest **speaks** calm and might
And carries to the shores that call my name.
I am the sea, its soothing song, and it
Is strength, and depth, and sky—and heart to me.

As used in the text, what does the word "speaks" most nearly mean?

A) **Imparts**

B) **Renounces**

C) **Agrees**

D) **Learns**

5

One way to measure the effectiveness of a marketing campaign is to _____ the number of times the campaign's advertisements are shared on social media. For example, a count of user shares shows that GreenLeaf's environmental campaign has been shared widely, indicating that its message resonates strongly with the audience.

Which choice completes the text with the most logical and precise word or phrase?

A) **limit**

B) **dispute**

C) **tally**

D) **predict**

6

Though Elias Carter, author of *The Prism of Time*, is not as widely recognized as some of the most celebrated contemporary scientists, influential figures have praised his work, including physicist Sarah Langston and biologist Raj Mehta. In her foreword to Carter's book *Shifting Dimensions*, Langston highlights Carter's innovative synthesis of theoretical and experimental approaches—showing how, contrary to traditional views, scientific research can effectively integrate both.

Which choice best states the main purpose of the text?

A) **To argue that all scientific research must rely equally on theoretical and experimental methods**

B) **To compare the work of a scientist with that of a researcher who praised him**

C) **To explain what inspired a scientist to pursue a specific line of research**

D) **To present a reason why a prominent scientist admires a certain book**

CONTINUE

7

Citizen journalism, which involves members of the public collaborating with professional journalists to report on events, is often a powerful and inclusive way to gather news. It allows communities to bring attention to overlooked stories, foster civic engagement, and increase the diversity of perspectives in the news. This method was integral to the success of a project led by journalist Maria Torres, documenting the impact of urban development on local neighborhoods, which included contributions from dozens of residents in Chicago.

Which choice best describes the overall structure of the text?

A) **It introduces the topic of a journalism project, describes the project's significance, and then presents its findings.**

B) **It argues for a new approach to journalism, comments on the public's opinion about the approach, and then describes how that approach was applied in a specific project.**

C) **It identifies a particular approach to journalism, lists some benefits of that approach, and then mentions a project in which that approach was used.**

D) **It describes the development of a type of journalistic collaboration, shows how that collaboration has been used in a specific project, and then suggests future collaborative efforts.**

8

The following text is from *Reflections by the Sea* by a contemporary author. The narrator is spending time at the coast to unwind.

I strolled along the shore, the soft breeze carrying with it the salty tang of the sea. The rhythmic sound of waves crashing against the rocks calmed my restless mind. As I walked, I forgot the deadlines, the reports, the endless meetings, and instead thought of simpler times, days filled with laughter and curiosity. The vastness of the ocean before me seemed to hold endless possibilities for the future, while its gentle touch awakened vivid memories of childhood summers spent building sandcastles and chasing seagulls.

Which choice best states the main idea of the text?

A) **Having decided to leave behind a fast-paced lifestyle, the narrator is retreating to the seaside where he spent his childhood.**

B) **The narrator's coastal surroundings help him escape work-related stress by sparking reflections on childhood memories and hopes for the future.**

C) **The narrator is using the quiet of the seaside to brainstorm strategies for solving professional challenges.**

D) **The narrator becomes distracted by thoughts of youth, preventing him from addressing pressing work-related issues.**

9

Data Table: Average Ages of Fossil Samples from Select Excavations

Excavation Name	Year	Location	Approximate Age of Fossil Samples (millions of years)
Site Alpha	1950	North America	1.2
Site Beta	1965	South America	0.8
Site Gamma	1975	Africa	1.4
Site Delta	2020	Asia	0.3

The excavations at Site Alpha, Beta, and Gamma were conducted during the mid-20th century and yielded fossil samples from some of the oldest species known to researchers. More recently, Site Delta was excavated, revealing additional fossil specimens. Researchers have analyzed and dated the fossils, concluding that the fossils from Site Delta are significant because _____.

Which choice most effectively uses data from the table to complete the claim?

A) **they are significantly younger than the fossils discovered at any of the other sites.**

B) **they were discovered at the same location as the fossils from Site Alpha.**

C) **they are closest in age to the fossils discovered at Site Beta.**

D) **they helped confirm the predicted ages of fossils found at Site Gamma.**

10

In a study by researchers Smith and Lee, residents of Metropolis and Rivertown were surveyed about their use of local libraries. Of the 450 respondents from Metropolis, 60% indicated that they visit the city's libraries, and of the 600 respondents from Rivertown, 40% indicated using their libraries. Given that the percentage of Metropolis respondents who reported having access to other educational resources near libraries was much lower than that reported by Rivertown respondents, the difference in library use can't be explained by Metropolis residents having better access to additional educational resources near libraries.

Which choice best describes the main idea of the text?

A) Even though the study found that libraries in Rivertown are more likely to be close to other educational resources than libraries in Metropolis, Metropolis has more educational resources overall than Rivertown.

B) The study's findings suggest that an increase in the number of educational resources near libraries would likely increase library use in Metropolis but not in Rivertown.

C) The study's finding that a greater proportion of residents use libraries in Metropolis than in Rivertown is partly due to the greater prevalence of libraries in Metropolis.

D) Although the study found that a greater proportion of residents use libraries in Metropolis than in Rivertown, that difference isn't due to greater access to educational resources near libraries in Metropolis.

11

Defensive Behavior and Lifespan Traits of Select Mammal Species

Scientific name	Common name	Displays defensive bluff?	Average lifespan of offspring (years)	Number of offspring per year	Parental care involvement
Panthera leo	Lion	No	10	2	Female only
Ursus arctos	Brown bear	No	12	1	Shared
Suricata suricatta	Meerkat	Yes	18	4	Female only
Canis lupus familiaris	Domestic dog	Yes	25	6	Shared

In an extensive review of mammalian behavior, a team of researchers cataloged the prevalence of defensive bluff behaviors—such as feigned aggression or loud vocalizations—across various species. The findings suggest the behavior likely evolved independently multiple times, leading the team to take into consideration ecological and life history characteristics with putative links to the behavior's onset, including characteristics associated with future reproduction potential and reproduction investment. Based on their analysis, the team concluded that _____.

Which choice most effectively uses data from the table to complete the conclusion?

A) average lifespan, number of offspring per year, and parental care strategies are equally associated with the use of defensive bluff behaviors.

B) average lifespan and number of offspring per year are more strongly associated with defensive bluff behaviors than the parental care strategy is.

C) defensive bluff behavior is most often observed in species with fewer offspring per year due to longer parental care periods.

D) among species with shared parental care, defensive bluff behavior is associated with shorter average lifespans.

12

The golden eagle and the bald eagle are large birds of prey that inhabit mountainous regions and forests across North America. Researchers led by Dr. Alex Kim wanted to understand how these eagles select nesting sites. They analyzed factors such as proximity to water sources and elevation of nesting areas. They found that golden eagles prefer higher elevation sites with sparse vegetation, but this was not true for bald eagles, which preferred areas closer to water with dense tree cover. Based on their findings, the researchers concluded that land-management practices that involve increasing tree density in high-elevation areas are less likely to _____.

Which choice most logically completes the text?

A) attract birds that don't typically nest in high-elevation areas to the region than they are to encourage nesting by bald eagles or golden eagles.

B) extend the lifespan of golden eagles in the area than they are to increase the population of bald eagles in the area.

C) decrease the area's suitability for both golden eagles and bald eagles than they are to improve conditions for other species.

D) attract golden eagles to the area than they are to attract bald eagles to the area.

13

The River's Bend is a 1925 novel by Clara Jenkins. In one portion of the novel, Jenkins establishes a contrast between the protagonist's desire for change and the attitude of the protagonist's friend, Leah, writing, _____.

Which quotation from *The River's Bend* most effectively illustrates the claim?

A) "Leah stood still as the river flowed past, unmoving and unwavering. She had always been like that, at least to me."
B) "The sound of the wind rustling through the trees reminded me of times we laughed together. I wished the moment could last forever."
C) "[Leah] offered a quiet nod, a gesture that felt like approval but lacked any true commitment or passion."
D) "As time went on, [Leah's] contentment with routine began to irritate me; I longed for excitement. I left our small town before she even considered it."

14

Dyes give textiles their color. Indigo is a plant-based dye used to create shades of blue, while synthetic dyes are produced from chemical compounds. Plant-based dyes contain high levels of organic compounds, whereas synthetic dyes often contain trace amounts of heavy metals. In a 2023 study, researchers tested the blue dye found on textiles from an ancient settlement dated to approximately 4,000 years ago. The test revealed that the dye contained no heavy metals but had a high concentration of organic compounds. This finding led the researchers to conclude that _____.

Which choice most logically completes the text?

A) the dyes used by the ancient textile makers likely came from plants because synthetic dyes were unavailable.
B) the ancient textile makers preferred plant-based dyes because they were more vibrant than synthetic dyes.
C) the ancient textile makers used plant-based dyes rather than synthetic dyes to color some of the textiles examined in the study.
D) the textiles examined in the study are the oldest known examples of the use of plant-based dyes for coloring fabrics.

TEST 90

CONTINUE

15

Dr. Susan Morales, a sociologist at the University of Chicago, _____ community rituals in urban neighborhoods—specifically, how events such as block parties and parades serve as tools for fostering collective identity and strengthening social bonds.

Which choice completes the text so that it conforms to the conventions of Standard English?

A) have examined

B) examines

C) examine

D) are examining

16

Works by celebrated sculptors Maya Lin and Richard Serra were featured in the Museum of Modern Art's exhibition *Shaping Spaces: Modern Sculpture*. This 2015 exhibition showcased the innovative designs _____ artists who redefined spatial dynamics in modern art.

Which choice completes the text so that it conforms to the conventions of Standard English?

A) of;

B) of:

C) of,

D) of

17

On March 14, 2023, the research vessel **Endeavor** set sail for the Pacific Ocean, beginning _____ two months and fifteen days, the journey concluded when the ship docked at Pearl Harbor in Hawaii.

Which choice completes the text so that it conforms to the conventions of Standard English?

A) Expedition-22, spanning

B) Expedition-22, it spanned

C) Expedition-22 spanning

D) Expedition-22. Spanning

18

Agriculture was essential to the Maya civilization, which flourished in Mesoamerica from around 250 CE to 900 CE. Its people _____ maize, beans, and squash to sustain their large populations. In return, they developed complex trade systems that brought them obsidian, jade, and other valuable resources.

Which choice completes the text so that it conforms to the conventions of Standard English?

A) are cultivating

B) cultivate

C) cultivated

D) will cultivate

19

The Great Library of Alexandria is often considered one of the most significant libraries of the ancient world. In 48 BCE, a fire _____ during Julius Caesar's siege of the city, destroying part of the library and its priceless collection of scrolls. Many works were never recovered, marking a tragic loss to history.

Which choice completes the text so that it conforms to the conventions of Standard English?

A) has erupted

B) erupted

C) will erupt

D) erupts

20

As a pioneer in the field of aviation in the early 1900s, Bessie Coleman of _____ an essential role in inspiring future generations of pilots, particularly women and people of color.

Which choice completes the text so that it conforms to the conventions of Standard English?

A) Chicago. Achieved

B) Chicago: achieved

C) Chicago; achieved

D) Chicago achieved

21

Maya Angelou's 1969 memoir **I Know Why the Caged Bird Sings**, a powerful narrative about the early life of _____ offers a deeply personal perspective on race, identity, and resilience in America.

Which choice completes the text so that it conforms to the conventions of Standard English?

A) Angelou, and

B) Angelou and

C) Angelou,

D) Angelou

22

Renowned for its unique design, the Millennium Bridge in London is a pedestrian suspension bridge spanning the River Thames. However, tests conducted during its opening in 2000 revealed excessive swaying when large crowds crossed. _____ engineers temporarily closed the bridge to address the structural issues and redesign it for public safety.

Which choice completes the text with the most logical transition?

A) In contrast,

B) As a result,

C) For instance,

D) Likewise,

TEST 06

23

When a species is no longer found living in the wild or in captivity, it is considered extinct. _____ the dodo, a flightless bird native to Mauritius, became extinct in the late 1600s due to hunting and habitat destruction.

Which choice completes the text with the most logical transition?

A) Therefore,

B) Admittedly,

C) For example,

D) In conclusion,

24

While researching a topic, a student has taken the following notes:

- Fossilized tree resin, known as amber, has been discovered in various regions of the world.
- Some pieces of amber contain preserved organisms, such as insects and small plants.
- A particularly famous piece of amber from Myanmar contains a 99-million-year-old dinosaur tail with feathers.
- This discovery has provided valuable insights into the evolution of feathers and their role in dinosaur biology.

The student wants to provide an example of a notable piece of amber. Which choice most effectively uses relevant information from the notes to accomplish this goal?

A) Amber is fossilized tree resin, and it has been discovered in many regions worldwide.

B) Some amber pieces contain preserved organisms, including insects and plants.

C) A famous piece of amber from Myanmar contains a 99-million-year-old dinosaur tail with feathers.

D) Amber provides insight into prehistoric life, including the evolution of feathers in dinosaurs.

25

While researching a topic, a student has taken the following notes:

- Chinese astronomer Zhang Heng studied celestial phenomena and invented devices to measure seismic activity.
- He proposed a geocentric model of the universe in which Earth is at the center, surrounded by celestial spheres.
- Zhang Heng published his geocentric model in 132 CE.

The student wants to specify when Zhang Heng published his geocentric model. Which choice most effectively uses relevant information from the notes to accomplish this goal?

A) In 132 CE, Zhang Heng published his geocentric model of the universe, proposing that Earth is at the center surrounded by celestial spheres.

B) Zhang Heng, who studied celestial phenomena, invented devices to measure seismic activity and proposed a geocentric model.

C) Zhang Heng was a Chinese astronomer who made significant contributions to the study of celestial phenomena.

D) A Chinese astronomer who studied celestial phenomena, Zhang Heng proposed that Earth is at the center of the universe surrounded by celestial spheres.

26

While researching a topic, a student has taken the following notes:

- The Nobel Prize in Physics is awarded annually for groundbreaking contributions to the field of physics.
- Albert Einstein won the award in 1921 for his explanation of the photoelectric effect.
- Marie Curie won the award in 1903 for her pioneering research on radioactivity.

The student wants to emphasize the order in which Marie Curie and Albert Einstein won the Nobel Prize in Physics. Which choice most effectively uses relevant information from the notes to accomplish this goal?

A) Albert Einstein and Marie Curie both won the Nobel Prize in Physics for their significant contributions to science.

B) Marie Curie won the Nobel Prize in Physics in 1903; Albert Einstein won it later, in 1921.

C) In 1921, Albert Einstein won the Nobel Prize in Physics for his explanation of the photoelectric effect.

D) It was in 1903 that Marie Curie won the Nobel Prize in Physics.

27

While researching a topic, a student has taken the following notes:

- Early photography required the use of large and cumbersome equipment.
- Anna Atkins is credited with being one of the first women to create photographic images.
- Atkins produced a series of cyanotype prints of plants from 1843 to 1853.
- Julia Margaret Cameron became known for her artistic portraits and photographs of literary figures starting in 1864.

The student wants to emphasize the order in which Anna Atkins and Julia Margaret Cameron began their photographic work. Which choice most effectively uses relevant information from the notes to accomplish this goal?

A) From 1843 to 1853, Anna Atkins used cyanotype photography to document plants, followed by Julia Margaret Cameron's work starting in 1864.

B) Julia Margaret Cameron started her career in photography years after Anna Atkins had already created cyanotype prints.

C) Anna Atkins' photographic work began in 1843, while Julia Margaret Cameron's began in 1864.

D) Early photography required bulky equipment, as demonstrated by the work of Anna Atkins and Julia Margaret Cameron.

 CONTINUE

Module 1 answer

1

Correct Answer: B) Considering

 Why it's correct:

"Contemplating" in this context refers to a thoughtful, deliberate mental process. The artist isn't *arguing* or *daydreaming*, but quietly and deeply reflecting on her color choices. "Considering" captures this nuance with precision—it implies weighing options with care, which aligns with the artist's introspective mood.

⟨?⟩ **Why the others are wrong:**
- **A) Debating** – Suggests a back-and-forth or conflict between options. "Contemplating" may involve reflection, but not the conflict implied by "debating."
- **C) Disregarding** – The *antonym* of what the sentence shows. She's not ignoring the colors—she's giving them full attention.
- **D) Hoping for** – Implies desire rather than thought. She's not wishing for certain colors; she's evaluating them thoughtfully.

2

Correct Answer: B)

 Why it fits:

"Acclaim" refers to enthusiastic and public praise—exactly what is appropriate for an innovative chef admired for her work. It matches both tone and logic.

⟨?⟩ **Why the others fail:**
- **A) Criticism** – Opposite meaning. The sentence is clearly positive.
- **C) Empathy** – Refers to understanding emotions, which is irrelevant to culinary recognition.
- **D) Instruction** – Suggests teaching, not receiving praise. It doesn't logically follow the context of public appreciation.

3

Correct Answer: B) Collectively

📝 Why it works:
"Collectively" denotes a group receiving something as a unit—perfect for describing a shared award. It mirrors "jointly recognized" and emphasizes collaboration.

💬 Why others miss the mark:
- **A) Retroactively** – Means "after the fact," unrelated to sharing an award.
- **C) Symbolically** – Would suggest the award isn't literal or substantive, which it clearly is.
- **D) Unintentionally** – Implies an accident, conflicting with the Academy's deliberate decision.

4

Correct Answer: A)

📝 Why it's right:
In poetic diction, "speaks" often means *to express* or *communicate*. The waves "speak" calm and might not through literal speech, but by *imparting* those qualities through their movement and sound.

💬 Why the others drown:
- **B) Renounces** – To reject or disown—utterly out of place here.
- **C) Agrees** – "Speak" here doesn't imply agreement, but rather expression.
- **D) Learns** – Waves aren't sentient; they cannot learn. The metaphor is about communication, not cognition.

5

Correct Answer: C)

📝 Why it fits:
"Tally" means to *count or record*, perfectly suited to the context of measuring shares. The sentence even says "a count of user shares," reinforcing that numerical tracking is the goal.

The rest don't measure up:

- **A) Limit** – To restrict, which is not the intent here.
- **B) Dispute** – To argue against, unrelated to measurement.
- **D) Predict** – To forecast, but we already have the *actual* count; no prediction is needed.

6

Correct Answer: D) To present a reason why a prominent scientist admires a certain book

Why it is correct:

The passage revolves around physicist Sarah Langston's **foreword** in Carter's book, praising his integration of theory and experimentation. The focus is not on Carter's biography or the specifics of his methods, but rather *why a prominent scientist admires his book*. This aligns perfectly with answer D.

Why the other choices fail:

- **A)** Claims *all* science must equally rely on theory and experimentation—a **universal claim** not supported by the text. The passage discusses one example, not a mandate.
- **B)** No comparison is made between Carter and Langston as *researchers*. Langston is a commentator, not the subject.
- **C)** The passage doesn't explore **Carter's inspiration** or his motivation—only the response to his work.

7

Correct Answer: C) It identifies a particular approach to journalism, lists some benefits of that approach, and then mentions a project in which that approach was used.

Why it is correct:

The structure is quite clear:

1. **Introduction** of *citizen journalism* (the approach),
2. **Benefits listed** (attention to overlooked stories, civic engagement, diverse perspectives),
3. **Example project** (Maria Torres's work in Chicago).

This is a textbook "concept → benefits → example" structure—perfectly encapsulated by C.

📱 **Why others fail:**

- **A)** Implies that the project is introduced **first**, which it is not—it appears **last**.
- **B)** Suggests a strong **argument** for a new approach and discussion of public opinion, which isn't in the text.
- **D)** Mentions **development** and **future suggestions**, which are not present—the text is descriptive, not speculative.

8

Correct Answer: B) The narrator's coastal surroundings help them escape work-related stress by sparking reflections on childhood memories and hopes for the future.

📝 **Why it is correct:**

The narrator is clearly overwhelmed by professional life and finds solace at the sea. The text is rich with imagery of both **childhood memories** and **a hopeful, open future** ("endless possibilities"). This answer gracefully captures both themes: *release from stress* and *reflective inspiration*.

📱 **Why others miss the mark:**

- **A)** Suggests a **deliberate life change** ("having decided to leave behind"), which isn't confirmed in the text. There's no evidence that this is a permanent retreat.
- **C)** Incorrect tone—the narrator isn't *brainstorming work strategies*, but escaping them.
- **D)** Misrepresents the narrative's emotional tone. The memories aren't a **distraction**; they are a source of **comfort and reflection**.

9

Correct Answer: A) they are significantly younger than the fossils discovered at any of the other sites.

📝 **Explanation:**

This is directly and precisely supported by the table:

- **0.3 million years** is the **youngest** value in the entire column.
- The use of "significantly" is supported by the fact that 0.3 is **less than half** the next youngest sample (0.8 at Site Beta).
- This answer **best aligns** with the claim that researchers found something "significant" about these fossils based on **age**.

💬 **Why the Other Options Are Incorrect:**

- **B) "They were discovered at the same location as the fossils from Site Alpha."**

  -**Wrong:** Site Alpha = **North America**, Site Delta = **Asia** → **Different locations.**

- **C) "They are closest in age to the fossils discovered at Site Beta."**

  -**Wrong:** Site Delta = 0.3 million years, Site Beta = 0.8 → **0.5-million-year difference.**

  -Site Delta is **not** closest in age to any other—it's the most distant in terms of age.

- **D) "They helped confirm the predicted ages of fossils found at Site Gamma."**

  -**Wrong:** There is **no data or claim** in the passage or table connecting Site Delta with Site Gamma, nor any mention of **predictions.**

  -Also, Site Gamma fossils are **older (1.4 million years)**—no support for "confirmation."

10

Correct Answer: D) Although the study found that a greater proportion of residents use libraries in Metropolis than in Rivertown, that difference isn't due to greater access to educational resources near libraries in Metropolis.

📝 **Why it's correct:**

- **Fact 1:** More residents in **Metropolis** (60%) use libraries than in **Rivertown** (40%).
- **Fact 2: Rivertown** has **greater access** to educational resources *near libraries.*
- **Inference:** Since Rivertown has better access but lower library use, that variable can't **explain** the difference.

This answer perfectly captures that structure:

Difference in use ✔

But **not** explained by access ✔

💬 **Why others are wrong:**

- **A)** Invents a claim: Metropolis has "more educational resources overall"—**not stated.**
- **B)** Misinterprets the conclusion—it doesn't say increasing resources **would** increase library use in Metropolis.
- **C)** Claims the difference is due to **prevalence of libraries**—**not mentioned at all** in the passage.

Answer: B)

📝 **Observations:**

• Species with **bluff behavior** have **higher lifespans and more offspring**.

• Parental care is **not a clear predictor**: both Yes and No groups are split between "shared" and "female only".

Hence, lifespan and offspring correlate better with bluffing than parenting style.

💬 **Why others are wrong:**

• **A)** Says all three traits are **equally** associated—clearly not true.

• **C)** Claims bluffing is linked to **fewer** offspring—not supported; dogs and meerkats (bluffers) have more.

• **D)** Implies short lifespan + shared care = bluffing—not consistent with the data (dogs have long lifespan).

Correct Answer: D) Attract golden eagles to the area than they are to attract bald eagles to the area.

📝 **Why it's correct:**

• **Golden eagles** prefer: **high elevation + sparse vegetation**

• **Bald eagles** prefer: **low elevation + dense tree cover**

• So if you **add trees to high elevation**, it makes it **less appealing to golden eagles** (goes against their preference), but **possibly more appealing to bald eagles**.

The answer correctly compares **relative likelihood** of attracting one species over the other based on habitat alteration.

💬 **Why others are wrong:**

• **A)** Introduces a third group of "birds that don't nest in high elevations"—irrelevant.

• **B)** Talks about **lifespan**, which is not discussed.

• **C)** Suggests **both eagle types** would find it unsuitable—**not supported**; only golden eagles are negatively affected.

13

Correct Answer: D) "As time went on, [Leah's] contentment with routine began to irritate me; I longed for excitement. I left our small town before she even considered it."

📝 **Why it's correct:**

This quote provides a **direct contrast**:

• The **narrator desires change** and **leaves**.

• **Leah remains**, content with **routine**.

It **explicitly demonstrates** the divergence in their attitudes—exactly what the question describes.

💬 **Why others are wrong:**

• **A)** Describes Leah's character, but doesn't highlight the narrator's desire for change.

• **B)** Focuses on nostalgia, not contrasting desires.

• **C)** Is too vague—"approval without passion" doesn't clearly show the **contrast** in motivations.

14

Correct Answer: C) The ancient textile makers used plant-based dyes rather than synthetic dyes to color some of the textiles examined in the study.

📝 **Why it's correct:**

• The dye had **no heavy metals** (common in synthetic)

• It had **high organic compounds** (common in plant-based)

• Therefore, it's **logical** to conclude that plant-based dyes were used—especially given that **synthetic dyes weren't available 4,000 years ago**.

This choice is **precise** and **evidence-based**, avoiding overreach.

💬 **Why others are wrong:**

• **A)** Is *mostly* true, but it adds speculation about **availability**, which isn't the main basis of the conclusion.

• **B)** Claims **preference**—not supported; the conclusion is based on **chemical composition**, not taste.

• **D)** Claims these are the **oldest known** examples—**not mentioned** in the passage.

TEST 06

289

15

Correct Answer: B)

 Why it's correct:

- **Subject:** *Dr. Susan Morales* → singular.
- We need a **present tense, singular** verb to match.
- "Examines" is the third-person singular present tense of "examine" → correct form.

   ⚡ **Why the others are wrong:**
   - **A) have examined** → plural verb; doesn't agree with singular subject.
   - **C) examine** → base form/plural; again, wrong agreement.
   - **D) are examining** → present progressive *plural* form.

16

Correct Answer: D)

 Why it's correct:

- The phrase is simply "the designs **of artists**."
- No punctuation is necessary between "designs" and "of"—they're part of the same noun phrase.
- Clean and grammatically correct.

   ⚡ **Why the others are wrong:**
   - **A) of;** → semicolon is used to connect **two independent clauses**—not the case here.
   - **B) of:** → colon should follow a complete clause when listing/explaining. Not appropriate here.
   - **C) of,** → the comma interrupts the noun phrase unnecessarily.

17

Answer: D)

📝 **Why it's correct:**

- "Expedition-22" ends the first sentence.
- What follows is a **new sentence**, adding detail about the time.
- "Spanning" begins a **participial phrase**, and must be set off as part of a new, descriptive sentence.

Why others are wrong:

- **A)** Improper punctuation with a comma splice.
- **B)** Awkward, grammatically incorrect structure.
- **C)** Missing punctuation between independent clauses.

18

Answer: C) cultivated

📝 **Why it's correct:**

- The sentence is in **past tense** ("was essential," "flourished").
- "Cultivated" matches that tense perfectly.

 Why others are wrong:

- **A) are cultivating** – present progressive → wrong tense.
- **B) cultivate** – present → doesn't match past context.
- **D) will cultivate** – future → illogical and incorrect in a historical context.

19

Answer: B) erupted

📝 **Why it's correct:**

- Again, this is a **historical event** being described → needs past tense.
- "Erupted" is the simple past, correct form.

📝 **Why others are wrong:**

- **A) has erupted** – present perfect → not appropriate for distant past.
- **C) will erupt** – future → doesn't fit a 48 BCE event.
- **D) erupts** – present → not logical for historical narration.

TEST 06

20

Answer: D)

 Why it's correct:

- "Bessie Coleman of Chicago achieved⋯" is a simple, correct subject-verb construction.
- No punctuation is necessary between "Chicago" and "achieved."

    Why others are wrong:
    - **A) Chicago. Achieved** – creates a sentence fragment; the subject and verb are split incorrectly.
    - **B) Chicago: achieved** – colon incorrectly used; no list or explanation.
    - **C) Chicago; achieved** – semicolon between subject and verb → grammatically incorrect.

21

Answer: C)

 Why it's correct:

- The phrase is "...early life of Angelou, [it] offers..."
- We need a **comma** to separate the dependent clause ("about the early life of Angelou") from the independent clause that follows.
- Without the comma, it reads as a run-on.

    Why others are wrong:
    - **A) Angelou, and** – "and" wrongly joins clauses; no compound structure here.
    - **B) Angelou and** – again, no second element for "and" to connect.
    - **D) Angelou** – missing necessary comma to separate the clauses.

22

Answer: B) As a result,

 Why it's correct:
This is a classic **cause-and-effect** transition.

- Cause: Tests revealed a problem.

- Effect: Engineers closed the bridge.
- Thus, **"As a result"** is the most logical connector.

  ⌨ **Why others fail:**
  - **A) In contrast** – Signals opposition, which doesn't fit the flow.
  - **C) For instance** – Introduces examples, not effects.
  - **D) Likewise** – Suggests similarity, but the action is **responsive**, not similar.

23

Answer: C) For example,

 Why it's correct:

The second sentence illustrates the definition given in the first.
- A **specific case** of extinction (the dodo) follows a **general definition**.
- Perfect use case for "**For example.**"

  ⌨ **Why others fail:**
  - **A) Therefore** – Suggests a conclusion, not an illustration.
  - **B) Admittedly** – Used to concede a point, which isn't happening here.
  - **D) In conclusion** – Wraps things up; too final for this spot.

24

Answer: C) A famous piece of amber from Myanmar contains a 99-million-year-old dinosaur tail with feathers.

 Why it's correct:

This directly names **a specific, notable** piece and gives **details**:
- Location (Myanmar)
- Content (dinosaur tail)
- Age (99 million years)
- This is the strongest, most focused example.

TEST 90

Why others fail:

- **A)** Too general—doesn't cite a specific piece.
- **B)** Mentions preserved organisms but not the dinosaur tail.
- **D)** Talks broadly about amber's insights, not a concrete example.

25

Answer: A) In 132 CE, Zhang Heng published his geocentric model of the universe, proposing that Earth is at the center surrounded by celestial spheres.

📝 **Why it's correct:**
It **clearly identifies the year** and ties it directly to the action (publication).
It also includes the core concept (Earth at center, celestial spheres).

 Why others fail:

- **B)** Doesn't mention **132 CE**, which is essential.
- **C)** General bio info—missing the **main focus** (date of model).
- **D)** Gives his theory, but omits the **year of publication**.

26

Answer: B) Marie Curie won the Nobel Prize in Physics in 1903; Albert Einstein won it later, in 1921.

📝 **Why it's correct:**
This sentence:
- Gives both **dates**
- Uses **"later"** to **highlight sequence** Perfect for emphasizing **order of events**.

 Why others fail:

- **A)** Groups them equally, doesn't show **who came first**.
- **C)** Focuses only on Einstein; leaves Curie out.
- **D)** Mentions Curie but ignores Einstein—**no comparison**.

27

Answer: C) Anna Atkins' photographic work began in 1843, while Julia Margaret Cameron's began in 1864.

 Why it's correct:

This is a **clear, side-by-side comparison** that:

• Includes **both names**
• Gives **specific start years**
• Uses **"while"** to connect events logically

 Why others fail:

• **A)** Is technically okay, but **less direct** than C and introduces extra info.
• **B)** Is vague—"years after" doesn't give the full picture.
• **D)** Talks about equipment, not timing or order of work.

Page Intentionally Left Blank

Module 2

Reading and Writing
27 Questions, 32 Minutes

The questions in this section address a number of important reading and writing skills. Each questions includes one or more passages, which may include a table or graph. Read each passage and question carefully, and then choose the best answer to the question based on the passage(s).

All questions in this section are multiple-choice with four answer choices. Each question has a single best answer.

1

Databases such as the Global Biodiversity Information Facility are vast collections of electronically stored data that can be used to analyze the distribution of _____ species. (specialized species that inhabit isolated or inaccessible regions, on the other hand, tend to be poorly represented.) A database could reveal, for example, that the monarch butterfly is one of the most widely distributed butterfly species in North America.

Which choice completes the text with the most logical and precise word or phrase?

A) trivial

B) conventional

C) profound

D) accidental

2

Obligate carnivores are animals that depend solely on animal flesh for their nutritional needs. Their dietary reliance is why obligate carnivores can be _____ those that are facultative carnivores (able to digest both animal and non-animal food): the facultative red fox can thrive on a varied diet, but its survival does not depend exclusively on consuming other animals, as does that of the obligate tiger.

Which choice completes the text with the most logical and precise word or phrase?

A) demarcated from

B) reconstituted as

C) derived from

D) conflated with

3

"In 2020, Dr. Elaine Roberts and her team revealed a faint signal detected by a deep-sea sonar system as definitive proof of a new species of marine life, which some experts had argued was too elusive to identify. Comprehensive computational modeling helped preclude doubts about the signal's _____, verifying the discovery with an accuracy rate of over 98%."

Which choice completes the text with the most logical and precise word or phrase?

A) subtlety

B) ambiguity

C) likelihood

D) inconspicuousness

4

Although Dr. Karen Torres, a biologist, is not as well recognized as the most prominent scientists of the last few decades, her research has had significant backing from renowned experts, including ecologist Dr. Anne Patel and conservationist Dr. Michael Brooks. In his preface to Torres's study *Biodiversity in the Tropics*, Brooks argues that the work masterfully integrates what ecologist Paul Ehrlich described as descriptive and predictive methodologies—while Ehrlich viewed studies as either descriptive (documenting observations) or predictive (forecasting outcomes), *Biodiversity in the Tropics* combines both approaches seamlessly.

Which choice best describes the overall structure of the text?

A) It accounts for a scientist's lack of widespread fame, cites a professional who appreciates that scientist, and summarizes the traits that make the scientist's work distinctive.

B) It describes a scientist's acclaimed career, mentions two professionals who supported that career, and explains why the scientist achieved success.

C) It refers to a scientist whose work is not widely known, highlights two experts who admire that scientist, and provides a reason why one of them values the scientist's work.

D) It portrays a scientist whose research is seen as complex, mentions two admirers of that scientist's work, and discusses information that might make the research more comprehensible to others.

 CONTINUE

5

Tokyo boasts efficient public transportation, but replicating a feature of Tokyo associated with commuter satisfaction—e.g., its high frequency of trains—may not necessarily result in improved satisfaction levels in other cities. As transportation expert Hiroshi Tanaka explains, our understanding of commuters' preferences regarding public transit remains incomplete: some studies focus on **station accessibility**, others on **personal schedule flexibility**, and so forth, but commuting choices are influenced by a range of complex factors that vary among individuals.

Which choice best describes the function of the references to "station accessibility" and "personal schedule flexibility" in the text as a whole?

A) They are examples of factors that studies suggest are important in commuters' decision-making about public transit but that the text claims most people rarely consider when making commuting decisions.

B) They represent factors that have been identified as important influences on commuting decisions but that the text suggests are merely some of the many factors that may contribute to people's decision-making about public transit.

C) They illustrate factors that researchers believe commuters consider when making public transit decisions in most contexts but that the text argues are unique to commuting decisions made by people in Tokyo.

D) They identify factors that Tanaka argues have been overemphasized in studies of decision-making about public transit but that the text asserts are relevant to most commuters' decisions.

6

Text 1:

"Marie Curie, renowned for her groundbreaking discoveries in radioactivity, is celebrated despite her methodical and emotionless approach to scientific communication. Her reports are factual and avoid personal reflection, focusing solely on experimental results. That her work remains influential is a testament to her intellect—even if readers engage with her research for its implications rather than her narrative style, they will find much of value."

Text 2:

"Curie's communication style has been critiqued, but it is inappropriate to fault a scientist for neglecting an aspect that was never their goal. For instance, while Curie's writings primarily detail experimental data and avoid personal anecdotes, her aim was to present reproducible evidence to advance the scientific field, not to produce emotionally resonant accounts. Her avoidance of subjective commentary reflects her commitment to objectivity, which is central to her contributions to science."

Based on the texts, the author of Text 1 would most likely agree with the author of Text 2 on which point?

A) Curie's earlier papers are more representative of her communication style than her later works.

B) Curie's communication style is often unjustly criticized.

C) Curie's reports focus more on experimental results than on personal insights or reflections.

D) Curie's objectivity was essential to her success in advancing scientific knowledge.

TEST
06

299

7

"The following text is from Charles Dickens' 1861 novel *Great Expectations*. In the text, the narrator reflects on the relationship between Pip and his guardian, Mr. Jaggers, while addressing the reader directly.

It was fortunate for Pip that he did not, like others, fully understand the stern judgments Jaggers passed upon his clients. Indeed, what individual among us could bear to reconcile the ideals we hold of our character with the blunt truths others might reveal about us? We are frail beings sustained by the illusions of our own merit: pity us, if we were to encounter blows that shatter that fragile support! The very strength to endure would drain from us."

Which choice best states the main idea of the text?

A) While people strive to maintain a virtuous image, even minor criticisms can undermine their sense of self-worth.

B) People often focus excessively on whether others admire them, to the detriment of their own well-being.

C) It is better for individuals to remain unaware of the differences between their self-perception and others' opinions of them.

D) While honesty is valued, people generally hesitate to confront others about their flaws.

8

"**Some scientists** have suggested that the animal species of the Arctic Archipelago originated from surrounding mainland regions before the islands fully emerged approximately 15 million years ago. David Smith et al. determined that the lineage of Arctic foxes on the Archipelago dates back about 18 million years, while Emily Wong et al. estimated that the lineage of Arctic hares on the islands is only about 8 million years old."

Which statement about the view put forward by "some scientists" is best supported by information in the text?

A) The view could be true of the Arctic foxes but is not true of the Arctic hares.

B) The view has some empirical support but is contradicted by the findings of Smith et al.

C) The view suggests that the Arctic Archipelago may have emerged as early as 18 million years ago.

D) The view relies on incorrect assumptions about the origin ages of the lineages of Arctic foxes and Arctic hares on the Archipelago.

9

"Poetry in Ancient Tamil, a classical language of South India, often utilizes *uyir-kalvi*, a figurative pairing of nouns that traditionally represents a broader concept. For instance, the common *uyir-kalvi aaduvum puli* ('the goat, the tiger') conveys the meaning 'prey and predator.' The device serves both an artistic purpose—structuring the rhythm of lines—and a cultural one: the associations between the paired nouns and the concept they represent may seem opaque, as in the above example, and are usually intelligible only within the cultural symbolism prevalent in Tamil ceremonial traditions."

Which statement about the *uyir-kalvi aaduvum puli* is most strongly supported by the text?

A) Its regular use in Ancient Tamil poetry suggests it was well-understood by its original audience.

B) Its cryptic nature may lead its poetic function to be overlooked by modern readers unfamiliar with Tamil culture.

C) Its apparent ambiguity becomes clear when interpreted within its specific cultural framework.

D) Its symbolic meaning relies on the intrinsic relationship between the paired nouns in the *uyir-kalvi*.

10

"Tokyo Bay, Japan, has implemented engineered barriers along 70% of its shoreline to mitigate flooding and typhoon damage, a strategy known as coastal reinforcement. To examine the impact on fish populations, Takashi Mori et al. assessed fish communities at various sites using the Index of Aquatic Community Integrity (IACI), where higher scores indicate higher aquatic integrity. The researchers compared two common types of coastal barriers—sea walls and breakwaters—and found that sea walls were more negatively associated with aquatic community integrity than breakwaters."

Which finding, if true, would most directly illustrate the researchers' finding?

A) Fish communities at Yokohama, a site with a high percentage of shoreline consisting of sea walls and breakwaters, had lower average IACI scores than did fish communities at Kawasaki, a site with a low percentage of shoreline consisting of sea walls and breakwaters.

B) The difference in average IACI scores for fish communities at Chiba and Funabashi, two sites with a higher percentage of shoreline consisting of sea walls than of breakwaters, was statistically insignificant.

C) Fish communities at Funabashi, a site with a relatively high percentage of shoreline consisting of sea walls, had lower average IACI scores than did fish communities at Narita, a site with a relatively high percentage of shoreline consisting of breakwaters.

D) Fish communities at Yokohama, a site with equal percentages of shoreline consisting of sea walls and breakwaters, had higher average IACI scores than did fish communities at Narita, a site with different percentages of shoreline consisting of sea walls and breakwaters.

TEST
06

11

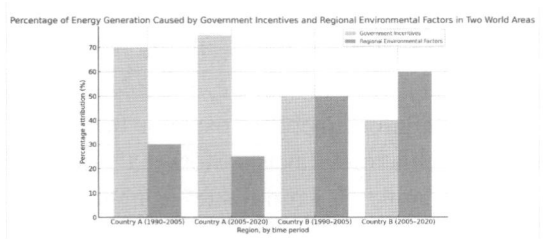

Percentage of Energy Generation Caused by Government Incentives and Regional Environmental Factors in Two World Areas

In a study on renewable energy adoption, Layla Moreno et al. conducted a meta-analysis of more than 200 countries to determine whether the composition of renewable energy sources in national energy portfolios was more strongly influenced by government incentives or by regional environmental factors. Moreno et al. propose that absent other factors, the share of energy attributed to regional environmental factors would increase relative to the share attributed to government incentives in countries as governments implement efficient subsidies. If true, this suggests the possibility that _____."

"Which choice most effectively uses data from the graph to complete the statement?"

A) countries in Country A experienced a slower rate of renewable energy adoption in the period from 2005 to 2020 than countries in Country B did, despite increasing government subsidy in Country A.

B) national governments of countries in Country A provided less efficient incentives in the period from 2005 to 2020 relative to the period from 1990 to 2005.

C) national governments of countries in Country A and in Country B generally provided more effective incentives in the period from 2005 to 2020 than in the period from 1990 to 2005, but at different rates.

D) national governments of most countries in Country B provided more effective incentives in the period from 2005 to 2020 than they had in the period from 1990 to 2005, but those of several countries in this region did not.

12

Crafted by culinary innovators, the EcoChef Collection emphasizes the growing demand among chefs for environmentally sustainable cooking practices. One way to achieve this is through the use of locally sourced ingredients, which promotes a balance between the ecological impact of food sourcing and the nutritional quality of the meals. Chefs who are committed to this approach meticulously plan every detail of their recipes, from ingredient selection and storage methods to preparation techniques and plating aesthetics. Thus, _____

Which choice most logically completes the text?

A) culinary teams like those in EcoChef strive to incorporate distinct ingredients into every recipe that they create.

B) culinary teams like those in EcoChef typically work with extensive inventories to reduce preparation times for new recipes.

C) locally sourced ingredients are considered throughout both the planning and preparation of a new dish.

D) using locally sourced ingredients focuses more on the ecological benefits of farming practices than on the nutritional quality of the final dish.

13

The morphological distinctiveness of echinoderms—marine invertebrates exhibiting radial symmetry, often resembling a star-shaped configuration centered around a singular axis—complicates comparative analyses with most other animal taxa, where bilateral symmetry along an anterior-posterior axis is the norm. Sea stars, in particular, pose a conundrum, having seemingly abandoned a head configuration despite their evolutionary roots in bilateral organisms. Leveraging genomic insights from *Hemichordus griseus* acorn worms (proximal relatives of sea stars, presumed to share homologous markers in anatomical development), Maria Konrad et al. discerned gene expression patterns exclusive to anterior genes in *Luidia clathrata* sea stars across the entire body, with limited posterior gene activity localized to peripheral regions. These findings imply that _____.

Which choice most logically completes the text?

A) notwithstanding the predominance of anterior gene expression in the genetic framework of sea stars, posterior genetic activity confined to peripheral regions predominantly accounts for the starlike morphology that differentiates sea stars from other echinoderms.

B) although the two species exhibit phylogenetic proximity, there is only marginal congruence in the genetic determinants of head, tail, and trunk development between *L. clathrata* sea stars and *H. griseus* acorn worms.

C) rather than undergoing evolutionary modifications culminating in the complete loss of head structures in their radial anatomy, as previously hypothesized, sea stars' morphological evolution led to the absence of a defined trunk and a composition dominated by anterior structures.

D) contrary to assertions that their morphology derives from bilateral ancestors, sea stars emerged with an anomalous structural blueprint devoid of both bilateral and radial symmetry.

14

As historian Dr. Elaine Murrow explains, **oral history (OH)** and **documented history (DH)** take distinct approaches to preserving cultural narratives. OH refers to the spoken stories and experiences of individuals passed down through generations, and DH _____ to the written records and archival materials that offer a formal account of events.

Which choice completes the text so that it conforms to the conventions of Standard English?

A) are referring

B) refers

C) have referred

D) refer

15

Romeo, a popular restaurant in New York City, has a seating capacity of 120, which accounts for approximately 30 percent of the venue's maximum occupancy. Having limited seating options _____ common for establishments in the area.

Which choice completes the text so that it conforms to the conventions of Standard English?

A) are

B) is

C) were

D) have been

TEST 09

303

16

The Andromeda Galaxy, a neighboring galaxy with billions of stars similar to those in the Milky Way, _____ like many celestial objects, visible to the naked eye from Earth under the right conditions.

Which choice completes the text so that it conforms to the conventions of Standard English?

A) are,
B) were,
C) have been,
D) is,

17

J.K. Rowling's *Harry Potter* series first debuted in 1997 with *The Philosopher's Stone*, a single volume that gained immense popularity and would lead to the creation of a global phenomenon. These transformative _____ the publication of six additional books, multiple movie adaptations, and the establishment of a worldwide fan base.

Which choice completes the text so that it conforms to the conventions of Standard English?

A) creations would include
B) creations, include
C) creations included
D) creations, including

18

Though she has written several acclaimed novels, including *Beloved* and *The Bluest Eye*, author Toni Morrison may be best known for her time as an editor at Random House. She did not begin her writing career until her mid-thirties, _____ released her debut novel after years of editing others' works.

Which choice completes the text so that it conforms to the conventions of Standard English?

A) however. She
B) however and she
C) however, she
D) however she

19

With the adoption of sustainable farming practices that use land and water more efficiently, the overall depletion of these resources might be expected to decrease. Researchers have observed that increases in efficiency often correlate negatively with resource _____ efficiency improvements, reducing the cost of production, may lead to greater overall consumption.

Which choice completes the text so that it conforms to the conventions of Standard English?

A) conservation; though
B) conservation, though,
C) conservation, though
D) conservation, though;

20

On March 14, 2018, scientists observed a volcanic eruption on a remote Pacific island, causing significant geological shifts in the region. The explosive event _____ from the buildup of pressure beneath the Earth's crust, releasing lava and ash into the atmosphere at incredible speeds.

Which choice completes the text so that it conforms to the conventions of Standard English?

A) results
B) resulting
C) had resulted
D) resulted

21

The Sphinx is a monumental limestone statue in Egypt that combines the body of a lion with the head of a human. _____ many other ancient sculptures also feature hybrid creatures, but the Sphinx is distinguished by its colossal size and the mystery surrounding its origins; standing near the Great Pyramid of Giza, it continues to captivate archaeologists and tourists alike.

Which choice completes the text with the most logical transition?

A) Of course,
B) However,
C) Specifically,
D) Moreover,

22

On November 22, 1963, John F. Kennedy was assassinated while riding in a motorcade in Dallas, Texas. This was just one of a number of tragic incidents that shaped American history during the 20th century. _____ between 1901 and 2000, four sitting U.S. presidents were assassinated while in office.

Which choice completes the text with the most logical transition?

A) Hence,
B) In other words,
C) Nevertheless,
D) In sum,

23

In 2022, researchers at a marine biology institute determined the migration path of a rare species of sea turtle, tracking its journey across thousands of miles of open ocean. Their findings were far more precise than those of a similar study conducted in 1950. _____ this earlier study relied on crude observation methods, such as physical tagging and manual tracking.

Which choice completes the text with the most logical transition?

A) Of course,
B) Ultimately,
C) Likewise,
D) To that end,

TEST 09

305

24

The Hoover Dam, located on the border of Nevada and Arizona, generates approximately 4 billion kilowatt-hours (kWh) of electricity annually. _____ the Three Gorges Dam in China, the largest hydroelectric dam in the world, generates over 100 billion kWh of electricity each year.

Which choice completes the text with the most logical transition?

A) For instance,

B) As a result,

C) That is,

D) By comparison,

25

While researching a topic, a student has taken the following notes:

- Generally, an increase in altitude reduces air pressure.
- The thinning of air at high altitudes is referred to as atmospheric rarefaction.
- A 2018 study conducted by NASA and ESA examined the effects of atmospheric rarefaction on various materials.
- When tested at high altitudes, Material A's tensile strength decreased by 15%.
- When tested at high altitudes, Material B's tensile strength decreased by 25%.

The student wants to emphasize a similarity between Material A and Material B. Which choice most effectively uses relevant information from the notes to accomplish this goal?

A) Both Material A and Material B experienced reduced tensile strength at high altitudes, according to a 2018 study.

B) Researchers determined that Material B's tensile strength decreased more than that of Material A at high altitudes.

C) In 2018, a research team observed the effects of atmospheric rarefaction on various materials, including Material A and Material B.

D) Atmospheric rarefaction refers to the thinning of air at high altitudes, which can reduce the tensile strength of certain materials.

26

While researching a topic, a student has taken the following notes:

- Alan Turing (1912–1954) was a mathematician, logician, and cryptanalyst born in London, England.
- He was one of the pioneers of computer science and artificial intelligence.
- In 1936, Turing published a paper introducing the concept of a "universal machine," later known as the Turing Machine.
- During World War II, he worked at Bletchley Park, where he played a key role in cracking the Enigma code.
- His work during the war contributed significantly to the Allied victory.

The student wants to emphasize the order in which Turing's key achievements occurred. Which choice most effectively uses relevant information from the notes to accomplish this goal?

A) Alan Turing made significant contributions to both theoretical and practical fields, such as his 1936 paper on the Turing Machine and his wartime work on the Enigma code.

B) Alan Turing's 1936 paper laid the foundation for his later achievements, including his role in cracking the Enigma code during World War II.

C) During World War II, Turing cracked the Enigma code, an achievement that preceded his groundbreaking 1936 publication introducing the Turing Machine.

D) Turing's wartime work at Bletchley Park demonstrated the practical application of his 1936 theoretical concepts, such as the Turing Machine.

27

While researching a topic, a student has taken the following notes:

- *Eclipse* is a 1915 photograph by American artist Edward Weston.
- It features the silhouette of a tree against a partially obscured sun.
- Silver gelatin and platinum are two common photographic printing techniques.
- Silver gelatin printing uses light-sensitive paper coated with a silver salt emulsion.
- Platinum printing uses light-sensitive paper coated with a platinum solution.

The student wants to contrast silver gelatin printing and platinum printing. Which choice most effectively uses relevant information from the notes to accomplish this goal?

A) In contrast to silver gelatin printing, in which the paper is coated with a silver salt emulsion, platinum printing is a common photographic printing technique.

B) Platinum printing, rather than silver gelatin printing, is the technique Weston used to create the 1915 photograph *Eclipse*.

C) Platinum printing is silver gelatin's opposite: the paper is coated not with a silver salt emulsion but with a platinum solution.

D) In both silver gelatin printing and platinum printing, light-sensitive paper is used, allowing images to be developed.

TEST
06

 CONTINUE

Module 2 answer

Answer: A)

📝 Why A) "trivial" is correct:

- The passage contrasts **"specialized species"** that are **"poorly represented"** with another kind of species that are **well-represented** in a database. The monarch butterfly is given as an example of the well-represented type.
- The use of "trivial" here does **not** mean "unimportant" in a derogatory way. Instead, it points to **common, widespread species**—those that are **easily found and documented**.
- In databases, **commonplace or ubiquitous species** are overrepresented simply because they are easier to observe and record.

  #### 🗨 Why not the others?
  - **B) conventional** – Suggests something *traditional* or *standard in method*, not in distribution. Doesn't fit the context of species' **geographic availability**.
  - **C) profound** – Illogical here. "Profound species"? That phrase is semantically odd. "Profound" usually refers to depth or complexity, not distribution.
  - **D) accidental** – Misleading. Accidental distribution implies randomness or lack of pattern—irrelevant and confusing in this contrast.

Answer: A)

📝 Why A) "demarcated from" is correct:

- "Demarcated from" means **clearly distinguished or set apart** from something else.
- The sentence sets up a **comparison and contrast**: obligate vs. facultative carnivores.
- Because of their strict diet, obligate carnivores can be **clearly separated (demarcated)** from those with more flexible diets.

Why not the others?

- **B) reconstituted as** – "Reconstitute" means to rebuild or restore, usually from parts. Makes no sense here; obligate carnivores aren't being reassembled into something else.
- **C) derived from** – That would mean obligate carnivores **came from** facultative ones, which is **not the point of the sentence**.
- **D) conflated with** – Means "mixed up with" or "mistaken for," which contradicts the logic. The sentence explains why they can be **distinguished**, not confused.

3

Correct Answer: B)

📝 **Why B) "ambiguity" is correct:**

- The sentence deals with verifying a **previously uncertain** or **questionable** signal.
- "Preclude doubts" means to **eliminate uncertainty**, which means they are eliminating **ambiguity**.
- Thus, the best completion is **"ambiguity"**—a state of uncertainty or multiple interpretations.

 Why not the others?

- **A) subtlety** – A subtle signal can still be valid; the issue here isn't *how faint* it is, but whether it's ambiguous.
- **C) likelihood** – Doesn't make logical sense. You don't "preclude" doubts about **likelihood**; that would imply the signal's existence is too likely, which isn't the concern.
- **D) inconspicuousness** – Means "hard to notice," which would support skepticism, not resolve it. Modeling wouldn't preclude that.

4

Correct Answer: C)

📝 **Why C) is correct:**

- The passage structure is **1) acknowledgment of lesser fame, 2) mention of support from two prominent scientists, 3) detailed praise from one of them (Brooks).**
- Thus, the passage highlights admiration from experts and then **explains why** Brooks admires the work, especially regarding its integration of descriptive and predictive methodologies.

Why not the others?

- **A)** is **almost** right but slightly off: It says it "cites a professional," implying just one, whereas the passage cites **two**.
- **B)** inaccurately says Torres had an **acclaimed career**, which the passage does **not** support—it only says her work is praised by a few, not widely recognized.
- **D)** is incorrect because the passage does **not** say the research is hard to understand or that its **complexity needs explanation**—just that it integrates two approaches.

5

Correct Answer: B)

Explanation:

- The sentence **lists these factors** ("station accessibility" and "personal schedule flexibility") as **examples** of what different studies emphasize.
- However, **Tanaka's key point** is that *no single factor explains everything*; decisions about commuting are complex and individual.
- Therefore, **these examples are part of a larger, multifactorial view**: the text acknowledges them as **important** but **not exhaustive**.

 Why others are wrong:

- **A)** falsely claims the text says people **"rarely consider"** these factors—there is no such assertion.
- **C)** is incorrect because the text doesn't say these factors are **unique to Tokyo**—in fact, it generalizes beyond Tokyo.
- **D)** misrepresents the passage—it does **not** say the factors were **overemphasized** in studies, just that they're **part of the picture**.

6

Correct Answer: C)

Why C) is correct:

- Text 1 says Curie's writing is "methodical," focused on "experimental results" and not "personal reflection."
- Text 2 explains that this style was **intentional** and central to her **scientific goals**.

• So, both **agree she focused on reporting results over personal anecdotes**.

 Why others are wrong:

• **A)** mentions "earlier vs. later works," which is **not discussed** in either text.

• **B)** discusses *criticism*, but Text 1 is **neutral**, not defending her from unfair critique.

• **D)** is close—but while Text 2 emphasizes **objectivity**, Text 1 doesn't explicitly connect objectivity with her **scientific success**, only her **influence**.

7

Correct Answer: C)

📝 **Why C) is correct:**

• The narrator argues that people **survive on illusions** of their own virtue.

• Harsh truths could **break** their self-esteem—so **ignorance may be protective**.

• Thus, **remaining unaware of how others view us protects our self-concept**.

 Why others are wrong:

• **A)** implies even *minor* criticisms break self-worth—but the text talks about **shattering illusions**, not *minor* damage.

• **B)** introduces a theme about *admiration*, which is never mentioned.

• **D)** says people **hesitate to criticize**—the narrator doesn't discuss others' hesitations, only the **impact of truth** on ourselves.

8

Correct Answer: A)

📝 **Explanation:**

• Some scientists" say animals came from the mainland *before* islands emerged (~15 mya).

• Arctic **foxes' lineage = 18 mya** → fits this view.

• Arctic **hares' lineage = 8 mya** → evolved **after** islands emerged.

• Thus, **the view works for foxes but not hares**.

📖 **Why others are wrong:**
- **B)** wrongly says Smith et al. *contradict* the view—they actually **support** it.
- **C)** implies the view adjusts the date of the **Archipelago's emergence** (to 18 mya), which the scientists do **not claim**.
- **D)** claims the view is based on **incorrect assumptions**—but the passage doesn't accuse these scientists of being wrong, only **partially accurate**.

9

Correct Answer: C)

📝 **Explanation:**
- The text says the meaning of these pairings may seem "**opaque**" and are usually only understood **within Tamil ceremonial tradition**.
- Hence, while seemingly ambiguous, **they become clear in context**.

📖 **Why others are wrong:**
- **A)** says the device was **well-understood**—this is **not stated**, and the "opaqueness" suggests otherwise.
- **B)** assumes modern readers *overlook* the poetic function—this is speculative and unsupported.
- **D)** says the symbolic meaning comes from an *intrinsic* relationship—however, the text stresses **cultural symbolism**, not literal relationships.

10

Correct Answer: C)

📝 **Explanation:**
- The study showed **sea walls** harm aquatic integrity **more** than **breakwaters**.
- C) directly compares a **sea wall–heavy** site (Funabashi) to a **breakwater–heavy** site (Narita) and shows **lower IACI scores** for the former.
- This **illustrates** the conclusion perfectly.

312

💬 **Why others are wrong:**

- **A)** muddles the comparison—Yokohama has both sea walls and breakwaters; Kawasaki's shoreline type is **unspecified**.
- **B)** compares **two sea wall–heavy** sites with **no meaningful variable difference**—thus, it doesn't support the sea wall vs. breakwater claim.
- **D)** introduces **equal percentages** in one site and a **vague contrast** in the other, diluting the clarity of a direct causal link.

Answer: B)

📝 **Explanation:**

Fits the data: In **Country A**, government incentives became **more dominant** in 2005–2020 (75%), and **environmental influence declined**, contradicting the expected effect of efficient subsidies.

→ Therefore, we infer that **incentives became *less efficient*** over time.

💬 **Why the other choices are incorrect:**

- **A)**

  "Countries in Country A experienced a slower rate of renewable energy adoption..."

  ✗ Not supported: The graph says **nothing about the rate of adoption**, only the **influence attribution** (not absolute adoption or speed).

- **C)**

  "Governments... generally provided more effective incentives... but at different rates."

  ✗ False for Country A: In **Country A**, regional influence **decreased**, which **contradicts** the effect of more efficient incentives.

- **D)**

  "Most countries in Country B provided more effective incentives... but several did not."

  ✗ The graph only shows **averages**, not **subgroup variation**. We cannot say "most" vs. "several" countries based on **aggregate bars**.

12

Correct Answer: C)

📝 **Explanation:**

- The passage sets up a **cause-effect relationship**:
  - **Premise:** EcoChef is about **sustainability**, particularly through **locally sourced ingredients**.
  - **Support:** Chefs **plan meticulously**, from ingredient selection to plating.
- **Conclusion:** It logically follows that **local ingredients are woven throughout the entire creative process—from planning to preparation**.

  ❓ **Why the other options are incorrect:**
  - **A)** "incorporate distinct ingredients"
    - ✗ *"Distinct"* is vague and unrelated to **sustainability** or the **planning process** emphasized in the paragraph.
  - **B)** "work with extensive inventories to reduce preparation times"
    - ✗ Inventory and prep time are **irrelevant** here. The focus is on **ingredient origin and ecological impact**, not efficiency.
  - **D)** "focuses more on ecological benefits... than on nutritional quality"
    - ✗ Contradicts the passage, which explicitly says local sourcing promotes **balance** between **ecological** and **nutritional** concerns—not a preference for one.

13

Correct Answer: A)

📝 **Acknowledges the Evidence:**

1. ✔ Begins with a concession: although **anterior genes dominate**, this matches the findings.
2. **Connects Morphology to Gene Expression:**
3. ✔ The clause "posterior genetic activity confined to peripheral regions..." points directly to a **spatial correlation**: the arms or "points" of the star shape lie at the **edges**, where **posterior gene expression occurs**.
4. ✔ The phrase "accounts for the starlike morphology" answers the **core question**: *what causes the sea star shape?*
5. **Aligns with Evolutionary Developmental Biology:**
6. ✔ In embryology, **body patterning** often results from where certain genes are expressed.

7. ✔ Since **posterior genes** are only active **in peripheral zones**, those zones become **morphologically distinct** (i.e., arms or projections), forming the **starlike structure**.

8. **Conclusion**: A) provides both a **biological mechanism** (spatial gene expression) and a **logical implication** (resulting morphology), directly matching what "these findings imply."

💬 **Why the other options are incorrect:**

B)

"Although the two species exhibit phylogenetic proximity, there is only marginal congruence in the genetic determinants of head, tail, and trunk development..."

✔ **Why it fails:**

• The passage **does not focus** on comparing **L. clathrata** and **H. griseus** in terms of congruence.

• *H. griseus* is mentioned as a **reference** to identify homologous genes, not as the **focus** of divergence.

• This choice **shifts the topic** to **cross-species comparison**, which is **not what the findings are about**.

C)

"Rather than undergoing evolutionary modifications culminating in the complete loss of head structures... sea stars' morphological evolution led to the absence of a defined trunk and a composition dominated by anterior structures."

✔ **Why it falls short:**

• This answer **accurately summarizes gene expression**, but it **doesn't explain the star-like shape**.

• It provides an **internal description** of sea star anatomy—no trunk, anterior-heavy—but **stops short** of connecting that to **why sea stars look like stars**.

• It misses the **central implication**: how posterior genes **at the periphery** shape the **morphology**.

D)

"Contrary to assertions that their morphology derives from bilateral ancestors, sea stars emerged with an anomalous structural blueprint devoid of both bilateral and radial symmetry."

✔ **Why it's factually incorrect:**

• The passage **explicitly states** that sea stars evolved from **bilateral organisms**—this is a **given**, not refuted.

• Also, sea stars **clearly exhibit radial symmetry**. Saying they lack both **bilateral and radial** symmetry is biologically **false**.

• This answer **contradicts the text** and fundamental echinoderm biology.

14

Answer: B)

📝 Why B is correct:

This sentence uses a **parallel construction**: "OH refers... and DH refers..." The verb must match in tense and structure. "OH" is singular (oral history), and so is "DH" (documented history). The verb "refers" agrees with a **singular subject** and keeps the present tense to maintain parallelism.

> ### ❓ Why not the others:
> - **A) are referring** – Wrong tense (present progressive), and it's plural. "DH" is singular.
> - **C) have referred** – Present perfect tense introduces an unnecessary past perspective.
> - **D) refer** – Incorrect subject-verb agreement. "DH" is singular; "refer" is plural.

15

Answer: B)

📝 Why B is correct:

The subject is **"having limited seating options,"** which is a **gerund phrase** and treated as singular. So, the singular verb "is" matches the subject.

> ### ❓ Why not the others:
> - **A) are** – Incorrect; "are" is plural, while the subject is singular.
> - **C) were** – Past tense, but the sentence is in the present tense.
> - **D) have been** – Present perfect plural, but again, the subject is singular and the sentence doesn't need perfect aspect.

16

Answer: D)

📝 Why D is correct:

"The Andromeda Galaxy" is singular. The verb must match the subject: **"is"** is singular and present. The comma is required before "like" as it sets off a nonrestrictive clause.

Why not the others:
- **A) are,** − Plural verb; incorrect.
- **B) were,** − Past tense; shifts away from the present description.
- **C) have been,** − Present perfect; unnecessary complexity.

17

Answer: A)

Why A is correct:
The context is future-in-the-past: "would lead to the creation..." so to match that implied conditional/future past, **"would include"** aligns with "would lead." "Creations" is the subject of "would include."

Why not the others:
- **B) creations, include** − This is a comma splice and creates a fragment.
- **C) creations included** − Shifts to simple past, misaligning with the conditional "would lead."
- **D) creations, including** − "Including" creates a participial phrase, not a complete verb clause. It's grammatically off unless rewritten differently.

18

Answer: A)

Why A is correct:
We need a full stop (**period**) between two independent clauses:
"She did not begin..." and "She released..." "However" is used as a **conjunctive adverb**, and must either start a new sentence or be preceded by a semicolon—not a comma alone.

Why not the others:
- **B) however and she** − "And" makes the sentence a run-on; grammatically jarring.
- **C) however, she** − Comma splice. "However" alone with a comma can't join two independent clauses.
- **D) however she** − Lacks punctuation and reads like a dependent clause. It's not grammatical here.

TEST
06

317

19

Answer: D)

✎ Why D is correct:
We need a **semicolon** to join two independent clauses:

1. "Researchers have observed that increases in efficiency often correlate negatively with resource conservation,"
2. "Efficiency improvements... may lead to greater consumption."
3. The word **"though"** functions here as an interrupter and must be offset with **commas or semicolons**. The semicolon elegantly separates the two clauses while allowing "though" to transition.

？ Why not the others:
- **A) conservation; though** – "Though" hangs without any punctuation after it. Incomplete.
- **B) conservation, though,** – Creates a comma splice.
- **C) conservation, though** – Missing the punctuation needed after "though" before launching into an independent clause.

20

Answer: C)

✎ Why C is correct:
This describes a **past perfect** situation: an event **had resulted** from prior buildup. Since the "eruption" is in the past (March 14, 2018), the cause of it (the buildup) had happened even earlier. Thus, past perfect is required.

？ Why not the others:
- **A) results** – Present tense; inconsistent with the past timeframe.
- **B) resulting** – This would make a fragment; needs a subject and verb.
- **D) resulted** – Simple past, but doesn't reflect the proper sequence of past events (cause before effect).

21

Answer: A)

 Why A is correct:

The sentence acknowledges that **many ancient sculptures also feature hybrid creatures**, so it's not denying that fact—it's affirming it before shifting focus to **what makes the Sphinx unique**. "Of course" serves to **acknowledge shared knowledge** and smoothly introduce a **contrast of emphasis**, not contradiction.

Why not the others:
- **B) However,** – Signals a contradiction or counterpoint, but no contradiction exists.
- **C) Specifically,** – This implies a narrowing of focus, but the sentence is comparing, not specifying.
- **D) Moreover,** – Adds information of the same kind, but here the goal is to *contrast* the Sphinx's uniqueness.

22

Answer: B) In other words,

Why B is correct:

The phrase **restates or clarifies** the previous idea: JFK's assassination is one tragic event among others. "In other words" signals a **rephrasing** of a general idea into a more specific and dramatic statistic.

Why not the others:
- **A) Hence,** – Indicates a conclusion or result, which isn't appropriate here.
- **C) Nevertheless,** – Signals contrast, which doesn't fit.
- **D) In sum,** – Suggests a summary or conclusion, but this isn't the end of a paragraph or idea.

20

Answer: A)

Why A is correct:

This transition **lightly concedes** the obviousness of the earlier study's limitations. It sets the stage for an explanation *why* the modern results were better—because the earlier methods were primitive. "Of course" fits the **tone of expectedness**.

319

Why not the others:

- **B) Ultimately,** – Refers to a final result, not the comparison being made here.
- **C) Likewise,** – Suggests similarity, but this sentence is contrasting.
- **D) To that end,** – Indicates purpose or intent, which is not the function here.

24

Answer: D) By comparison,

 Why D is correct:

The sentence draws a **clear quantitative comparison** between two dams. "By comparison" is the perfect transitional phrase to show contrast in magnitude.

Why not the others:

- **A) For instance,** – Suggests an example, but this isn't an example of Hoover Dam—it's a comparison.
- **B) As a result,** – Suggests causality, which is not the case.
- **C) That is,** – Used to clarify or rephrase, but no clarification is needed here.

25

Answer: A) Both Material A and Material B experienced reduced tensile strength at high altitudes, according to a 2018 study.

Why A is correct:

It clearly and directly **compares the effects** on both materials, emphasizing the **shared outcome**: reduced tensile strength.

Why not the others:

- **B)** – Focuses on contrast, not similarity.
- **C)** – Introduces background information, not comparison.
- **D)** – Explains a concept, not a similarity between results.

320

26

Answer: B) Alan Turing's 1936 paper laid the foundation for his later achievements, including his role in cracking the Enigma code during World War II.

 Why B is correct:

It clearly shows **chronology**: theory came first (1936), followed by practical application during WWII. The word **"foundation"** supports the idea of sequence.

⟨?⟩ **Why not the others:**
- **A)** – Lists both achievements but not in an order-emphasizing structure.
- **C)** – Incorrect chronology; says WWII came *before* 1936.
- **D)** – Suggests direct application of his theory to war efforts, which overstates the link.

27

Answer: C)

 Why C is correct:

This sentence **clearly contrasts** the two methods by focusing on their **key difference**: the chemical coating.

⟨?⟩ **Why not the others:**
- **A)** – The sentence structure is awkward and doesn't focus clearly on contrast.
- **B)** – Incorrect assumption; the notes never say Weston used platinum printing.
- **D)** – Points out similarity, not contrast.